DECISIONS OF THE
MARYLAND CAMPAIGN

OTHER BOOKS IN THE COMMAND DECISIONS IN AMERICA'S CIVIL WAR SERIES

DECISIONS
OF THE
MARYLAND CAMPAIGN

The Fourteen Critical Decisions
That Defined the Operation

Michael S. Lang
Maps by Tim Kissel

COMMAND DECISIONS
IN AMERICA'S CIVIL WAR
Matt Spruill and Larry Peterson,
Series Editors

The University of Tennessee Press / Knoxville

Library of Congress Cataloging-in-Publication Data

Names: Lang, Michael S., author. | Kissel, Tim, cartographer.
Title: Decisions of the Maryland Campaign : the fourteen critical decisions that
defined the operation / Michael S. Lang ; maps by Tim Kissel.
Description: First edition. | Knoxville : The University of Tennessee Press, [2022] |
Series: Command decisions in America's Civil War | Includes bibliographical
references and index. | Summary: "The Maryland Campaign represented Gen.
Robert E. Lee's first invasion of the North. Opposing Lee was Gen. George B.
McClellan, who had just retreated from Lee's onslaught during the Seven Days Battles. While Lee and McClellan fought a preliminary battle at South Mountain, and
would engage again at Shepherdstown as the Confederate Army withdrew across
the Potomac, the full force of both armies would meet at Antietam, and the subsequent battle would prove to be the bloodiest single-day battle of the war. *Decisions
of the Maryland Campaign* introduces readers to critical decisions made by Confederate and Federal commanders throughout the campaign. Michael S. Lang examines
the decisions that prefigured the action and shaped the contest as it unfolded. Complete with maps and a guided tour, this book is Lang's second contribution and the
thirteenth volume in a series of books that explores the critical decisions of major
campaigns and battles of the Civil War"—Provided by publisher.
Identifiers: LCCN 2022033516 | ISBN 9781621907480 (paperback)
Subjects: LCSH: Maryland Campaign, 1862. | Strategy—History—
19th century. | Maryland—History—Civil War, 1861–1865—Campaigns. |
United States—History—Civil War, 1861–1865—Campaigns.
Classification: LCC E474.61 .L36 2022 | DDC 973.7/336—dc23/eng/20220713
LC record available at https://lccn.loc.gov/2022033516

CONTENTS

ILLUSTRATIONS

Photographs

Maps

PREFACE

The more I study the Civil War, the more I am convinced that 1862 was possibly the most transformative year of that conflict. From Fort Donaldson to Stones River, from Hampton Roads to Fredericksburg, the chasm between where the nation was at the year's beginning and end is remarkable. Hand in glove with this transformation was Lee's first great invasion of the North—the 1862 Maryland Campaign and the vicissitudes it brought about. This book was written specifically to guide you through the critical decisions of that campaign.

As is the case with the other volumes in the Command Decisions of the American Civil War series, *Decisions of the Maryland Campaign* applies critical decision methodology. This approach is designed to allow someone who understands "what happened" to move to the next level and ask, "Why did it happen, or what caused it to happen?" When the critical decision concept is understood, it can be applied to any battle or campaign in any war.

The Maryland Campaign did not happen as a result of random chance. Events occurred as they did because of the decisions made at all levels of command on both sides. Some of these were the routine decisions made during any campaign or battle. A smaller number were important decisions. At the top of the decision hierarchy, a select number of actions shaped how the campaign and battle unfolded. These were the critical decisions.

Critical decisions cover the entire spectrum of war: strategic, operational, tactical, logistical, personnel, and organizational. Initially, some decisions that appear to be minor are actually critical decisions that significantly impact future events.

It is essential that you, the reader, understand the concept of a critical decision. Without this understanding, this book will appear to be only a short and selected narrative history of the Maryland Campaign. This work does something different, exploring how battles and campaigns developed as they did—examining the why instead of the what.

This chart shows the decisions hierarchy. At the bottom are the many and various decisions, above those are a lesser number of important decisions, and at the top are a very few critical decisions.

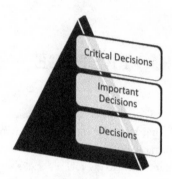

Decisions Hierarchy

The fourteen critical decisions made during the Maryland Campaign are arranged in three specific time periods.

> The Campaign Begins, September 3–13, 1862
>> Lee Invades the North
>> McClellan Takes Command
>> Henry Halleck Does Not Evacuate Harpers Ferry
>> Lee Divides His Army
>> Sugar Loaf Mountain is Occupied
>> McClellan Responds to Special Orders 191
>
> South Mountain, Harpers Ferry, and the Eve of Antietam,
> September 14–16, 1862
>> Lee Stands at South Mountain
>> Pleasonton Sends Willcox to Turner's Gap
>> Franklin Delays at Crampton's Gap

Miles Surrenders Harpers Ferry
Lee Offers Battle at Sharpsburg
McClellan Launches His Attack

The Aftermath of Antietam, September 18–20, 1862
McClellan Does Not Attack
Lee Withdraws to Virginia

The criterion for a critical decision is that it is of such magnitude as to shape not only the events immediately following it, but also the campaign or battle from that point on. If these critical decisions had not been made, or if different actions had been taken, the sequence of events for the Maryland Campaign would have been significantly different.

I chose the critical decisions based on my years of study of the Maryland Campaign and extensive experience on the ground where the fighting occurred. Other historians might select different critical decisions, depending on their background. However, I believe these core choices shaped the campaign.

This book looks at decisions made both during the battles and before and after the fighting. While South Mountain and Harpers Ferry are significant in their own right, these engagements are parts of the sum that is the 1862 Maryland Campaign. In addition, this work is not intended to be a complete retelling or reinterpretation of the campaign. For example, I only briefly reference the very complicated and relevant political aspects of the campaign, and I touch on but a few material points of the overall narrative. Any number of excellent books provide a more detailed analysis of those topics. They are not listed here, so the reader should refer to the bibliography as an introductory study guide. This book covers just those events and details relevant to the various critical decisions discussed.

The reader will quickly notice that this volume does not go into those decisions made during the Battle of Antietam. This is by design—my stand-alone manuscript *Decisions at Antietam* will guide the reader through these actions. If you have read *Decisions at Antietam* before this volume, you will note that some of the decisions are repeated in both works. This was also by design, as individual critical decisions can be viewed as both campaign related and battle related. For example, Lee's decision to stand at Sharpsburg not only impacted the battle by helping inaugurate it, but also furthered the overall campaign. The reader can enjoy both of these books separately or together.

As you read, you will notice that the Union and Confederacy used similar but often differing methods to identify units. Both sides identified units at the company, battalion, and regimental level in the same manner. Companies were distinguished by a letter—e.g., A Company, B Company, and so on. Regiments and battalions were usually designated by a number—e.g., Fifth (or 5th) Texas, Nineteenth (or 19th) Indiana. Above the regimental level, the Union and Confederacy took different approaches to identify individual units.

The official designations of Union brigades, divisions, and corps were numeric and began with a capital letter. Examples include First Brigade, Third Division, Second Corps, or Brig. Gen. John C. Caldwell's First Brigade, Maj. Gen. Israel B. Richardson's First Division, Maj. Gen. Jesse L. Reno's Ninth Corps. When referring to a brigade or division belonging to or commanded by an individual, lowercase letters are used. Examples include Crawford's brigade, Richardson's division, Reno's corps, and so on.

Early in the war, the Confederacy simultaneously used both numbering and naming systems for unit designations. The numbering system was employed far less often than the naming system as the war progressed. Confederate brigades, divisions, and commands/corps were officially designated by the commanders' last names, followed by Brigade, Division, Command, or Corps. Examples include Kershaw's Brigade, McLaws's Division, and Longstreet's Command. Identification can also be problematic because multiple generals and colonels named Anderson, Hill, and Jones led units in the Army of Northern Virginia at that time.

The Confederate Congress did not authorize the designation of corps until September 18, 1862. Subsequently, Robert E. Lee did not organize his army into corps until November 6, of that year. Longstreet and Jackson unofficially had "commands" during the campaign. However, after-action reports and various manuscripts alternately refer to these commands as corps and wings.

It is also not uncommon for various sources to identify the same Confederate unit by the name of the former commander, the name of the current commander, or both. For instance, source material sometimes refers to Lawton's Division as Ewell's Division. Maj. Gen. Richard S. Ewell commanded this unit at Second Bull Run. He was wounded at that fight; thus, Brig. Gen. Alexander Lawton led this division during the campaign. Of course, as with most things related to the Civil War, these rules always have exceptions. Additional details on unit designations and leadership are referenced in the order of battle located in appendixes ll and lll of this manuscript.

As is the case with many Civil War battles, the fighting at South Mountain has more than one name. Several early Southern accounts identified the Battles of South Mountain as the Battle of Boonsboro Gap. Southerners tended to name engagements for the closest town, while Northerners tended to name them for the nearest water bodies. There were exceptions to this rule as well. To avoid identifying every battle twice in this book, I am sticking with the Northern naming convention going forward.

Determining the specific facts and events that occurred during the Civil War can be extremely problematic. As a result, understanding the precise number of combatants on each side of the conflict becomes a very circular discussion with no clear answer. To further complicate this situation, new research contradicting earlier assertions seems to be published every day. Additionally, as many students of the war understand, exact and standard timekeeping was not generally practiced in the nineteenth century. Therefore, readers should increase or decrease every headcount by 15 percent and add or subtract an hour from every stated time. Appendix IV of this manuscript contains additional details on the two armies' strengths and casualties.

A complete and thorough grasp of mid-nineteenth-century warfare often requires studying the ground where these events took place. Topography plays a critical role in comprehending a decision or event, and knowing what a decision-maker saw can often provide valuable insight that is otherwise obscured. Exploring the geographic area where the Maryland Campaign took place perfectly illustrates this fact. To better facilitate such understanding, I have included a guide with tour stops that correlate with many of the critical decisions (appendix I). This brief guide has a specific practical purpose: to help a reasonably well-informed reader follow the campaign on the ground and develop further insights into the fighting and the critical decisions' effects.

I sincerely hope you find this work a beneficial addition to your library and your study of this most decisive campaign of the American Civil War.

ACKNOWLEDGMENTS

I wish to publicly acknowledge my good friends Matt Spruill and Larry Peterson. As the series coeditors, Matt and Larry have provided me with invaluable feedback throughout the creation of this manuscript.

I would like to also acknowledge the talented individuals at the University of Tennessee Press. Specifically, Thomas Wells. He and his team have been extraordinarily helpful to me during this process.

I wish to also thank the men and women who make up the United States National Park Service and those at the Antietam National Battlefield. I have lost count of the number of times I have visited the tremendously beautiful and moving battlefield of Antietam. With every visit, I learn something new. These dedicated and knowledgeable custodians of this hallowed ground are some of the finest I have encountered.

Additionally, I wish to acknowledge the many new friends I have made over the years who are avid fans of Antietam as I am. These include members of SHAF (Save Historic Antietam Foundation), Antietam Battlefield Guides, and the Antietam Institute.

During the process of creating this manuscript, I found many like-minded Antietam devotees on social media. While too numerous to mention, many of these newfound friends are very talented amateur and professional photographers alike. Among these is my friend Matt Brant. Matt, an extremely gifted photographer, was kind enough to contribute to this book. Several of his stunning photos grace the pages of this manuscript.

INTRODUCTION

Thursday, September 25, 1862, dawned crisp and clear on the Confederate camps along the Opequon Creek near Smoketown, Virginia. Throughout the villages and farmlands of northern Virginia, the mercury was now dipping to fifty degrees at night, as the warm summer weather had begrudgingly given way to far cooler autumn nights. Near this now long-forgotten crossroads west of Martinsburg, Confederate general Robert E. Lee made his headquarters.[1]

Within his tent's relative seclusion, Lee dictated a melancholic message to Confederate president Jefferson Davis in Richmond. As both his wrists were still splinted from a nasty fall almost four weeks prior, Lee had been forced to rely on his staff for even the most basic of tasks. In addition to having to dictate most of his communications, the general needed help dressing and eating. He was forced to ride in an ambulance during the recent campaign or sit on horseback with an orderly holding the reins. In fact, it would be almost another three weeks before Lee could perform his regular routine without the cumbersome splints and accompanying pain.[2]

Throughout his campaign in Maryland, Lee had regularly communicated with Davis, keeping him abreast of his progress. Eight days had now passed since the horrendous clash along the Antietam Creek, and three weeks had elapsed since the Confederate army first crossed the Potomac into the North. In this latest communication, Lee recounted the current condition of his forces. He also advised the president that although the Federal army north of the Potomac was mostly quiet, Union forces had reoccupied Harpers Ferry.

Gen. Robert Edward Lee, Commanding, Army of Northern Virginia, circa
1860-1865. Library of Congress.

After falling back from Sharpsburg on the eighteenth, the Rebels recrossed
the Potomac. Following a sharp battle at Shepherdstown (September 19
and 20) and an aborted attempt to reenter Maryland via Williamsport, they
had essentially remained in this vicinity. Once Lee sent his most grievously
wounded men south, he paused near Smoketown to gather up as many stragglers as possible. These soldiers had been wandering back into the ranks for
ten days. Field returns three days earlier had shown forty-one thousand men
now present for duty in the Confederate army.[3]

Lee informed Davis that he still believed his best course of action was
to recross the Potomac and advance his army to Hagerstown, Maryland, despite its diminished strength. However, Lee's soldiers had other designs. The
Confederate army was exhausted, hungry, and footsore. More significantly,
the Army of Northern Virginia was dramatically afflicted by the casualties
resulting from its recent battles. The fourteen thousand casualties suffered
during the campaign was an inescapable reality now facing Robert E. Lee.[4]

"I am, therefore, led to pause,"[5] he confessed in his typical understated
way. In doing so, the general acknowledged what should have been obvious
to him for days—his first great campaign into the North had come to an end.
The next day, Lee issued orders for the Army of Northern Virginia to move
up the Shenandoah Valley to Winchester. Here they would rest and recover.
All the while, Lee had to be wondering if and when the Union army would
cross the Potomac River and pursue them.[6]

One cannot help but wonder how much time the Confederate commander now devoted to evaluating the course events had taken over the past three weeks. Did Lee commit to any moments of quiet contemplation second-guessing his own decisions and those of his lieutenants? What mistakes had he made, and what lessons had he learned? If Lee somehow had the chance to relive the events of the past three weeks, would he follow the same path as before? Would Lee still choose to cross over the Potomac and invade Maryland? Would he still decide to divide his forces in an effort to dislodge the Union garrison at Harpers Ferry? Would he still choose to stand and fight along the banks of the Antietam Creek?

In the subsequent eight months, Lee's Confederates would meet the Army of the Potomac two more times under two separate Union commanders. Both of these battles (Fredericksburg and Chancellorsville) were undisputed Confederate victories. These triumphs emboldened Robert E. Lee to try his hand at a second invasion of the North in June and July 1863.

September 25, 1862, also saw developments on the north bank of the Potomac. Union Maj. Gen. George B. McClellan had his headquarters near Sharpsburg, Maryland. The Union Fifth and Ninth Corps had made their camps between Sharpsburg and the Potomac. The Sixth Corps, along with Couch's division and part of the cavalry, had marched to Williamsport to counter Lee's attempt to cross back over the Potomac. Meanwhile, the First, Second, and Twelfth Corps had reoccupied Maryland Heights and the town of Harpers Ferry. [7]

The Union commander was also taking stock and contemplating his own course from the past several weeks. McClellan was likewise laboring to see what the future held for himself and the Army of the Potomac. That day, he wrote to his wife, Mary Ellen. He mentioned the colder nights and the feeling that his men's morale seemed to be improving. He also expressed his opinion about his intended course of action, stating, "My own judgment is to watch the line of the Potomac until the water rises, then to concentrate everything near Harpers Ferry—reorganize the army as promptly as possible & then if secesh remains near Winchester to attack him—if he retires to follow him & attack him near Richmond." Furthermore, he issued this prediction: "It is very doubtful I shall remain in the service after the rebels leave this vicinity."

As a conservative Democrat who felt he was fighting exclusively for the preservation of the Union, McClellan confessed, "I cannot make up my mind to fight for such an accursed doctrine as that of servile insurrection—is too infamous."[8] This last comment was in reference to Lincoln's Emancipation Proclamation, made public just three days before.

Maj. Gen. George Brinton McClellan,
Commanding, Army of the Potomac,
circa 1861. Library of Congress.

What McClellan did not tell his wife was how badly his own army had suffered in the recent conflicts. The Army of the Potomac counted over 15,000 casualties in the battles fought since September 14. This number did not include the 12,000 Union soldiers captured when the garrison at Harpers Ferry fell. However, on September 20, 1862, returns for the Army of the Potomac showed 164,000 men present for duty. Of these, roughly 92,000 were within fifteen miles of McClellan's headquarters at Sharpsburg. By all accounts, the Union commander likely had somewhere between 70,000 and 78,000 combat effectives available to him that day.[9]

Was George McClellan now prone to any moments of reflection of his own? Did he spend any time retracing his own steps from the last few weeks? Did he question himself in any way or have any moments of self-doubt? Were the decisions to attack at South Mountain and Antietam still the correct ones?

Since the end of the Battle of Shepherdstown (September 19 and 20), McClellan had declined to advance his army south to pursue Lee. Other than cavalry incursions and those forces in Harpers Ferry proper, the Union army remained north of the Potomac in Maryland. McClellan alluded to several reasons for his decision, but a glaring lack of supplies and healthy horses was the most obvious.

Over the next several weeks, conversations at the Union command's highest levels had one conspicuous theme. The War Department and the Lincoln administration insisted McClellan move south and pursue Lee and his Army of Northern Virginia, while McClellan argued the myriad of reasons he could not.[10] On October 26, 1862, forty days after the Battle of Antietam ended, and following continual haranguing by the Lincoln administration, McClellan finally sent his army across the Potomac River in force. After twelve days, the Army of the Potomac progressed just over forty miles to Warrenton, Virginia, although no significant battle resulted from this advance.[11]

Meanwhile, in Washington, DC, some fifty-odd miles from the post-Antietam drama along the upper Potomac, the war had taken a dramatic turn. Determined to change the conflict's character, Abraham Lincoln released the Preliminary Emancipation Proclamation to the Northern papers on September 22. Under his war powers as commander in chief, the president seized on the Union victory at Antietam as a catalyst for arguably the most substantive social and political change in the republic's history. The war that Lincoln had long insisted was about the preservation of the Union was suddenly and irreversibly transformed into a more virtuous cause. That cause was the elimination of the institution of slavery.

The quarrel between McClellan and the administration finally came to a head in early November. After almost fifteen months of command, the Union commander's military assets no longer outweighed his political liabilities in Lincoln's eyes. On a snowy November 7, 1862, Maj. Gen. Ambrose Burnside, accompanied by Brig. Gen. Catharinus P. Buckingham, arrived at McClellan's headquarters, now located between Upperville and Rectortown, Virginia. Dispatched from Washington two days before, Buckingham's orders were to relieve McClellan and inform Burnside he was to take command of the Army of the Potomac.[12] The removal of George Brinton McClellan from command of the Army of the Potomac put the final punctuation mark on the Maryland Campaign of 1862 and closed this turbulent chapter of the war.

Unquestionably, the events that brought these two army commanders and their respective presidents to this point in time were not preordained. There was no divine hand steering the course of events here—even if many on both sides of the conflict believed this to be the case. On the contrary, the historical journey that brought these men to face one another from opposite sides of the Potomac at this exact moment was the direct and observable result of more than a few human beings making more than a few very critical decisions—including the choices of Robert E. Lee, George B. McClellan, and Abraham Lincoln.

To fully understand this journey, we must set the chronometer back to the first days of September 1862. At that time, the momentum of the war's Eastern Theater was arguably as one-sided as it would ever be for the Confederacy.

As summer waned the Civil War took on a decidedly gloomier tenor for the Union.

In March 1862, McClellan landed his massive army on the Virginia Peninsula. After several battles, three months, and dozens of miles marched, McClellan was finally within sight of Richmond. On June 31, the Confederate commander Joe Johnston was wounded, at the Battle of Seven Pines. Jefferson Davis immediately selected Robert E. Lee to take his place. On July 25 Lee attacked the Army of the Potomac. Throughout the Seven Days' Battles, this new aggressive Confederate commander drove McClellan's forces back from Richmond's gates and across the peninsula to the banks of the James River. This led general-in-chief Maj. Gen. Henry Halleck to order the evacuation of the Army of the Potomac. Eliminating that threat to the Confederate capital, Lee then advanced his army north, defeating Maj. Gen. John Pope's Army of Virginia at Cedar Mountain (August 19) and then at the Second Battle of Bull Run (August 28–30).[13] In a driving thunderstorm on September 1, Lee tried once again to get on Pope's flank near Chantilly, Virginia. After this inconclusive battle, Pope's Army of Virginia retreated into the defenses of Washington, DC. Lee, determined that he could no longer pursue the Federal troops, ordered his divisions to concentrate north toward the Potomac near a small Virginia crossroads called Dranesville. As the curtain came down on the Second Bull Run Campaign, the stage was now set for the next act. That act would be the Maryland Campaign of 1862.

In a mere two months, Lee's Army of Northern Virginia had accomplished one of the most remarkable reversals of fortune seen during the war.[14] On June 26 McClellan and the Army of the Potomac were five miles from the Confederate capital's outskirts at Richmond, and after battling two separate Union forces, Lee and his army were now twenty miles from the defensive works of Washington, DC.

One of Lee's most ardent enthusiasts described a defining quality of this new Confederate commander: "If there is one man in either army, Confederate or Federal, head and shoulders above every other in audacity, it is General Lee! His name might be Audacity. He will take more desperate chances, and take them quicker than any other general in this country, North or South; and you will live to see it, too."[15]

In the Western Theater, Union forces had made significant gains in the first half of 1862. The Tennessee and Cumberland Rivers had been opened by the Union after the victories at Forts Henry and Donelson in February. After two bloody days in April, the Confederates fell back from Shiloh, and by the end of May, they also evacuated Corinth, Mississippi. With much of Western Tennessee under Union control, New Orleans, the Confederacy's largest city at that time, was captured by the Federals on May 1. Consequentially, protecting the Confederate strongholds like Vicksburg on the Mississippi River became a top priority for the Confederacy. By August Confederate forces in the West were back on the offensive. In an attempt to reverse Federal gains of the previous spring, and to divert Union attention away from Vicksburg and Chattanooga, forces under Rebel commanders Gen. Braxton Bragg and Maj. Gen. Edmund Kirby Smith attempted to outflank Union major general Don Carlos Buell by launching an invasion deep into Kentucky.[16]

In Washington, DC, an overly optimistic Secretary of War Edwin Stanton had closed many Northern recruiting stations in April. Like many in the North, Stanton assumed that Confederate defeat in the spring of 1862 was a foregone conclusion, and that Union armies had all the men they would ever need. It was not until July 1 that he fully comprehended how wrong he was.[17] In the White House, pressure on the Lincoln administration was emerging from all sides. The 1862 midterm elections were slated for November, and any setback by the upstart Republican Party could upset the balance of political power. Abraham Lincoln had the dual challenge of fighting a Civil War while combating factions of Northern opposition. Some of the most vigorous of these adversaries were, in fact, Republicans just like Lincoln.

In August 1862, abolitionist and publisher Horace Greeley printed a scathing 2,200-word editorial titled "The Prayer of Twenty Millions." The article took Lincoln to task for numerous sins, including his general conduct of the war and his inaction regarding Southern slavery's destruction. Greeley accused the president of being "strangely and disastrously remiss in the discharge of . . . official and imperative duty." In addition, Lincoln was "unduly influenced by the counsels, the representations, the menaces, of certain fossil politicians hailing from the Border Slave States."[18]

Northern Democrats were not above hurling their own brand of hyperbolic rhetoric at the president. Like many of his fellow Democrats, Copperhead leader and former governor of Connecticut Thomas H. Seymour despised the administration and any Democrat who supported it. He charged these individuals with, in his words, "helping Lincoln carry on a war which is wicked and infamous beyond that of any previous war since the time of the Goths!"[19]

Perhaps the worst of all of the president's critics dwelled within his own party. The so-called Radical Republicans believed Lincoln was far too indulgent toward slavery and the South. Ohio senator Benjamin F. Wade, one of the faction's leaders, once referred to the president's views on slavery as follows: "[These notions] could only come of one born of poor white trash and educated in a slave State." Wade once callously referred to Lincoln's assassination as an opportunity for more determined leadership.[20]

President Abraham Lincoln, sixteenth
President of the United States. Library
of Congress.

While the Radical Republicans did not constitute a majority in the party, many sat on critical congressional committees like the Joint Committee on the Conduct of the War. The radicals' primary mission was to seek out and remove incompetent and disloyal officers. However, they absolutely reviled secessionists, slavery, and any Democrat whom they perceived as lenient toward the traitorous South, including George B. McClellan and his devotees.[21]

If all these circumstances were not enough for Lincoln to worry about, rumors abounded that Great Britain and France were poised to formally recognize the Confederacy. Such a decision threatened to bring an unwelcome shift in power to the conflict, one the Union was unlikely to recover from.

As the struggle at Manassas reached its climax, the Lincoln administration was facing yet another great calamity unfolding before its very eyes. Scores of defeated Union soldiers streamed into Washington, DC, in the wake of yet another humiliating defeat. A Confederate army that had seemingly been on the threshold of capitulation had somehow seized the initiative and was now on the offensive twenty miles from a capital on the verge of panic. The calamity facing the Union war effort was as dire as possible and worsening with every passing day.[22]

As one can imagine, the mood in Richmond was the exact opposite. In three months, Jefferson Davis had stopped asking where the Confederate government's seat should relocate to once Richmond fell and started asking Robert E. Lee what his next offensive move might be. History began to record Lee's storied reputation, which only grew over the next three years and beyond.[23]

On September 2, a jubilant Jefferson Davis issued a statement to the Confederate Congress extolling the army's virtues and commander.

> I have the gratification of presenting to Congress two dispatches from General Robert E. Lee, commanding the Army of Northern Virginia, communicating the result of the operations north of the Rappahannock. From these dispatches it will be seen that God has again extended his shield over our patriotic army, and has blessed the cause of the Confederacy with a second signal victory on the field already memorable by the gallant achievement of our troops. Too much praise cannot be bestowed upon the skill and daring of the commanding general who conceived, or the valor and hardihood of the troops who executed, the brilliant movement whose result is now communicated. After having driven from their intrenchments an enemy superior in numbers, and relieved from siege the city of Richmond, as heretofore communicated, our toil-worn troops advanced to meet another invading army re-enforced not only by the defeated army of the General McClellan, but by the fresh corps of Generals Burnside and Hunter. After forced marches, with inadequate transportation, and across streams swollen to unusual height, by repeated combats they turned the position of the enemy, and forming a junction of their columns in the face of greatly superior forces, they fought the decisive battle of the 30th, the crowning triumph of their toil and valor.[24]

Armed with renewed confidence and enthusiasm, the Confederate Army of Northern Virginia and its resolute commander were now poised to embark on one of the most critical Civil War campaigns. The decisions made over the course of the next three weeks would bring McClellan and Lee to battle three times in the farmlands of Maryland and Virginia, but they would also bring these officers to decidedly different ends once the campaign was over. The two men faced choices that would dramatically affect not only the outcome of the war, but also the course of the nation for decades to come.

CHAPTER 1

THE CAMPAIGN BEGINS,
SEPTEMBER 3–13, 1862

The Maryland Campaign of 1862 encompassed the Battle of Antietam and the Battles of South Mountain (Turner's, Fox's, and Crampton's Gaps), the Battle/Siege of Harpers Ferry, and the Battle of Shepherdstown. To fully comprehend these engagements, we must first understand the decisions that facilitated the two armies' movements beforehand. While not as well documented, the decisions reached from September 3 to September 13 are essential to comprehending this key Civil War campaign.

If you have skipped the preface, please return to it and read the definition of a critical decision to better understand the format in which this book is presented.

Lee Invades the North

Situation

By the beginning of September 1862, Robert E. Lee had been in command of the Army of Northern Virginia for a total of three months. During this time, he drove McClellan off the Virginia Peninsula and then defeated Pope at Cedar Mountain and Second Bull Run. In the process, Lee managed to shift the fighting in the Eastern Theater from Richmond's outskirts to the very fringes of Washington, DC. He had accomplished all of this in the face of an enemy that, at least on paper, outmatched him in almost every significant way: numbers of men, small arms, artillery, horses, and so forth. Northerners and Southerners who spoke openly of Confederate defeat at the beginning of 1862 now believed this new aggressive Rebel commander would likely bring the war into the very heart of the Union. In the early days of September 1862, this is precisely what Lee was considering.

After one last attempt to harass/attack Pope's flank at Chantilly, Lee and the Army of Northern Virginia compelled the Union Army of Virginia to fall back to the relative safety of the defensive works surrounding Washington, DC. Now positioned near Dranesville, Virginia, the Confederate commander contemplated his next move as his opponent continued east.[1]

His first task was to reinforce his army. Augmented by some twenty-five thousand men brought from Richmond, Lee now had about seventy thousand men of all arms as his army gathered south of the Potomac. To supplement the force that fought at Second Bull Run, Lee added the divisions of Maj. Gen. D. H. Hill, Maj. Gen. Lafayette McLaws, and Brig. Gen. John G. Walker; four battalions of reserve artillery; and the cavalry brigade of Brig. Gen. Wade Hampton. These reinforcements more than made up for Lee's losses at what came to be known as the Second Bull Run or Second Manassas Campaign.[2]

The army Lee led in September 1862 was organized into the "command" structure that had served him so well during the previous campaign. Longstreet's Command was led by Maj. Gen. James Longstreet, and it consisted of the three divisions commanded by Maj. Gen. Richard H. Anderson, Brig. Gen. David R. Jones, and Brig. Gen. John Bell Hood, in addition to an independent brigade under Brig. Gen. Nathan G. "Shanks" Evans. Jackson's Command was led by Maj. Gen. Thomas J. "Stonewall" Jackson, and it included the three divisions of Brig. Gen. Alexander R. Lawton, Maj. Gen. A. P. Hill, and Brig. Gen. John R. Jones. Lee also had three unattached divisions commanded by Maj. Gen. D. H. Hill, Maj. Gen. Lafayette McLaws, and Brig. Gen. John G. Walker.

A cavalry division under Maj. Gen. J. E. B. Stuart consisted of the brigades of Brig. Gen. Fitzhugh Lee, Brig. Gen. Wade Hampton, and Col. Thomas T. Munford, as well as the horse artillery commanded by Capt. John Pelham. Lee's reserve artillery was commanded by Brig. Gen. William N. Pendleton. This cadre of mostly skilled and experienced commanders formed the nucleus of Lee's army.[3]

Additionally, Lee's army had approximately 292 pieces of artillery as he staged his troops for the next campaign. These were primarily organized into eighty batteries attached to the various divisions and five battalions in the artillery reserve.[4]

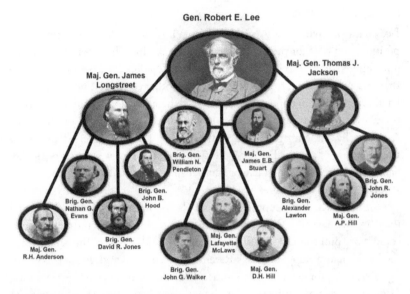

Army of Northern Virginia Organization, September 1862.

By Lee's own admission, the Army of Northern Virginia was not in the best physical shape as it was readied for its next move. For months many of his units had been fighting and marching almost continuously. Conversely, the Rebel commander's army was made up almost entirely of combat-tested veterans. Fifty-two percent of the army's infantry regiments had fought in three or more major battles, and 81 percent had fought in two or more. All of the 184 infantry regiments in Lee's army were veterans of at least one major engagement.[5]

To reduce his transportation needs on the next campaign, Lee took steps to strip his army down to all but the barest of essentials. Excess baggage, clothing, and equipment were to be left behind, as well as broken wagons and unfit horses.[6]

Options

With the Second Bull Run Campaign now complete, Lee had five operational choices available to him. He could stay in northern Virginia, withdraw to Richmond's vicinity, move to the Shenandoah Valley, cross the Potomac River and drive north, or march on Washington. Each of these options presented varying degrees of risk and possible reward. Robert E. Lee now had the very first of several critical decisions to make.

Option 1

Lee could stay where he was in northern Virginia, reinforce, strengthen his position, and wait for the Union forces to attack him. That area of north Virginia offered no real strategic advantage to the Confederates besides a location that was a day's march from Washington. Another consideration was that any Union forces sent to oppose Lee could outflank a position in the region using the Chesapeake Bay on one side or the Potomac upstream fords on the other. Additionally, remaining in the area would keep Lee that much farther away from his base of supply. Fairfax County, where his army was now positioned, had been occupied by one force or another since 1861 and had been completely stripped of food and forage.

Additionally, Lee's supply line from Richmond was 110 miles long, and the Virginia Central Railroad and the Orange and Alexandria Railroad could move provisions only sixty miles to the Rapidan River. The bridges over the Rapidan and Rappahannock Rivers had been destroyed. From this point, supplies, food, forage, and ammunition had to be transported the remaining distance by wagon. Unfortunately, Lee did not have the needed wagons or animals to sustain such a supply line. [7]

Option 2

Lee could decide that it was best to withdraw his forces to just south of the Rappahannock River or all the way to the vicinity of Richmond and go into a defensive posture to protect the Confederate capital. This option would undoubtedly solve his issues relating to logistics and position, as it had done for Confederate general Joe Johnston back in March.[8] On the downside, this decision would squander all the blood and treasure the Confederates had expended driving the enemy away from Richmond. If the Army of Northern Virginia abandoned the area north of the Rappahannock, the Federals would likely move to reoccupy the region. Moreover, if Lee and his men fell back from northern Virginia, they would give up all the advantages of initiative they had gained up until that point.

Option 3

Lee could move west into the Shenandoah Valley to rest and refit his wearied army. The valley offered plenty of food and shelter, and as Stonewall Jackson had shown the previous spring, it was a place where Southern troops could stand a reasonably good chance of gaining a defensive advantage against any Union advance. At this point in the war, the Shenandoah Valley had a tenuous communication line to Richmond. The line ran up the valley to Staunton from

Winchester, where the Virginia Central Railroad connected it to the Confederate capital. Lee could also use the valley as a potential avenue of invasion into the North, as he would do in 1863. Stonewall favored this course of action. Like Option 2, this plan would relinquish the Rebel initiative and leave any forces at Richmond beyond Lee's immediate support, and at this point in the war, the Confederate capital might be the objective of any future Federal offensive.[9]

Option 4

Lee could decide to move north and take the fight into the heart of the Union. From a strictly logistical standpoint, this was the riskiest of the five options because it would require the commander to significantly extend his supply lines, but his troops could potentially forage in the abundant and fertile farmlands of Maryland and Pennsylvania. This course of action would also leave Richmond with only a token force to guard it. However, by forcing the enemy to respond to his offensive, Lee could possibly prevent the Union from launching a renewed counteroffensive against a lightly defended Confederate capital. Moreover, moving his soldiers north would also allow Lee to keep the strategic initiative he had worked so hard to gain.

Option 5

Finally, Lee could march his army east and attack Washington, DC. Being a meticulous commander, the general would undoubtedly have considered this option. I speculate that he might have regarded the Union capital as a fantastic and tempting prize. While this enticing plan would not solve any of the aforementioned logistics problems, capturing the city would allow Lee to maintain the initiative.

The principal problem with this option was that Washington, DC, was heavily defended. A ring of fortified, interconnected strongpoints encircled the city, and over six hundred heavy guns guarded it. Lee no doubt knew the smaller caliber of his own field artillery would be wholly outmatched in such a contest. By this time, perhaps seventy thousand Union troops occupied the capital, not to mention the additional forty thousand soldiers of Pope's army who were now falling back into the city. Even if Lee did not know the exact number of these men and artillery, he undoubtedly believed it was substantial.[10]

Decision

Lee chose to invade the North (Option 4). The first three choices do not seem to have been practical options considering the style of offensive warfare he preferred. Possibly better than any other general in the war, Lee understood

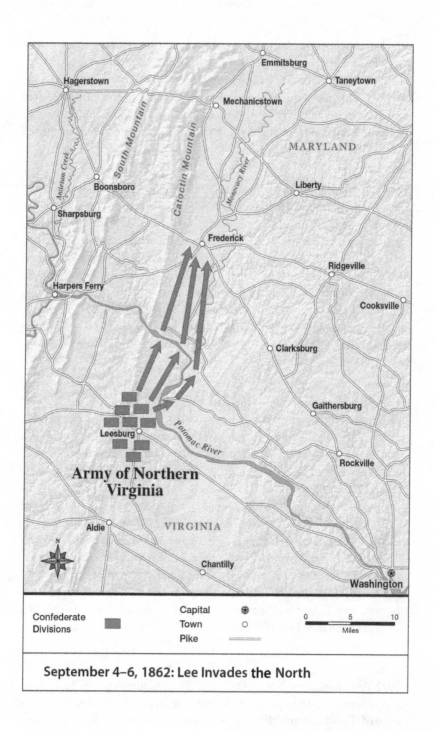

Emmitsburg

Hagerstown

Taneytown

Mechanicstown

MARYLAND

South Mountain

Catoctin Mountain

Antietam Creek

Boonsboro

Liberty

Sharpsburg

Monocacy River

Frederick

Harpers Ferry

Ridgeville

Cooksville

Clarksburg

Gaithersburg

Leesburg

Potomac River

Rockville

Army of Northern
Virginia

Aldie

VIRGINIA

N

Chantilly

Washington

Confederate
Divisions

Capital ⊛

Town ○

Pike ═══

0   5   10

Miles

September 4–6, 1862: Lee Invades the North

the advantages of gaining momentum and the means of maintaining it. He had worked hard to appropriate the initiative from McClellan and Pope, and he was not about to relinquish it. Options 1–3 would make it much simpler for the Union commander to reestablish his army's advantage.

Perhaps more clearly than any Confederate leader, Lee also understood that the South's hopes of victory and independence would not come from remaining on the defensive. His strategy suggests that he was unwilling to wait for the Union armies to come to him or box him in around or near Richmond. It is possible that Lee saw a static defense scenario as an open invitation for the Union to overwhelm Confederate troops with the superior weight of its war machine. Lee's actions also indicate that his chosen strategy, and the only chance for Confederate victory, was an aggressive offense: forcing whichever Union commander he encountered to react to him and his army, then dealing the Federals a fatal blow at the appropriate time.

It is likely Lee dismissed Option 5 out of hand. Even if the general believed that his men's mettle outweighed their physical condition, he surely understood that conducting a campaign of maneuver and a siege of a heavily fortified city were two very different things. In the end, he could sow nearly as much panic and consternation in the Northern populace just by being in proximity to Washington, and he could do so with far less risk to his army.

After contemplating all his options, Lee sent a dispatch to Confederate president Jefferson Davis on September 3, 1862, announcing his intention to take the war to the North:

> The present seems to be the most propitious time since the commencement of the war for the Confederate army to enter Maryland. . . . We cannot afford to be idle, and though weaker than our opponents in men and military equipments, must endeavor to harass if we cannot destroy them. I am aware that the movement is attended with much risk, yet I do not consider success impossible. [11]

Lee believed that the Army of the Potomac's recent defeats had left it demoralized, unorganized, beaten, and not at all ready for renewed fighting. In the Northern papers, he also read that Federal forces had received some sixty thousand raw recruits. Surely it would take time to train, coordinate, and incorporate these new men into the army. Lee believed that several weeks would pass before the Union army could get organized and come out of the Washington defenses to offer him battle.[12] Indeed, there is little doubt in the general's confidence that he had plenty of time to move deep into Union territory and conduct his campaign of maneuver before the Army of the Potomac could march out and threaten him.

Lee's invasion offered additional opportunities for the Confederacy. Lee was naturally concerned with what kind of reception his soldiers would receive in Maryland. Would the Army of Northern Virginia be seen as liberators or conquerors? Would Marylanders join his ranks or fight him? He really did not know. While in Leesburg, the general did spend a fair amount of time questioning native Marylander Col. Bradley T. Johnson, an officer in his army. Lee gleaned critical topographical information on Maryland from Johnson, and he also listened intently to the colonel's appraisal of the Maryland citizenry's general mood and feelings about the Confederacy. Johnson painted a somewhat gloomy picture for the Confederate commander, implying a frosty welcome for the Rebels in Maryland.

On the other hand, Lee had requested that exiled Maryland governor Enoch Louis Lowe accompany his troops into the state. Lowe might validate the Confederates' invasion and serve as a symbol to rally Marylanders to the Southern cause. Whatever reception Lee foresaw in Maryland, he determined to move forward. This suggests that he gave the appropriate consideration to the opinion of a single Maryland citizen. While eager to help, Lowe would not join Lee in time to influence anyone in the Old-Line State.[13]

Although modern scholarship debates this point, some evidence suggests that a Rebel victory on Northern soil would go a long way toward inducing European recognition of the Confederacy, possibly leading to some military aid or intervention. A politically savvy general, Lee also saw a potential victory north of the Potomac as a convenient way to sow discontent and fear in the Northern population, thereby influencing the upcoming midterm elections.

Most importantly, and above all other considerations, Lee wanted and needed a decisive military victory over the Union army. This was the point of the campaign. Even though he was keenly aware of political implications, it is essential not to lose sight of the fact that the military goals undergirding those political objectives were paramount in Lee's mind. He reasoned that advancing far enough into Maryland or possibly Pennsylvania could turn the Federals out of their Washington defenses. This development would compel Union forces to pursue him, traveling far from their base of supply and support. Lee would then deliver a knockout blow to make all the aforementioned objectives possible. As a result, the Confederacy would be holding all the cards and could negotiate separation from the Union from a position of strength. Lee further rationalized that this victory would undermine Northern morale, thus collapsing popular support for continuing the war.[14]

The general revealed his thinking in a September 8 letter to Davis written from Frederick, Maryland:

> Such a proposition, coming from us at this time, could in no way be regarded as suing for peace; but, being made when it is in our power to inflict injury upon our adversary, would show conclusively to the world that our sole object is the establishment of our independence and the attainment of an honorable peace. The rejection of this offer would prove to the country that the responsibility of the continuance of the war does not rest upon us, but that the party in power in the United States elect to prosecute it for purpose of their own. The proposal of peace would enable the people of the United States to determine at their coming elections whether they will support, those who favor a prolongation of the war, or those who wish to bring it to a termination, which can but be productive of good to both parties without affecting the honor of either.[15]

After the war, when an interviewer quizzed the former commanding general on the campaign in Maryland, Lee stated succinctly, "I went into Maryland to give battle, and could I have kept Gen. McClellan in ignorance of my positions and plans a day or two longer, I would have fought and crushed him." While other considerations were significant, it is evident from this statement that the Rebel commander had but one primary goal in mind for the invasion—a military victory on the field of battle, thus according the Confederacy a dominant political advantage.[16]

Results/Impact

Any number of events, not the least of which was a battle to be fought at Sharpsburg in two weeks, were tied to Lee's decision. The next decision resulted directly from the general's advance into the North. Part of the reason that McClellan was put in command and Pope dismissed was the Rebel incursion into Maryland, which placed extreme pressure on the Lincoln administration. When Lee crossed the Potomac into Maryland, he posed a real threat to the Union and consequently changed the course of future events. Had the Confederate general not done so, Pope might have remained in command of some portion of the army for several more weeks or months. The two principal eastern Union armies might not have been combined into one. Most importantly, this first decision of the campaign was perhaps the most critical of all. Had it not been made, there would have been no Maryland Campaign,

The Army of Northern Virginia crossing the Potomac, circa 1862. Harpers Weekly.

Battles of South Mountain, Battle of Harpers Ferry, and Battle of Antietam. All other critical decisions going forward flowed from Lee's first decision.

On September 4, 1862, Lee's Army of Northern Virginia began to cross the Potomac River near Leesburg at White's and Cheek's Fords, and near Point of Rocks about twenty-five miles upstream from Washington, DC. Lee's decision gives us great insight into his thought processes, how he fought the war from this point forward, and how he had mostly been fighting it since the start of the Seven Days' Battles. When given a choice, the Rebel commander preferred aggressiveness. As Lee urged his army across the Potomac River's chilly waters, he inaugurated what came to be known as the Maryland Campaign of 1862.[17]

Alternate Decision/Scenario

Had Lee concluded that his army was far too weak and used up to conduct a prolonged campaign in Maryland, he might have decided to move into the Shenandoah Valley to rest and refit (Option 3). Any number of scenarios could have evolved from that choice. Lee might have left in place some of the reinforcements added before the campaign to defend Richmond, then moved the rest of his army to Winchester. En route, he might have detached a force to capture Harper's Ferry. Lee could conceivably have remained unmolested in the valley for several weeks while the Lincoln administration sorted out

Potomac River at White's Ford, Virginia Side, modern image. Author.

its own military situation and determined its next move. Without the added pressure of a large Confederate force north of the Potomac, this process could possibly have taken several weeks. We might have seen a renewed Union advance toward Richmond or some other Federal offensive scenario as a result. In fact, we might have seen almost anything except what actually happened. Alternatively, Lee could have rested in the valley until he felt his army was in prime fighting shape and advanced on Maryland via the Shenandoah as he did in May and June 1863.

McClellan Takes Command

Situation

By September 1, 1862, the full breadth of the Federal military disaster at Second Bull Run was revealed to the Lincoln administration and the Northern population at large. Pope's defeated Army of Virginia was now retreating into Washington. This circumstance, combined with McClellan's recent Peninsula Campaign debacle, quickly evolved into the president's worst-case scenario. Some twenty miles from the nation's capital, the Army of Northern Virginia was now free to roam wherever it pleased, and the Union army was seemingly powerless to stop it. This outcome did not generate the same level of panic as the Union's first retreat from Manassas thirteen months before, but it was extremely problematic in its own right. Adding to Lincoln's miseries, Confederate forces were also advancing into Tennessee and Kentucky. He was now facing some of the darkest days of his presidency.[18]

The Federals' first priority was to defend Washington, DC. In retrospect, we know that the likelihood of Lee attacking Washington was nonexistent. However, no amount of logical argument would have persuaded those living in the city in September 1862 otherwise. At the forefront of those overly concerned with a Rebel attack on the capital was Union general-in-chief Henry Wager Halleck. Halleck was convinced that the Union capital was the target of Lee's invasion, and that the Confederate plan was to dupe McClellan into an advance northwest and then double back on the capital. Halleck held this belief almost up until the clash at Sharpsburg began.[19]

With each passing day, the tension in the capital city and the nation as a whole grew. As Lee began his crossing on September 4, 1862, rumors and panic in the North increased with every mile the Rebels marched. The *New York Times* called the Confederate offensive "a Barbarian Invasion of the North." Lawyer and diarist George Templeton Strong noted, "I fear our army is in no condition to cope with Lee's barefooted, ragged, lousy, disciplined, desperate ruffians. They may get to Philadelphia or New York or Boston, for fortune is apt to smile on audacity and resolution." And on September 5, Henry Halleck seemed to confirm the administration's worst fears, stating, "I think there can now be no doubt that the enemy are crossing the Potomac in force."[20]

Beset from all sides by detractors and military catastrophes, Lincoln had to do something. The president was under ever-increasing pressure to make a command change. One more reverse, especially on Union soil, could be disastrous. To further add to his troubles, Lincoln encountered crisis within his administration. Led by Secretary of War Edwin M. Stanton and Secretary of the Treasury Salmon P. Chase, a number of the president's cabinet members demanded McClellan's dismissal for disobeying orders and failing to adequately support Pope at Second Bull Run. Lincoln was feeling additional pressure from antiwar Democrats and Radical Republicans, who often criticized his every move. Meanwhile, presumably sitting in a drawer someplace in the White House, the Emancipation Proclamation was symbolically waiting for the political and military opportunity to give itself life.

McClellan assumed authority over Pope's forces by presidential edict as they fell back into Washington, DC. Halleck and Lincoln had ordered McClellan to take command of the capital's defenses and all the troops therein. As it was becoming more and more apparent that a Union force would eventually have to march out and meet the Confederate invaders, one question

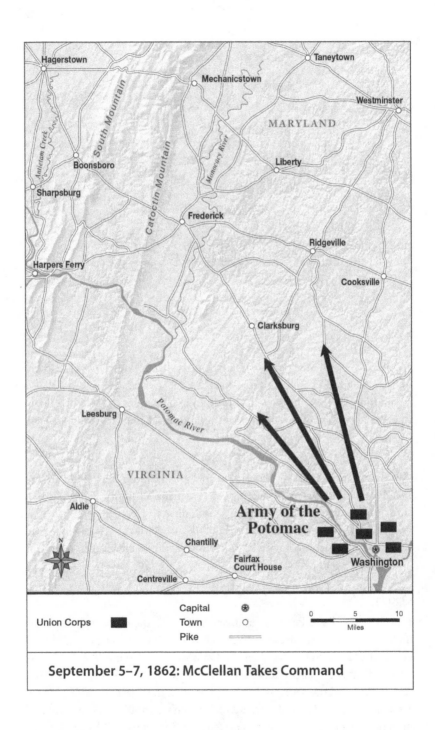

Hagerstown

South Mountain

Antietam Creek

Boonsboro

Sharpsburg

Harpers Ferry

Mechanicstown

Taneytown

Westminster

MARYLAND

Monocacy River

Liberty

Catoctin Mountain

Frederick

Ridgeville

Cooksville

Clarksburg

Potomac River

Leesburg

VIRGINIA

Aldie

Chantilly

Fairfax
Court House

Centreville

**Army of the
Potomac**

Washington

N

Union Corps	■	Capital	⊛	0		5		10
		Town	○			Miles		
		Pike	═══					

September 5–7, 1862: McClellan Takes Command

President Abraham Lincoln, 16th
President of the United States.
Library of Congress.

remained on everyone's mind. That question was, "Who would lead this army?" When combined with the Washington garrison, this force swelled to over 140,000 men. Who was capable of leading this host, or at least a part of it, out of the safety of the city's defenses to confront Lee's invading legions?[21]

Options

Abraham Lincoln had several options open to him: keeping Pope in command and combining the two armies under his authority, looking to the corps commander for a replacement, combining all forces under McClellan, or giving the assignment to Henry Halleck, or. With the Confederate invasion growing more oppressive by the moment, President Lincoln now had a critical decision to make.

Option 1

Lincoln could leave Pope in command and place the corps of both armies under him. Pope was already commanding the Army of Virginia and those attached units from the Army of the Potomac. It would not have been challenging to add the remainder of the Army of the Potomac's corps to his command. Pope had the necessary rank and position in the army, and he was also a staunch Republican and a friend of Lincoln's from his days in Illinois. It must be remembered that politics played a significant role in the conflict. The

Joint Committee on the Conduct of the War was enormously active, looking for conspiracies and disloyal officers wherever it could find them. Although Lincoln usually kept his own counsel as to who would command his armies, he certainly understood the nature of the current political climate, which was unfriendly to those who appeared disloyal to the Union.

While tarnished by his recent defeat, Pope might be a politically safe choice for Lincoln. Moreover, Pope was the preferred choice among Republicans in the North who favored conducting the war with the Rebels sans the kid-gloves policy they perceived McClellan engaged in. [22]

Option 2

Lincoln could select his next army commander from the pool of current corps commanders. A list of potential candidates might include Maj. Gen. Fitz John Porter, Maj. Gen. William B. Franklin, Maj. Gen. Jesse Reno, Maj. Gen. Joseph Hooker, or even Maj. Gen. Ambrose Burnside. Of these, only Burnside had ever held an independent command. It was also thought that Burnside had no real political ambitions, although he and McClellan were close friends. Both McClellan confederates, Porter and Franklin, were accused by Pope of failure to obey orders and were subject to court-martial.[23]

Option 3

Lincoln could conclude that giving McClellan overall command of the combined force was his best option. Some students of the Civil War mistakenly believe that McClellan was relieved of his command of the Army of the Potomac; he was not. He was simply a commander with a significantly smaller army to lead, as it was stripped away from him a piece at a time to reinforce Pope and the perceived threat to the capital. Some forces did remain under McClellan's command after the Peninsula Campaign ended. Additionally, by September 2, he already had control of the Washington garrison that defended the city and Pope's forces currently falling back from Bull Run and Chantilly.

McClellan certainly had the men's confidence from the Army of the Potomac; they preferred him, to be sure. On the other hand, McClellan was a Democrat, and the list of his political adversaries in Washington was growing longer every day.[24]

Option 4

Lincoln could order general-in-chief Maj. Gen. General Henry W. Halleck to take command of the field army. There is good evidence to indicate that

Lincoln considered giving control of this force to Halleck. Authors D. Scott Hartwig and Curt Anders suggest that when the president issued orders on September 3 to "organize an army for active operations"[25] but named no specific person to lead it, he hoped Halleck would take the hint and command it himself. No one knows if this was indeed the case, but Lincoln might have been looking for a less controversial option. Halleck certainly had the requisite rank and experience for command at this level, although he was often regarded as a better military theorist than an actual practitioner of operations in the field. John Pope, who was no fan of McClellan, also asked that Halleck step in and take a field command role. However, evidence also suggests the stress of his new position as general-in-chief had taken a toll on Halleck. His letters to his wife denote a reluctance to take on even more responsibility than his current job involved.[26]

Decision

Abraham Lincoln initially offered the command to Ambrose Burnside (Option 2), who declined it. Perhaps feeling some commitment to his old friend while doubting his abilities, Burnside told Lincoln that McClellan was the only man for the job. The president ultimately placed McClellan in command (Option 3).

Pope was eliminated from consideration, no doubt due to his recent Second Bull Run defeat. It could be argued that McClellan had quite a bit to do with Pope's downfall, but Pope's mishandling of the recent campaign seems to have sealed his fate. As far as Fitz John Porter and Joe Hooker were concerned, difficulties arose. Porter was considered too deeply embroiled in politics to be a practical choice, and he had only recently been accused of insubordination by Pope. Hooker had a somewhat unsavory reputation that seemed to make him an unpopular candidate. Despite some very vocal opposition from his cabinet, Lincoln reluctantly put George B. McClellan in command of the field army. In a statement that sounded like he was settling for the best of the worst possible options, the president told his private secretary John Hay, "We must use the tools we have."[27]

Campaign scholars debate whether Lincoln or Halleck ordered McClellan to take field command and confront Lee's invasion, or whether this decision formally took place. This is because, to date, no written order signed by either Lincoln or Halleck and specifically directing McClellan to assume command has surfaced. Many correctly point out that there was no need for a formal written order because McClellan was never relieved of command of the Army of the Potomac.

A dispatch dated September 3, over the president's name, was sent to

Halleck by Stanton. It ordered the formation of an active army but made no mention of its commander or designation. Halleck relayed that directive to McClellan the same day. Communicating with McClellan on September 5, Halleck again discussed a field army's formation without specifying its commander. In his testimony before the Joint Committee on the Conduct of the War, Halleck asserted,

> I think General McClellan left Washington and established his headquarters at Rockville on the 7th of September. He left here sometime in the afternoon or the night of the 7th; whether he got to Rockville before midnight or not, I cannot say. He had been directed some days before by the President to take the field against the enemy in Maryland.[28]

McClellan sent a message to Halleck dated September 6 requesting the suspension of the arrests of Generals Porter and Franklin until the "current difficulty" was over, and likewise asking that Joe Hooker be given command of Irvin McDowell's Third Corps (redesignated the First Corps) from the Army of Virginia. Was this just part of McClellan fulfilling his mandate to create a "movable force," or was he merely taking steps to create a command structure within an army he knew he would eventually lead, and that was more to his liking?[29]

D. Scott Hartwig points to the president as the decision-maker as well. Hartwig describes a September 7 visit to McClellan's Washington headquarters by Lincoln and Halleck:

> On the morning of September 7, Halleck accompanied Lincoln to McClellan's home on H Street "about 9 o'clock in the morning." Halleck recalled that at first there was some discussion between the three men, and then the president told McClellan, "General, you will take command of the forces in the field." With this simple order the question of command was settled. [30]

McClellan himself liked to recall after the war how he took command and set out after Lee without official authorization from either the president or the general-in-chief and risked his life and reputation by doing so. On the other hand, Dr. Tom Clemens writes that Lincoln and Halleck named each other the decision-maker, perhaps indicating that each man sought to shield himself from blame should the campaign end in disaster. Ultimately, and despite all the speculations and contradictions, one has to believe that even if Lincoln deferred to Halleck to deliver the message of command to McClellan, he would indeed have made his preference known to the general-in-chief.[31]

Based on communications from September 7 to and from McClellan in the *Official Records*, there seems to be little doubt that Halleck was issuing orders as if McClellan was commanding the field army by that date. As events occurred in such a confusing manner in those early September days, a timeline is included here:

> August 30—The Second Battle of Bull Run ends.
>
> August 31—The remnants of Pope's army continue to retreat into Washington. Henry Halleck wires McClellan and asks him to report to Washington, DC, to help him in the current crisis.
>
> September 1—The Battle of Chantilly takes place. Lincoln and Halleck meet with McClellan to inquire as to accusations that McClellan deliberately withheld troops from Pope during the Battle of Second Bull Run. Lincoln asks McClellan to take command of the city's defenses and Pope's forces as they return. The reorganization of the armies into one begins.
>
> September 2—Lincoln informs his cabinet that McClellan's appointment is temporary because he is a good organizer, but the president believes the general incapable of offensive warfare. Official orders are issued giving McClellan command of the Washington fortifications. McClellan rides out from the capital to meet Pope, informing him of the change in leadership.
>
> September 3—Pope orally presents his report on the defeat at Second Bull Run to Lincoln. Orders are issued to organize an army for active field operations.
>
> September 4—The Army of Northern Virginia begins to cross the Potomac.
>
> September 5—Pope is officially relieved of command. Lincoln offers Burnside the position. Burnside declines and tells the president that McClellan is the man for the job. Corps commanders are ordered to prepare to march with three days' rations.
>
> September 6—McClellan sends a message to Halleck asking to have the arrests of Generals Porter and Franklin sus-

pended until the current crisis is over and requesting that Joe Hooker assume command of McDowell's corps.

September 7—McClellan is ordered to take command of the field army and confront Robert E. Lee. McClellan and his staff depart Washington, DC, that same evening. [32]

Results/Impact

McClellan's assumption of command was critical because he and his leadership style drove the campaign's course and the coming battles. Subsequent events were influenced in large part by the decisions the commanding general did or did not make. Additionally, the Army of the Potomac's organization for this campaign resulted directly from Lincoln's selection for commander. As we will discuss later on, McClellan's management of Federal troops even motivated several of Robert E. Lee's choices. The speed at which the army marched, the command and control the soldiers exhibited, the manner in which the battles unfolded, and the way the Union reserves were used or not used, were all tied directly to the decision to place McClellan in command.

When the clash at Antietam ended and the Confederates withdrew across the Potomac, McClellan saw this outcome as a complete success and the ultimate goal of his Maryland operation. This perspective was the exact opposite of Abraham Lincoln's. [33] On paper, McClellan had an army numbering just shy of 100,000 men of all arms, and 85,000 troops were under his direct command on September 17. On September 7, when he departed Washington, McClellan probably had 87,000 men in total and about 72,000 combat effectives. Best estimates indicate that he eventually had about 79,000 soldiers present at Sharpsburg, representing approximately 70,000 combat effectives. McClellan ultimately got roughly 56,000 engaged on September 17. This number does not include the garrisons of Harpers Ferry and Martinsburg that totaled around 14,000 men combined. Perhaps 20 percent of this Union force consisted of troops so green they had neither fired their weapons in anger nor learned the complicated maneuvers essential to Civil War–era armies.

McClellan's new command, still designated the Army of the Potomac, was organized into six corps. The First Corps, formerly the Army of Virginia Third Corps, was commanded by Maj. Gen. Joseph Hooker. The Second Corps was commanded by Maj. Gen. Edwin V. Sumner. Maj. Gen. Fitz John Porter led the Fifth Corps, which joined the Army of the Potomac after it left Washington, DC. Maj. Gen. William B. Franklin headed the Sixth Corps and its attachment from the Fourth Corps division of Maj. Gen. Darius N. Couch. The Ninth Corps, with the Kanawha Division attached, was commanded by Brig. Gen. Jesse Reno (Brig. Gen. Jacob D. Cox

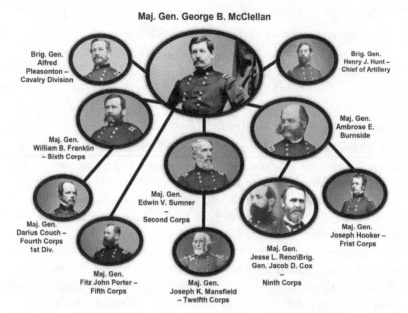

Maj. Gen. George B. McClellan

Brig. Gen. Alfred Pleasonton – Cavalry Division

Brig. Gen. Henry J. Hunt – Chief of Artillery

Maj. Gen. William B. Franklin – Sixth Corps

Maj. Gen. Ambrose E. Burnside

Maj. Gen. Edwin V. Sumner – Second Corps

Maj. Gen. Darius Couch – Fourth Corps 1st Div.

Maj. Gen. Joseph Hooker – Frist Corps

Maj. Gen. Fitz John Porter – Fifth Corps

Maj. Gen. Joseph K. Mansfield – Twelfth Corps

Maj. Gen. Jesse L. Reno\Brig. Gen. Jacob D. Cox – Ninth Corps

Union Army of the Potomac Organization, September 1862.

eventually took over after Reno was killed at South Mountain, and Burnside ostensibly commanded at Antietam). The First Corps Army of Virginia was renamed the Eleventh Corps, Army of the Potomac. It was left behind to rest and refit. The Twelfth Corps, formerly the Second Corps of the Army of Virginia, was led by Maj. Gen. Joseph Mansfield (Mansfield took command on September 15 after its former commander, Nathanael Banks was left behind to command the Washington garrison). Brig. Gen. Alfred Pleasonton headed McClellan's cavalry, and Brig. Gen. Henry Hunt was the army's chief of artillery.[34]

The herculean task McClellan faced in early September 1862 and the remarkableness of his performance are often downplayed. For all intents and purposes, he took parts of five separate commands,[35] including all those raw recruits, folded them into one capable fighting force, and then almost wholly restructured his army at the corps level. Furthermore, he accomplished all this organization, prepared this force for offensive operations in less than a week, and marched it out of Washington to face an enemy of unknown strength and intention. This metamorphosis was no small feat, and even Robert E. Lee did not believe it possible. The Confederate commander paid the price for underestimating his Union opponent.[36]

This latest version of the Army of the Potomac was now McClellan's once again, and its performance in the coming days is irrevocably linked to his legacy. The next two weeks' events unfolded as they did primarily because of the commanding general's actions or lack thereof.

Alternate Decision/Scenario

Had Burnside accepted the command, as he eventually did in November 1862, there is good reason to believe the Maryland Campaign's outcome would not have been the one history records. It is safe to say that Burnside was a very different leader than McClellan was. Had he agreed to Lincoln's offer, we would be looking at different operations and battles and at a different army organization altogether. While I could probably write a whole chapter on what might have happened had Ambrose Burnside commanded the army during the Maryland Campaign, I would instead ask you to read any number of accounts on the Battle of Fredericksburg and decide for yourself. While it is possible that Burnside's leadership might have still led to a clash at Antietam, one thing is certain: scores of tourists would now not be visiting Burnside Bridge at the Antietam Battlefield every year. As commander, Burnside might have reached many places on the field. But he would not have led the Ninth Corps to capture the iconic bridge that now bears his name.

McClellan and his staff, circa March 1862. Library of Congress.

Henry Halleck Does Not Evacuate Harpers Ferry

Situation

Henry Wager Halleck was born in 1815 to a father who was a veteran of the War of 1812. The younger Halleck graduated third in his West Point class of 1839 as a second lieutenant. After Gen. Winfield Scott sent him on a trip to Europe in 1844 to study the continent's fortifications, Halleck returned to America as a first lieutenant. Over the next several years, Halleck gave multiple lectures and wrote a number of books on military professionalism. His scholarly pursuits earned him the nickname "Old Brains," which was later used pejoratively.

During the Mexican War, Halleck was assigned to duty in California. He was awarded a brevet promotion to captain in 1847, then promoted to captain in the regular army on July 1, 1853. Halleck was later appointed military secretary of California and a major general of the California Militia by early 1861.

Once the Civil War broke out, Halleck was elevated to the rank of major general in the regular army in August 1861 and assigned to command the Department of the Missouri. During his time in the West, he established an uneasy relationship with Brig. Gen. Ulysses S. Grant. Halleck parlayed the Union's early success in the region into an opportunity to request overall command in the Western Theater. In 1862, his command was enlarged to

Maj. Gen. Henry W. Halleck, General-in-Chief, Union Army. Library of Congress.

include Ohio and Kansas and retitled the Department of the Mississippi. Impressed by Halleck's reputation as a military scholar and the recent victories in the West, President Lincoln summoned him to the East to become general-in-chief of all the Union armies in July 1862. While he was not an incompetent leader, Halleck was sometimes described as aloof. As general-in-chief he often had difficulty imposing discipline or direction on his field commanders. George B. McClellan, for example, who did not like Halleck, routinely ignored his advice and instructions.[37]

As Robert E. Lee began his advance into the North, he counted on several things happening so that his campaign would unfold as he had envisioned. First of all, given its current military situation, he relied on the Union army to be slow in its pursuit. Secondly, Lee assumed he could gather supplies for his army from the abundant Maryland farmlands. Lastly, he counted on the Union garrisons in the lower Shenandoah, including those at Harpers Ferry and Martinsburg, to follow proper military logic and evacuate once the Rebels outflanked their positions. Not withdrawing these garrisons proved one of the most critical decisions of the entire campaign.

Once Lee stepped into Maryland, it served his overall plan to push west over the Catoctin and South Mountain ranges. The mountains provided a natural barrier between the Confederates and their Union adversaries. It also drew the Federals that much farther away from the relative safety of the Washington defenses. Finally, Lee could use the Shenandoah Valley as his supply line and as a possible line of retreat. The Federal garrisons at Harpers Ferry and Martinsburg were now a genuine obstacle to that plan.[38]

As Col. Dixon S. Miles, the garrison commander at Harpers Ferry, was not directly under McClellan's command, McClellan could not order him to evacuate the position without permission from Halleck, the general-in-chief. According to McClellan, he advised Stanton and Halleck that the garrison be evacuated as early as September 4. As the Union commander was approaching Frederick, Maryland, on September 11, he sent the following in a dispatch to Halleck:

> I would also advise that the force of Colonel Miles, at Harpers Ferry, where it can be of but little use, and is continually exposed to be cut off by the enemy, be immediately ordered here. This would add about 25,000 old troops to our present force and would greatly strengthen us.[39]

The garrisons of Martinsburg and Harpers Ferry only totaled approximately fourteen thousand men when combined, but McClellan assessed the

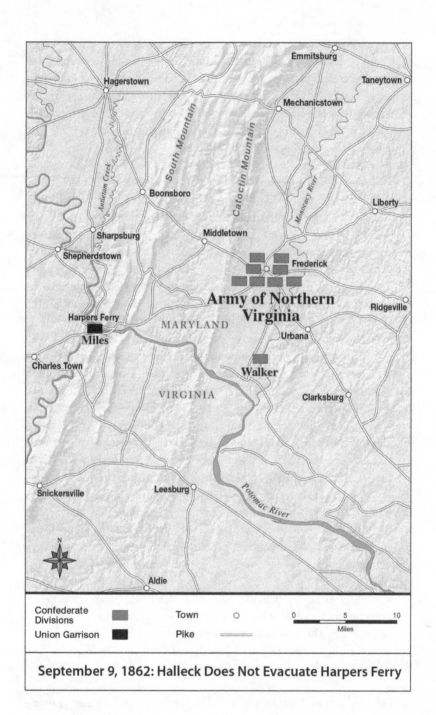

Emmitsburg

Taneytown

Hagerstown

Mechanicstown

South Mountain

Catoctin Mountain

Monocacy River

Antietam Creek

Boonsboro

Liberty

Middletown

Sharpsburg

Shepherdstown

Frederick

**Army of Northern
Virginia**

Ridgeville

Harpers Ferry

MARYLAND

Urbana

Miles

Charles Town

Walker

Clarksburg

VIRGINIA

Snickersville

Leesburg

Potomac River

N

Aldie

Confederate
Divisions

Town

Union Garrison

Pike

0   5   10
Miles

September 9, 1862: Halleck Does Not Evacuate Harpers Ferry

situation correctly. Miles reported to the department head, Maj. Gen. John E. Wool, who was his staunch supporter and friend. Yet it was Maj. Gen. Henry W. Halleck as general-in-chief who eventually made the decision concerning evacuation.[40]

Military doctrine specifies that a position should be evacuated once the enemy outflanks it; otherwise, the risk of the position being cut off or captured is magnified. Harpers Ferry was easily isolated, and it could be a complicated place to defend. Was it only a matter of time before the garrison fell and the fourteen thousand troops there became prisoners? On the other hand, could the protectors of Harpers Ferry somehow put up a reasonable defense and hold out until relief came? Could an intelligent and resourceful commander make a formidable stand from, for example, Maryland Heights? Halleck suggested this plan on September 5.[41]

Harpers Ferry was a logistically meaningful communication and transportation hub. It marked the confluence of two major rivers, and it controlled access to the lower Shenandoah Valley. More importantly, Harpers Ferry was situated at the junction of the Baltimore and Ohio and the Winchester and Potomac rail lines. Finally, the Chesapeake and Ohio Canal, which shadowed the Potomac River, ran adjacent to the town.[42]

Options

As general-in-chief, Halleck had two options from which to choose. He could evacuate the garrisons at Harpers Ferry and Martinsburg or leave them where they were.

Option 1

Halleck could order Miles and Brig. Gen. Julius White, the commander at Martinsburg, to abandon their posts and attempt to join McClellan's forces. The garrison at Winchester, Virginia, was already evacuated, so it seems army command deemed some Union posts in the lower Shenandoah less valuable than those who garrisoned them. Ironically, the commander at the Winchester post was General White. White was ordered to evacuate Winchester on September 2 and move his command to Martinsburg. As early as September 5, Halleck himself speculated that the Confederate plan might be to attack and overwhelm the garrison at Harpers Ferry. [43]

The farther west the Confederate army advanced, the more complicated an evacuation became for Harpers Ferry's men. This removal would be difficult, but it would not be impossible. As late as September 12, an escape route to the east was theoretically available to allow Miles to link up with Franklin's

Sixth Corps, advancing up the Potomac River's north bank.[44] Fourteen hundred cavalry troopers ostensibly led by Col. Benjamin Franklin "Grimes" Davis managed to escape Harpers Ferry on the night of September 14–15. Breaking out with fourteen hundred mounted men and escaping with what amounted to an entire infantry corps are two very different things, but the option was available to the Federals.[45]

This choice would abandon the critical Harpers Ferry junction to the enemy without a fight, but it would save the troops there to fight another day. Even if the Federals did relinquish Harpers Ferry, there was no reason to believe they could not capture it again. As a matter of fact, the town changed hands eight times between 1861 and 1865, and the Army of the Potomac retook control of the town only a few days after the Battle of Antietam. Did Halleck believe holding the position provided a distinct tactical or strategic advantage? Could these forces be in a position to aid McClellan should Lee double back on Washington?[46]

Option 2

Halleck could order the garrison to stay as it was and defend the position. This option might offer some advantage in being in Lee's midst to harass him or delay his plans, forcing him to deal with such a massive stronghold sitting in his rear. Halleck could conclude that ordering Miles to stay as he was might disrupt Lee's plans. The general-in-chief believed Washington was the real objective of the Confederate advance, and all else was a ruse. This idea might have been in his mind for some time, perhaps making him think the garrison was in no real danger.

Most importantly, Halleck had to consider real political issues that had nothing to do with the military situation. Given the recent string of Union defeats, he might be reluctant to relinquish what was a critical transportation hub without a fight. Giving up key territory to the Rebels might add to the administration's political and public relations woes. Vocal critics in the North eagerly exaggerated any mistake, real or imagined, committed by the Lincoln administration.

Decision

Halleck decided Harpers Ferry should be held, and he ordered Miles and his men to remain in place and defend the position (Option 2). Halleck was determined to maintain these positions for some reason known only to him. Perhaps he believed Harpers Ferry was just too critical to give up without a fight, or perhaps he thought McClellan would be able to save the garrison.

The general-in-chief could also have had an entirely different reason for his choice. Whatever the reason, once the Army of Northern Virginia outflanked and surrounded the garrison, the point was made moot.[47]

Results/Impact

Holding Harpers Ferry, one of the most critical decisions of the campaign, proved a pivotal moment. Robert E. Lee suddenly had to put his operation on hold and figure out how to solve this dilemma. He had to determine what, if anything, he needed to do about the Union forces along his lines of communication. Little did he realize that his course of action in early September set off an ongoing chain of decisions and events resulting in the battles at South Mountain and the siege of Harpers Ferry. In the end, Halleck's choice led both armies to the banks of Antietam Creek and to America's bloodiest day.

Halleck eventually gave McClellan responsibility for and authority over the garrison, but it was too late by then. McClellan was never able to effectively communicate with Miles and the ill-fated garrison troops to order them to do anything, and thus their fate was sealed. Halleck could not have imagined how far-reaching his decision would be.[48] Indeed, Halleck's determination to hold Harpers Ferry led Robert E. Lee to make a critical decision of his own. On September 9, Lee actively responded to the Harpers Ferry garrison, further shaping events. The root cause of the battle along the Antietam's banks on September 17 can be directly traced to Halleck's choice.

Alternate Decision/Scenario

Had Halleck decided to evacuate the garrisons, history might have been recalled very differently than it is now. It goes without saying that if Harpers Ferry and Martinsburg had been abandoned, Lee would not have been compelled to divide his army to deal with them. Given that circumstance, every event thereafter would inevitably have been altered. Lee might have moved his forces unimpeded and uninterrupted northwest to Hagerstown, or north to Chambersburg, Gettysburg, or possibly even Harrisburg. Without Harpers Ferry to contend with, a decisive battle in the waning days of the summer of 1862 might have been fought at any one of those locations. Or it might not have taken place at all.

Without the garrison in Lee's way, it is safe to assume that Special Orders 191 dividing his army and eliminating the garrison would not have been issued, lost, and subsequently found by the Union army. As all these events led the opposing forces to an eventual clash at Sharpsburg, would a Battle of Antietam even have occurred if Halleck had evacuated the garrison? If so,

Harpers Ferry from Maryland Heights, modern image. Author.

the fighting might have taken place several days later as Lee fell back from a possible battle in Pennsylvania. Had Halleck chosen differently, Sharpsburg might today be just one more nondescript, sleepy little town in western Maryland.

Interestingly, when Lee invaded the North again in 1863 during the Gettysburg Campaign, Harpers Ferry was at the forefront of the action once more. This time, the Rebel general advanced northward down the Shenandoah Valley, driving Union forces before him as he went. All indications were that he intended to ignore the Federal force at Harpers Ferry as his soldiers proceeded. Ironically, in June's last days, Henry Halleck was engaged in a running argument with Maj. Gen. Joseph Hooker, the current army commander, over Hooker's desire to evacuate the Harpers Ferry garrison and add those men to his army. Hooker eventually resigned his command over this quarrel. His replacement, George Meade, immediately made the same request of Halleck. This time it was granted, and Harpers Ferry was abandoned.[49]

Lee Divides His Army

Situation

One of the most analyzed and often overanalyzed episodes in Civil War lore concerns Lee's decision to divide his army and the fate of the so-called Lost Orders or Lost Dispatch, as it is sometimes known. To write a book, article, or paper on the Maryland Campaign or the Battle of Antietam without devoting at least some text or a passing mention to the Lost Orders would be committing historical blasphemy. This subject has become forever intertwined with the narrative of the campaign. Moreover, the questions and circumstances of Special Orders 191 have become one of history's most enduring mysteries. Why Lee did what he did, how the order was mislaid, and how McClellan supposedly failed to capitalize on the most significant intelligence find in military history are topics Civil War scholars and enthusiasts love to debate endlessly. As tempting as it would be to add a voice to this chorus, we will focus only on the critical decisions connected to the order's loss. Because it is impossible to state unequivocally how the document went astray, it is equally impossible to characterize that loss as a critical decision. Therefore, the subject of how the orders became misplaced is classified merely as an event, albeit a very significant one.

No sooner than it crossed the Potomac, Lee's army began to converge on Frederick, Maryland. For the next several days, the general paused to rest his men and attempt to secure supplies. Lee also wanted to use this time to see what, if anything, the Union army would do in response to his invasion.[50]

Because Lee now desired to move west of the Catoctin and South Mountain ranges, he needed to find a more secure route for communication and

Confederates in Frederick, Maryland, circa 1862. Historical Society of Frederick County (Maryland).

supplies. He had counted on greater availability of supplies from the citizens of Maryland. Because those supplies were not forthcoming, he was forced to bring his provisions up from the depot he had established at Winchester, Virginia. Lee also saw these mountains as a natural barrier ideally suited for defense. Additionally, as he knew the Union army would eventually have to come out to fight him, Lee desired to pull those troops as far from Washington, DC, as he could. Doing so would keep the Federals from quickly reinforcing from the capital city once the decisive battle began.[51]

There was, however, one small obstruction to this plan. The Union garrisons at Harpers Ferry and Martinsburg, which were in the lower Shenandoah, had not evacuated as Lee anticipated they would, leaving him to resolve a real dilemma. Also, given the size of Lee's invasion force, it might be hazardous for him to conduct his operation with such a significant number of Union troops operating in his rear and his intended communication line. The general's September 12 letter to Jefferson Davis provides some insight into Lee's thought process and the conundrum he faced:

> Before crossing the Potomac I considered the advantages of entering Maryland east or west of the Blue Ridge. In either case it was my intention to march upon this town. By crossing east of the Blue Ridge, both Washington and Baltimore would be threatened, which I believed would insure the withdrawal of the mass of the enemy's troops north of the Potomac. I think this has been accomplished. I had also supposed that as soon as it was known that the army had reached Fredericktown, the enemy's forces in the Valley of Virginia, which had retired to Harper's Ferry and Martinsburg, would retreat altogether from the State. In this I was disappointed.[52]

A long-held military axiom states, "No plan survives first contact with the enemy." While this statement refers explicitly to tactics and the variable nature of battle, its premise is the same one Lee encountered. The adage basically asserts that all plans are good provided an enemy does what is expected, which is not often the case. When opponents behave unexpectedly, military operations become a bit more problematic and subject to change. Throughout military history, commanders like Robert E. Lee have made well-thought-out and elaborate plans based on their enemies acting precisely as predicted. Lee was an excellent field commander and quite unflappable, but on September 9, 1862, he was forced to reexamine his operational plans before moving forward with his objectives. His enemy was behaving in a way he did not foresee.[53]

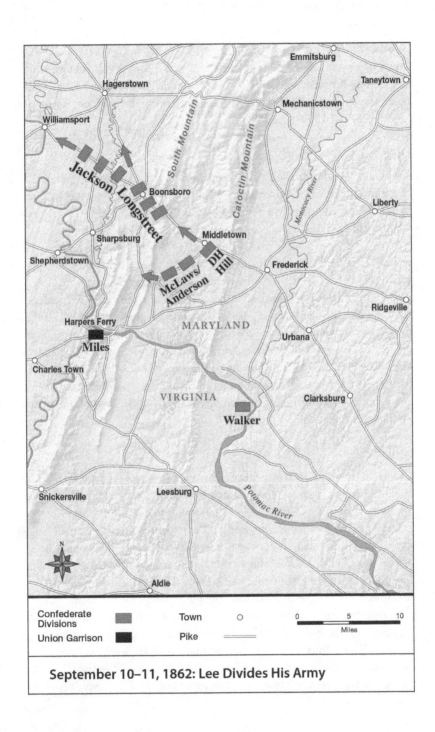

September 10–11, 1862: Lee Divides His Army

Options

Lee, who always considered his alternatives, had four options to choose from: abandoning his campaign, cutting off the Union garrisons and finding different supply routes, dividing his army and attacking the garrisons, or simply ignoring them.

Option 1

Lee could abandon his offensive campaign, retreat to Virginia, and seek a better time and place to strike again. While confident, the Confederate commander knew the nature of the risk he was taking. He had to ask himself whether this situation elevated that risk to unacceptable proportions.

Lee held the initiative and believed that time was still on his side. He was only five days into his offensive, so it seems unlikely that he would give it up at this point. Moreover, why would Lee invest all this time and energy into a campaign only to forsake it at the first sign of an obstacle? All evidence indicates that the Confederate general was under no pressure to accelerate his campaign or change his plans based on what he thought the Federals were doing. The Federal army was pursuing faster than Lee at first anticipated, but he gave no indication of being overly concerned by McClellan's initial moves. As we will see in the discussion of a future decision, Lee seriously considered abandoning his campaign on September 14 or 15, but he was not under that kind of pressure at this point.

Option 2

Lee could try to cut off and isolate the two garrisons and then see whether he could secure another route for his supplies and communications. This option was indeed viable, but it would be complicated to execute and perhaps impractical. First, how many men would Lee have to commit to such a plan—five thousand, ten thousand, or even more? Would those soldiers not be effectively lost for the balance of the campaign? Secondly, what other route was Lee going to use for his supplies and communications? Where else could he realistically go? As the Army of the Potomac moved west to follow the Confederate commander, Pleasonton's cavalry kept pace at a distance, and Franklin's Sixth Corps and Darius Couch's division followed a line parallel to the Potomac River. Thus, Lee could not maintain an open line back from where he came. Nor could he move his line farther west. The Shenandoah Valley runs at an angle from southwest to northeast, and the Allegheny Mountains prevented any such shift.[54]

Option 3

Lee could divide his army, send a force to attack, and capture or drive the garrisons off, thus opening his valley communication lines the way he had initially planned. In the meantime, the rest of the force could position itself someplace west of Frederick and wait, using the South Mountain range as a shield. With these feats accomplished, the army could reunite at Boonsboro or possibly Hagerstown.

Robert E. Lee still believed that the Union army was defeated, disorganized, and demoralized, and that his veterans were more than a match for the Union forces soon to be arrayed against them. This might be Lee's best option if he planned to continue his campaign. However, it was not without risk. The army would be divided not just in half but into several parts, the most substantial of these being committed to the Harpers Ferry operation. Lee counted quite heavily on the Union army commander (on September 9, Lee was likely unaware that McClellan was in command)[55] maneuvering his army at a slow pace while pursuing him. Additionally, the Confederate commander must have considered the opportunity to seize additional supplies, horses, and weapons from the Union garrison a tempting side benefit of its possible capture.[56]

Should Lee be successful, his communications would be secure, and he could once again concentrate on his main objectives. He could then maneuver his united force at will and pounce on the Federals whenever it suited him. History tells us that Lee was certainly not afraid to divide his army in the face of the enemy. He did it so often, in fact, that it seems to have been his go-to move. Lee had split up his forces before the Maryland Campaign, during the Seven Days' Battles, and at Second Bull Run. Afterward, he repeated the action during the Gettysburg Campaign and most famously at Chancellorsville.

Option 4

Lee could decide to bypass and ignore the garrisons and hope they would eventually leave. On its face, this would seem like an overly optimistic choice, but several points must be considered. Lee marched his army down the Shenandoah Valley as he was making his way to Pennsylvania in late June 1863. As he reached the vicinity of Harpers Ferry and its 1863 garrison, he bypassed and ignored the troops stationed there. As Lee's army moved north, it advanced on a line closer to Williamsport, and the general made no aggressive move against this Union garrison. As mentioned concerning the last decision, a squabble in the Union's high command over the garrison's state prompted Hooker to resign. When the new commander, George Meade, secured the force's evacuation, he unwittingly solved Lee's problem for him. While we can argue that Lee's actions regarding Harpers Ferry in 1863 directly resulted from the lessons learned in 1862, ignoring the garrison's troops was indeed an option open to him in September 1862.[57]

Decision

Lee ultimately determined to drive off the men stationed at Union garrisons or even capture these strongholds (Option 3). On September 9, 1862, after a conference with Longstreet and Jackson, Lee ordered his adjutant, Lieut. Col. R. H. Chilton, to pen Special Orders 191, make copies, and send them out to the various commands.[58] The directive sent Maj. Walter Taylor to Leesburg to not only help secure the lines of communication but also intercept Jefferson Davis, who indicated he was coming north to meet with Lee. Stonewall Jackson was ordered to take his command west toward Sharpsburg, cross the upper Potomac, and move on the garrisons from the west. Longstreet was to move to Boonsboro with his command and with the army's reserve, supply, and baggage trains.[59]

McLaws's Division and R. H. Anderson's were to move west and then south to Maryland Heights to seal off the Harpers Ferry garrison from the north. General Walker was to take his division and occupy Loudoun Heights, then cooperate with Generals McLaws and Jackson and intercept the enemy's retreat. D. H. Hill's division was to form the rear guard of the army west of South Mountain. General Stuart received orders to detach a squadron of cavalry to accompany the commands of Generals Longstreet, Jackson, and McLaws and cover the army's route. The main body of the cavalry would bring up all stragglers that might have been left behind. After all these tasks were accomplished, Lee ordered the army to reassemble at Boonsboro or Hagerstown on or about September 12.

Evidence suggests that Robert E. Lee never anticipated that the forces he was sending to capture the garrisons would have to lay siege to Harpers Ferry. In fact, Lee believed that once his troops converged on the enemy, the Union forces would flee to avoid being bottled up in the town. Their flight would then send them right into the waiting arms of Stonewall Jackson. These assumptions go a long way toward explaining why Lee set a seemingly ambitious timeline for completing the operation. However, for the second time, the Union forces at Harpers Ferry failed to act as the Confederate commander anticipated.[60]

Results/Impact

Lee's decision proved critical because it was the next step of the campaign's ever-altering course. In a direct response to Halleck's decision, Lee changed his plans, setting a new and radically different direction for the Confederate operation in Maryland. Like a stone thrown in a pond, the ripples of that choice had far-reaching effects.

This decision was vital in inaugurating the fighting at South Mountain and Harpers Ferry. Moreover, it led both armies to eventually meet at Sharpsburg, as Lee had to pause west of the mountains to allow time for the operation to be completed. It goes without saying that, had Lee opted not to divide his army, there would undoubtedly have been no order directing the army to split up. An order never written can be neither lost nor found. As we follow this narrative, we can see how this course of action altered the campaign. Robert E. Lee's calculated risk would expose his army to great danger and bring the two opposing forces one step closer to the clash at Antietam.

Alternate Decision/Scenario

Had Lee decided to abandon or postpone his campaign at this point, any number of possible scenarios could have resulted. The general would have had to move quickly to recross the Potomac at or near White's Ford or possibly upstream at Point of Rocks. Franklin's Sixth Corps and Couch's division

Lee's H.Q. Near Frederick, Maryland, September 6–10, modern image. Author.

moved along the river and would soon have been in his way. Franklin likely would not have been able to stop Lee all on his own, but this encounter might have given Halleck the proof he needed to substantiate his mistaken belief that Lee's objective had been Washington, DC, all along. McClellan might then have been able to converge on the Confederate commander, and we might have seen a battle along the banks of the Potomac. Lee would have more likely slipped back over the river and tried to recross upstream, possibly west of Harpers Ferry near Williamsport. This continued campaign would then have taken a very different course, both literally and figuratively.[61]

Sugar Loaf Mountain is Occupied

Situation

Some thirty miles northwest of Washington, DC, Sugar Loaf (Sugarloaf) Mountain is a 1,282-foot prominence just west of Parr's Ridge, about half-way between Urbana, Maryland, and the confluence of the Monocacy and Potomac Rivers. This solitary mountain has stood watch over this portion of North America for perhaps 1.1 billion years. Its name was derived from early settlers who thought it looked like a loaf of sugar. Today, a drive to the top of the mountain quickly reveals why both Union and Confederate forces sought to occupy it. On a clear day, you can see miles in every direction. From Sugar Loaf's peak, you can easily view Leesburg, Virginia, south of the Potomac; Frederick, Maryland, to the north; the South Mountain range to the north-west; Baltimore to the east; and Washington, DC, to the southeast.[62]

Although both Union and Confederate forces eventually employed what was known as the wigwag signaling system during the war, the United States Signal Corps got its unofficial start in May 1861. It would eventually include the United States Military Telegraph. The Signal Corps occupied a unique position within the army. While its members could quickly relay coded messages over great distances, they could also observe enemy movements because they were often positioned on the highest ground. With their telescopes, flags, and torches, the men of the Signal Corps had the means to quickly communicate their observations to key decision-makers.[63]

On August 30, 1862, a group of Union signalmen left Washington. Their assignment was to set up a line of signal/observation stations along the north bank of the Potomac, from Maryland Heights at Harpers Ferry to about twenty miles northwest of the capital. Additionally, a telegraph station was set up at Poolesville, Maryland, to quickly convey messages to Washington. From these positions, the Federals could observe every significant Potomac

Sugarloaf Mountain in distance, circa the 1920s. Courtesy of Heritage Frederick.

crossing point in the area. On September 3, 1862, one of these parties of signalmen, commanded by Lieut. Brinkerhoff N. Miner, climbed Sugar Loaf Mountain and set up a post. These Union soldiers were among the first to report the Confederate concentration of forces near Leesburg, Virginia, and the Rebel crossings of the Potomac several days later.[64]

This Union advantage, however, was not to last. On Saturday, September 6, just as the lead Confederate divisions began to converge on Frederick, Maryland, elements of Maj. Gen, J. E. B. Stuart's cavalry approached Sugar Loaf. Seeing the Rebel cavalry closing in on his position, Lieutenant. Miner and his outnumbered party quickly abandoned the mountain and were later captured. Understanding the value of Sugar Loaf's location, the Confederates, in turn, set up their own observation post there.[65]

Meanwhile, the Army of the Potomac continued its advance on three separate lines of march northwest from the capital. With orders to pursue the Confederates while protecting Washington and Baltimore, McClellan pressed them on a front almost thirty miles wide. The Union commander's fundamental problem was that no one was sure how many Confederates there were, where they were going, or what their intentions were. What McClellan did have in those early days of September was a veritable flood of often conflicting intelligence reports from every conceivable direction. He received communications from Pennsylvania governor Andrew Curtin, whose correspondence during the campaign often bordered on the hysterical. McClellan also received communications from the War Department in Washington and from Abraham Lincoln.

However, the primary source of the general's intelligence on the movements and numbers of the Rebels in Maryland was his cavalry, commanded by Brig. Gen. Alfred Pleasonton. Pleasonton's undermanned division did not have enough troopers to adequately cover the massive area he was responsible for.[66] Since J. E. B. Stuart and his Confederate cavalry prevented anything more than minimal direct observation by the Federals, Pleasonton's men received the bulk of their information by questioning local civilians and captured or deserted enemy soldiers. In modern intelligence parlance, this is referred to as "human intelligence." The inherent problem with this approach is that it is potentially inaccurate and misleading unless validated by other sources.[67]

Many of these civilians lived in an area of the country with a relatively low population density. For these Marylanders, a column of two thousand men no doubt looked like ten thousand men or more. These individuals likely had never seen that many people in one place at one time. Moreover, the same Confederate force on the march was quite often identified in two or three separate locations. Since civilian informants could not correctly identify them, the troops were reported to army headquarters as two individual units from two different sources.

Also, Rebel prisoners seemed to delight in spinning yarns for their Union captors about the Confederate army's size and intentions. In reported cases during the war, the Confederates deliberately sent selected men into the Federal lines to be captured and feed false information to the enemy. In other documented cases, Confederate commanders lied about their intentions when speaking to or near Marylanders several times during the campaign. When Stonewall Jackson was marching from Frederick to Harpers Ferry, he deliberately lied about his force's direction, knowing several locals were within earshot.[68]

We should not be overly critical of Pleasonton or his men, as they likely received no formal training in intelligence gathering. However, I can find no evidence that these troopers either vetted or filtered the information they collected. Instead, they passed all this raw intelligence right up the chain of command, where it no doubt fed directly into McClellan's misconceptions about the size of the forces he was facing. This conflicting and often confusing intelligence forced the Union army to feel its way along at a meticulous pace.[69]

On September 9, McClellan had his headquarters at Rockville, Maryland. As far as he was concerned, the overall state of military affairs in the state had only grown muddier. Conflicting details on the Confederate invasion force continued to filter in from every conceivable direction and every possible source. Two days before, Henry Halleck received a somewhat dubious report of Confederate general Braxton Bragg inexplicably marching forty thousand men over the mountains and down the Shenandoah Valley.[70]

That same day, McClellan forwarded several reports to army command that at least one hundred thousand Confederates were now in Maryland. However, an opportunity to provide operational clarity soon presented itself. If Union forces could recapture Sugar Loaf Mountain, the tactical situation might be made more manifest. McClellan had a number of units at hand to carry out such an operation. On that day, Union colonel John F. Farnsworth had stationed his cavalry brigade a few miles south of Sugar Loaf between Poolesville and Barnesville. Additionally, three corps of infantry were situated roughly ten miles southeast between Gaithersburg and the Potomac. Also, Couch's Fourth Corps division was almost due south on the Potomac near Seneca. Recapturing this key position might just give the Union commander the intelligence insight he so desperately needed.[71]

Options

McClellan had two options available to him. He could have Pleasonton use his available cavalry forces to recapture the mountain or order a more significant force to complete the task. With the future of his campaign hanging in the balance, McClellan had a critical decision to make.

Option 1

McClellan's first alternative was to have Pleasonton use whatever cavalry forces were at his immediate disposal to retake the mountain. The Union commander might have believed that Pleasonton had sufficient forces to capture Sugar Loaf. On the morning of September 9, McClellan knew that Pleasonton and Farnsworth's brigade had engaged Confederate cavalry at Poolesville, Maryland, and were advancing north to Barnesville. Col. John F. Farnsworth had about eight hundred troopers from his cavalry brigade, along with some horse artillery. Perhaps McClellan believed Sugar Loaf was thinly held; if so, it was not unreasonable for him to assume that his cavalry commander had more than enough strength to carry the assignment off.

Additionally, as Pleasonton was closer to the position on the mountain, McClellan would naturally rely on his feedback if a more significant force was required. For the last several days, the Union horsemen had advanced steadily from Washington, DC. When they did engage the enemy, the Confederates generally offered little more than token resistance, as they were under orders to not bring on a general engagement. Given the Union troopers'

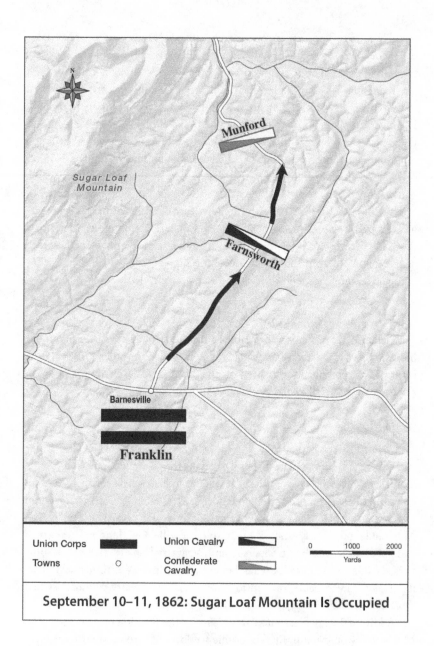

Union Corps	■■■■	Union Cavalry	▬▶
Towns	○	Confederate Cavalry	▬▶

0   1000   2000
Yards

September 10–11, 1862: Sugar Loaf Mountain Is Occupied

recent experience, their perception that the position on Sugar Loaf would fall easily was not unreasonable.[72]

Option 2

McClellan could send a more substantial infantry force to retake Sugar Loaf. Given the importance of the position on the mountain, McClellan could immediately order infantry from one of the nearby units to support the cavalry in its assignment. On the ninth, McClellan had three corps of infantry just over ten miles behind his cavalry. It would not require much hard marching to have a significant force within striking distance of Sugar Loaf by that evening or early on the morning of the tenth. Employing his infantry would give McClellan a tactical and numerical advantage in any clash with Confederate cavalry, as it is generally understood that cavalry forces were not able to deal with infantry deployed on a significant scale.

However, in his defense, over the next few days, McClellan received several erroneous reports that the mountain had been retaken when it had not. This confusion might have made the commanding general feel there was no urgency to send infantry support. The original dispatch from army headquarters to Pleasonton sent the morning of September 9 contained conflicting information. While it directed Pleasonton to try and take the position, it also included a confusing postscript:

> Brigadier-General Pleasonton.
> Poolesville:
> Major Myer, Chief Signal Officer, thinks the possession of Sugar Loaf Mountain as a signal station will be of great importance to us, and that its possession by the enemy is of great benefit to them. Will it be possible for us to get possession of it without incurring much risk?
>
> R. B. Marcy,
> Chief of Staff.
>
> P.S.—A Lieutenant Rowley, signal officer, says he was at the mountain a day or two ago, and that there was no enemy there on Saturday.
> R. B. M. [73]

Decision

McClellan ultimately decided to give Pleasonton and his cavalry the task of retaking Sugar Loaf Mountain. Given that Pleasonton was the commander at the point of the spear, one can argue that he, not McClellan, was in the best position to determine the strength of the force needed to occupy the mountain, and that he should have been the decision-maker. While this argument has merit, the outcome is the same.

On Tuesday, September 9, attacks by several companies of Farnsworth's brigade and a section of horse artillery drove a small contingent of Munford's Confederate troopers from the vicinity of Barnesville back to the base of Sugar Loaf. Reinforced, the Rebels held out until dark.

On September 10, reinforced Union cavalry tried again to dislodge the enemy holding the mountain, but the Confederates fighting dismounted made good use of the terrain and held them off for the balance of the day. That evening, Pleasonton called for support under the assumption he was confronting infantry. Darius Couch was ordered to send a brigade to his aid. William Franklin's Sixth Corps was much closer than Couch, and its men reached Barnesville first and prepared to join the fight. However, Franklin decided it was too late in the day to assault the position.

On September 11, William Franklin's Sixth Corps and a much larger contingent of Union cavalry made ready to attack Sugar Loaf. The Confederate troopers, witnessing Federal infantry bearing down on them, decided that the position had been held long enough. The Rebels retreated after delaying the Union recapture of the mountain by almost three full days. [74]

Results/Impact

This decision was critical for a fundamental reason. Because the mountain remained in Confederate hands for several vital days, there were no Union eyes on top of Sugar Loaf to help clarify the morass of confusing intelligence reports McClellan was receiving. The Federal commander lost a genuine opportunity to bring the operational situation into focus as his army approached Frederick. Consequently, the Union troops continued to grope along in their advance, and McClellan was forced to move forward with his force spread out over a wide arc to respond to any and all contingencies. This allowed Lee to carry out his Harpers Ferry operation unabated for several days, and it also left much of what was transpiring west of the mountains unconfirmed by McClellan. Both circumstances no doubt impeded the Army of the Potomac's advance from Washington.

A direct result of this slower march was that the Army of the Potomac did not arrive at Frederick and the base of the Catoctin Mountains until September 12, thus setting the timeline for the upcoming battles. Because the Union high command failed to quickly regain control of this valuable real estate, it was late on September 11 before McClellan was again receiving intelligence from the Sugar Loaf signal station. Only then could he confidently confirm that the Confederates had left Frederick and were moving west from the town. By then, McClellan was already convinced that the central Confederate thrust was, indeed, into the heart of Maryland. Various other sources also reported that the Rebels had departed Frederick, marching west and south. At that point, the information the Union commander received from the newly established signal station was far less valuable to him.[75]

Alternate Decision/Scenario

Had the Union deployed a more significant force and managed to retake Sugar Loaf on September 9 when the order was first issued, or even on the tenth, it might have changed the campaign's entire tenor. If Federal signalmen had been posted on the Mountain by the tenth, they would no doubt have clearly seen the Confederates executing the directives laid out in Special Orders 191. The signalmen would likely have seen the columns of Jackson, Longstreet, Hill, Walker, and McLaws as they marched in several directions away from Frederick. They might also have learned that only Confederate cavalry now stood between them and the town of Frederick.

If McClellan had been armed with this information, it is reasonable to assume that he might have pushed his own forces at a much speedier pace. As a result, knowing there was nothing other than Rebel cavalry in their way, the Army of the Potomac troops might have arrived in Frederick a day sooner than history records. If this action had moved up the fighting at South Mountain by a day as well, how significantly would the campaign have changed? If the battles at South Mountain had happened in the same way but on the thirteenth rather than the fourteenth, Lee might have been forced to abandon his operation. As we will learn in discussion of an upcoming decision, the main reason the Confederate commander consolidated his forces at Sharpsburg was because Jackson sent him a note on the morning of September 15 stating that the Harpers Ferry garrison would surrender that day. If the Army of the Potomac, including Franklin's corps, had been west of South Mountain the day before, Lee would likely have received that note as his forces were recrossing the Potomac back into Virginia.

Alternatively, Lee might have taken an entirely different action had McClellan been more aggressive. If the Army of the Potomac had pressed the Confederate cavalry force more determinedly, Stuart indeed would have notified Lee of the threat the Army of the Potomac posed. Lee executed his operation to eliminate the Harpers Ferry garrison believing he had ample time before any Union force could come out of Washington to pose a problem. Had the Federal army occupied Frederick by September 11, might Lee have been more concerned for the vulnerable state of his army? Might he have

Sugar Loaf Mountain, Maryland, modern image. Matt Brant.

disregarded the threat Harpers Ferry posed and instead chosen to consolidate his forces or perhaps call off his campaign?[76]

McClellan Responds to Special Orders 191

Situation

On Saturday, September 13, the events that led to Union and Confederate soldiers' inevitable collision at Antietam began to accelerate. For six days, McClellan had advanced his army along a front that was at times as much as thirty miles wide. He did so not only to facilitate his march but also to cover key Northern cities. Before September 11, the Union commander was unsure as to what Lee was doing and the direction in which he was traveling. McClellan thus advanced in a manner that shielded Washington and Baltimore as he progressed. Despite a deluge of intelligence, the general acknowledged for the moment that he had only the haziest notion of the Army of Northern Virginia's disposition and destination. In a September 8 communication to Pennsylvania governor Andrew Curtin, a frustrated McClellan wrote, "My information about the enemy comes from unreliable sources, and it is vague and conflicting."[77]

On September 11, Union signalmen on Sugar Loaf confirmed that the

Confederate army had left Frederick, Maryland. The Rebel forces were now busily carrying out the details of the plans Lee had laid out in his Special Orders 191. Learning that the Army of Northern Virginia was now mainly west of the Catoctin and South Mountain ranges and possibly divided into several parts, McClellan concentrated his forces at Frederick. [78]

On September 12, McClellan ordered Pleasonton to advance his cavalry, reconnoiter, and report on the enemy's dispositions. Situated west of Frederick and supported by elements of Reno's Ninth Corps, Pleasonton's men clashed with the Confederate rear guard along the National Road on the morning of the thirteenth. In a day's long-running battle, Pleasonton's force drove J. E. B. Stuart's men from the Catoctin range at Fairview Pass (Braddock Heights) through Middletown, and back to Turner's Gap.[79]

At approximately noon on the thirteenth,[80] Brig. Gen. Alpheus S. Williams's First Division of the Twelfth Corps approached Frederick, Maryland, from the southeast, marching from Ijamsville. As the division went into bivouac, two Union soldiers from the Twenty-Seventh Indiana Volunteers found a copy of Special Orders 191 in a field southeast of the town. The document was recognized for what it was, and it eventually made its way up the chain of command to McClellan, whose headquarters stood just west of Frederick. Along the way, an aide to Williams authenticated the signature on the document as that of Lieut. Col. R. H. Chilton, Lee's aide. According to one popular myth, upon receiving the orders, McClellan stated, "Now I know what to do!"[81]

By the time the dispatch fell under McClellan's eye, four days had passed since its official date stamp. The envelopment of Harpers Ferry was under way but behind schedule. Spread out over roughly 240 square miles, the Army of Northern Virginia was vulnerable. Six of its nine divisions were concentrated near Harpers Ferry, two were stationed at Hagerstown, and one was situated at Boonsboro. On the other hand, McClellan had his First, Second, and Twelfth Corps and one division of the Fifth Corps concentrated near Frederick, Maryland. The Union Ninth Corps was gathered west and south of Frederick in support of the cavalry operations. Finally, the Sixth Corps was stationed south of Frederick at Buckeystown, with Couch's Fourth Corps division south of it on the Potomac.[82]

If McClellan took the dispatch as gospel, his somewhat unfocused perception of the enemy's dispositions might sharpen. The exact time the copy of the Lost Order finally reached McClellan is up for debate. Some sources assert he read the document before noon, while others state the time as late as 3:00 p.m. When the orders did arrive, the general was reportedly conversing with a contingent of Frederick citizens, although recent scholarship indicates

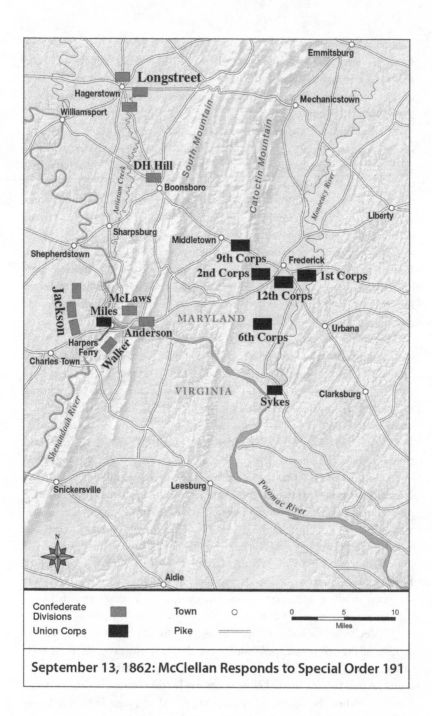

Emmitsburg

Longstreet

Hagerstown

Williamsport

South Mountain

Catoctin Mountain

Mechanicstown

DH Hill

Antietam Creek

Boonsboro

Monocacy River

Liberty

Sharpsburg

Middletown

9th Corps

Frederick

Shepherdstown

2nd Corps

1st Corps

Jackson

McLaws

12th Corps

Miles

MARYLAND

Urbana

Harpers
Ferry

Anderson

Walker

6th Corps

Charles Town

Shenandoah River

VIRGINIA

Sykes

Clarksburg

Snickersville

Leesburg

Potomac River

N

Aldie

Confederate
Divisions

Union Corps

Town   ○

Pike

0   5   10

Miles

September 13, 1862: McClellan Responds to Special Order 191

McClellan enters Frederick, Maryland, circa 1862.
Harpers Weekly.

he left the gathering and read the dispatch in the privacy of his headquarters tent.[83]

Options

After reading the now-famous Lost Orders, McClellan had three options: do nothing, wait for confirmation of its contents, or act immediately. Afforded what has been described as a "golden opportunity,"[84] the general faced perhaps his most critical decision of the campaign.[85]

Option 1

McClellan could do nothing and ignore the alleged order. He had several valid reasons to believe the dispatch was not the intelligence gift it appeared to be. First of all, there was a possibility, however slight, that Confederates had planted the order to deceive the Union commander—the conditions under which it was discovered could be considered almost too good to be true. Also, considering the length of time since the order had been written, the information it contained could be out of date and unreliable. According to the dispatch, the Confederate operation was to be completed by Friday, September 12, the day before. If this was true, the information it conveyed could be completely useless.

The copy of the order that made its way to McClellan was not a complete version of SO 191. The document the Union commander was now holding started at part\paragraph three and began with Roman Numeral three. McClellan had to wonder what information the first two parts contained and why this version omitted them. [86]

Furthermore, some of the order's contents conflicted with some of McClellan's current intelligence on the enemy's position. For example, in the days leading up to the Union army entering Frederick, McClellan received information from several sources that Stonewall Jackson was leading a Rebel force north, heading to Hagerstown and Pennsylvania. The dispatch had Jackson marching in the opposite direction and participating in the effort to capture Harpers Ferry.[87]

Finally, while it provided possible insight into the enemy's disposition, the communication shed no light on the whole Confederate force's size or its individual parts. For all McClellan knew, the "Main Body" as referenced in the document could be at Boonsboro or Hagerstown. Moreover, this force might be just as large as his own. The dispatch also referred to "Commands" several times but shed no light on what made up a command. In any case, McClellan could continue on his current course of advance without acting on this information. Other than the statement of General Williams's aide, nothing confirmed the document's authenticity. This unparalleled opportunity posed as many questions as it answered.[88]

Option 2

McClellan could wait while he confirmed all the information contained in the document and then decide on a course of action. He could order Pleasonton to press his pursuit of J. E. B. Stuart and report on what enemy forces lay beyond the South Mountain passes. In addition, the Union commander could sift through the previous day's intelligence reports to see how much of the information in the orders he could verify. Several reports made it to McClellan's headquarters that could confirm some of the contents of Special Orders 191. Jackson was reported at Williamsport and then at Martinsburg, but the dispatch indicated he was to cross the Potomac near Sharpsburg. Confederates were also reported in Pleasant Valley (McLaws and R. H. Anderson) and in Boonsboro and Hagerstown (D. H. Hill and Longstreet), and a Rebel force was said to be crossing the Potomac near Point of Rocks

(Walker). McClellan might already have remembered all of this; we do not really know. At that moment, he was aware that Harpers Ferry was already under siege. Given enough time, McClellan could confirm many of the items in the orders based on information within his immediate reach, then determine his plan. However, by the time he had done so, it might be too late to act on the information.[89]

Option 3

Finally, McClellan could act immediately. If he took the intercepted orders as gospel, a bold move could allow him to strike at Lee's army while it was divided and vulnerable. In doing so, McClellan might negate the superior numbers he assumed he was facing. That afternoon he had three of his corps (First, Second, and Twelfth) positioned in and around Frederick. The Ninth and the cavalry were in the Middletown Valley, and the Sixth and Couch's division were located within twelve miles of the thinly held Confederate line at Crampton's Gap. If McClellan believed a relatively small force now defended the passes through South Mountain, quick action might seize the gaps before they could be reinforced.

Although the Union commander did not know it, Maj. Gen. D. H. Hill's division, Stuart's cavalry, and a couple of brigades from Brig. Gen. Lafayette McLaws's division were all the Confederate forces currently in a position to defend the three passes. An immediate and aggressive attack could conceivably sweep them aside and place Lee in a very precarious position. Before he received the copy of Special Orders 191, McClellan had already issued orders to have Brig. Gen. Jacob D. Cox's Kanawha Division support elements of Pleasonton's cavalry, which was advancing from Frederick on the National Pike, to probe the South Mountain passes. Also, McClellan had already directed his forces to move on September 13 to scout an enemy he now believed to be west of South Mountain. Acting immediately would seem to be a logical extension of actions he had previously put in motion. Finally, as an experienced field commander, McClellan also knew the situation that revealed itself in the Lost Order could easily change with every passing hour.[90]

Decision

McClellan was convinced of the order's authenticity almost at once, and he acted accordingly (Option 3). That afternoon, he was waiting to hear what Pleasonton could confirm in his front. At that moment, supported by Ninth Corps infantry, Pleasonton's cavalry was advancing up the National Road west of Frederick on McClellan's orders. At 6:00 p.m., the Union commander tired of waiting for a reply and directed his lieutenants to advance and seize the opportunity that now presented itself. The army attacked Crampton's and Turner's Gaps the following morning. Much has been written about the speed at which McClellan and the Army of the Potomac moved, but this nearly immediate decision irrevocably altered the campaign's course. For the moment, McClellan had the initiative. He might be criticized for not moving more of his attacking force closer to the gaps during the night, for not supervising Franklin more closely, and for allowing his men to light campfires that Confederate colonel Alfred H. Colquitt ultimately observed from South Mountain. But McClellan did act straightaway. Even Robert E. Lee acknowledged that the Union army was now moving much faster than he had anticipated.[91]

In his "final report" written on August 4, 1863, McClellan stated, "On the 13th an order fell into my hands, issued by General Lee, which fully disclosed his plans, and I immediately gave orders for a rapid and vigorous forward movement."[92] To Lincoln, McClellan wrote the following:

> I have the whole rebel force in front of me, but am confident, and no time shall be lost. I have a difficult task to perform, but with God's blessing will accomplish it. I think Lee has made a gross mistake, and that he will be severely punished for it. The army is in motion as rapidly as possible. I hope for a great success if the plans of the rebels remain unchanged. We have possession of Catoctin. I have all the plans of the rebels, and will catch them in their own trap if my men are equal to the emergency. I now feel that I can count on them as of old. All forces of Pennsylvania should be placed to co-operate at Chambersburg. My respects to Mrs. Lincoln. Received most enthusiastically by the ladies. Will send you trophies. All well, and with God's blessing will accomplish it. [93]

McClellan also wrote to Halleck:

> An order from General R. E. Lee, addressed to General D. H. Hill, which has accidentally come into my hands this evening—the authenticity of which is unquestionable—discloses some of the plans of the enemy, and shows most conclusively that the main rebel army is now before us, including Longstreet's, Jackson's, the two Hills', McLaws', Walker's, R. H. Anderson's, and Hood's commands. That army was ordered to march on the 10th, and to attack and capture our forces at Harper's Ferry and Martinsburg yesterday, by

surrounding them with such a heavy force that they conceived it impossible they could escape. . . . Unless General Lee has changed his plans, I expect a severe general engagement to-morrow.[94]

Based on his communications, it seems reasonable to assume that McClellan believed that he held an authentic document providing some valuable insight into what lay ahead of him. Additionally, McClellan still assumed that Lee outnumbered him, and he expected a severe engagement the following day.

Results/Impact

Experienced readers know that much has been written about this event. The traditional view is that McClellan responded too slowly to this once-in-a-lifetime intelligence gift and let a chance to destroy Lee slip away. However, a more recent perspective argues that the Lost Order's finding had no significant impact on the Battles of South Mountain. This view contends that the dispatch only told the general details he already knew. However, these positions fail to consider the following points.

The order did validate some of the intelligence McClellan had been receiving until that point, including the fact that Lee had divided his forces and was now moving in two directions. As the day wore on, the Union commander became increasingly confident that he held the advantage, and he was more aggressive in his attack at Turner's Gap than he might otherwise have been. Ordering the First Corps to begin its march well before dawn on September 14 is an example of this.

McClellan discussed the dispatch's finding extensively in his writings, including his September 13 communications, his after-action report, and his accounts written in 1863. By that measure, the event clearly affected his thoughts and actions. If it did not influence the campaign or McClellan's thinking, why did he reference it so often? Why mention the order at all if its existence did not alter his view of the situation or his intentions?[95]

Additionally, we can only argue that the dispatch had no material effect if McClellan received it after sending Franklin orders on the thirteenth. This would mean that Franklin's corps would have advanced the necessary distance for a full-scale attack at Crampton's Gap irrespective of discovering the mislaid document. We know that McClellan sent orders to Franklin well after reading the Lost Orders.[96]

All this debate aside, McClellan's immediate action remains a critical decision for the following reasons. On September 14, the general used the dispatch's information to defeat the Confederate defenders at South Mountain.

Before dawn on September 14, McClellan advanced his army at the three South Mountain gaps. After an all-day clash, the Union controlled all three passes and was poised to deluge the Confederate defenders once the sun rose on the fifteenth. Lee, who had sent Longstreet's forces back to Boonsboro to support D. H. Hill, determined he could not hold his position, and he was eventually forced to fall back to Sharpsburg. The Confederate commander seriously considered abandoning his campaign upon realizing the genuine threat that the suddenly more bellicose Union army presented. Eventually, Lee began to consolidate his widely scattered forces and contemplate where he might make a stand next. Even if Lee considered a delaying action at South Mountain a foregone conclusion, he did not anticipate an assault that was as aggressive as McClellan's. McClellan's decision brought on the Battles of South Mountain, the subsequent Confederate retreat, and the Union advance the next day, leading both armies to the clash at Antietam.

Alternative Decision/Scenario

The first option, doing nothing, might have slowed the Army of the Potomac's advance, or at least caused it not to accelerate. Given this circumstance, McClellan might not have pressed his advance on South Mountain until the later on the fourteenth or possibly the fifteenth. Lee would then have had time to consolidate his army sooner and potentially provide a more vigorous defense at the mountain passes. In turn, subsequent events might have unfolded at a different pace, and the ultimate clash at Sharpsburg might have happened a day later.

Speculate for a moment—say that events happened as they did only one day later due to McClellan's delay. Think of every significant event that occurred between the moment McClellan was handed the Lost Order and the September 17 battle, and consider how many of those events unfolded as history records them due to pure timing. Assume Lee had had an additional day to consolidate his forces at South Mountain and then at Sharpsburg. An attack at the South Mountain passes on the fifteenth instead of the fourteenth means Lee might have had a much stronger force to defend his positions there. Alternatively, he might have been able to conduct a delaying action, then consolidate his army at Sharpsburg or possibly Hagerstown.

Moreover, what would have happened at Antietam had the battle been fought on September 18? If Lee had not had his whole army up and rested, including A. P. Hill, would the contest have been fought differently? Could Lafayette McLaws's men have been more effective with an additional day of rest? For that matter, could the whole Confederate army have been more ef-

Frederick, Maryland, circa 1862. *Harpers Weekly.*

ficient with that extra downtime? Think of how many more men would have been available to Lee had the fighting at Antietam happened one day later.

Conversely, wouldn't McClellan have had a more significant force available to him as well? The possibilities are numerous and potentially consequential. Last of all, we must remember that Lee's plan was predicated on the Union army advancing at a predictable pace. After September 13, by Lee's own admission, it was not.[97]

Lee Stands at South Mountain

Situation

September 13 was a pivotal day for the Confederate commander and the Army of Northern Virginia. In fact, Lee was now facing one of the most critical moments of his relatively short leadership tenure. Just nine days into his campaign, Federal forces were closing in from the east, his Harpers Ferry operation was behind schedule, and time was running out. It is possible that even the unflappable Lee was starting to feel as if he had pressed his luck a bit too far.

Two days earlier, on September 11, Lee had received word that a Union force was at or near Hagerstown, Maryland. He further divided his army

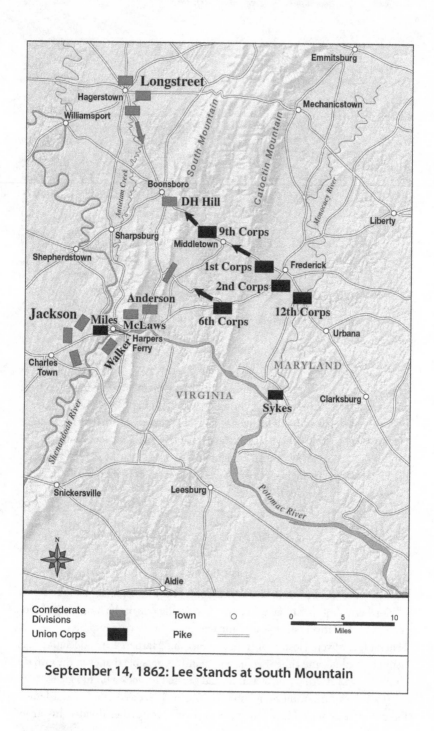

September 14, 1862: Lee Stands at South Mountain

in response, sending the divisions of Brig. Gen. David R. Jones and Brig. Gen. John B. Hood and the brigade of Brig. Gen. Nathan G. Evans under Longstreet from Boonsboro to counter this new threat.[98] At this moment, Lee still believed that the Union forces east of South Mountain were not an immediate hazard to his plans. After the war, the Rebel commander stated that "McClellan's army, widely extended, with its left on the Potomac, was moving only a few miles every day, feeling its way with great caution."[99]

This perspective changed dramatically over the next several days.

By noon on September 12, Lee learned that the Union army was concentrating at Frederick. By contrast, his own command was widely extended. The Army of Northern Virginia was now separated into four parts, with no one element in a position to immediately support any of the others. Four of Lee's nine divisions were now south of the Potomac, two were in Hagerstown, and two were on Maryland Heights and in Pleasant Valley. That left only D. H. Hill's eight-thousand-man division and one brigade of Stuart's cavalry standing between roughly forty-five thousand Federals in four infantry corps and Lee's rear guard at Turner's Gap.

D. H. Hill had his five brigades at or near Boonsboro, and on the thirteenth, he initially sent two brigades of infantry (Garland and Colquitt) and four batteries of artillery to Turner's Gap at the behest of J. E. B. Stuart. These units were to be followed by a third brigade (Anderson) the day after. In his after-action report, D. H. Hill outlined the dilemma he faced:

> On the 13th, I was ordered by General Lee to dispose of my troops so as to prevent the escape of the Yankees from Harper's Ferry, then besieged, and also to guard the pass in the Blue Ridge near Boons-borough. Major-General Stuart reported to me that two brigades only of the Yankees were pursuing us, and that one brigade would be sufficient to hold the pass. I, however, sent the brigades of Garland and Colquitt, and ordered my other three brigades up to the neighborhood of Boonsborough.
>
> An examination of the pass, very early on the morning of the 14th, satisfied me that it could only be held by a large force, and was wholly indefensible by a small one. I accordingly ordered up Anderson's brigade. A regiment of Ripley's brigade was sent to hold another pass, some 3 miles distant, on our left. I felt reluctant to order up Ripley and Rodes from the important positions they were holding until something definite was known of the strength and design of the Yankees.[100]

Pushed out of the Middletown Valley by Pleasonton, Stuart and his troopers were now feeling more significant pressure from Union cavalry and infantry. Stuart believed he could not defend the gaps with only his single brigade of cavalry. As he had sent the Jeff. Davis Legion to Crampton's Gap that afternoon, the Confederate cavalry commander now called on D.H. Hill for support. Once Hill's infantry was in place, Stuart moved the balance of his command, minus one regiment and a battery of horse artillery, south to support McLaws at Crampton's Gap, which he concluded was the position most at risk. Stuart outlined the situation in his after-action report:

> On reaching the vicinity of the gap near Boonsborough, finding General Hill's troops occupying the gap, I turned off General Hampton, with all his cavalry except the Jeff. Davis Legion, to re-enforce Munford, at Crampton's Gap, which was now the weakest point of the line. I remained myself at the gap near Boonsborough until night, but the enemy did not attack the position. This was obviously no place for cavalry operations, a single horseman passing from point to point on the mountain with difficulty. Leaving the Jeff. Davis Legion here, therefore, and directing Colonel Rosser, with a detachment of cavalry and the Stuart Horse Artillery, to occupy Braddock's Gap, I started on my way to join the main portion of my command at Crampton's Gap, stopping for the night near Boonsborough.[101]

By the afternoon of the thirteenth, indications were that something was happening on the eastern side of South Mountain. By that evening, it was clear to Robert E. Lee that the enemy was "advancing more rapidly than was convenient from Fredericktown."[102] Later that night, Lee received alarming and somewhat contradictory dispatches about the enemy's disposition and intentions. First was a message from Stuart that contained two critical pieces of information. Stuart indicated that he was sending the bulk of his men to support the forces currently occupying Crampton's Gap, which he believed would be the focal point of any Federal offensive. Secondly, Stuart informed Lee of an unnamed Southern sympathizer who had been present when McClellan was handed a copy of Special Orders 191. It is doubtful that McClellan would have been so careless as to reveal the dispatch contents to a relative stranger. The informant might have guessed through observation that the paper was of some importance and divulged some critical information heretofore unknown to the Union commander. While there is some doubt Stuart himself knew about the Lost Order, he indicated to Lee that he thought the Harpers Ferry operation was now compromised. Stuart also suggested that McClellan would launch his main attack to relieve the garrison.

Confederate Generals: Maj. Gen. Daniel H. Hill, Maj. Gen. James E.B. Stuart, and Maj. Gen. James Longstreet. Library of Congress.

Almost immediately after reading the message from Stuart, Lee received an urgent dispatch from D. H. Hill. Hill asserted that J. E. B. Stuart's earlier estimate of at most two brigades of Federal infantry in his front was incorrect. To support this contention, Hill relayed a message from brigade commander Col. Alfred H. Colquitt stating that hundreds of enemy campfires were now clearly visible east of his position in the Middletown Valley. In his communication Colquitt politely said, "Genl Stuart must have been mistaken as to the strength of the enemy." Hill now believed that McClellan and the main Federal force were in his front, directly east of Turner's Gap.[103]

Meanwhile, the Confederate trap was closing in on the Union garrison at Harpers Ferry. McLaws had taken Maryland Heights, and Walker had occupied Loudoun Heights. After chasing the Martinsburg garrison into Harpers Ferry, Jackson's three divisions closed in from the west.[104]

As Lee pondered his next move, he was attempting to manage a very complex operational juggling act. First of all, he eventually needed to induce the Federal army to move west of South Mountain to make that terrain an obstacle to any additional Union support. However, this could not happen before Lee could bring his own army back together. Therefore, the general had to make sure his force at Turner's Gap was strong enough to conduct a successful holding action. The vulnerability of McLaws's and Anderson's Divisions gave him the most concern. If not addressed, the units' positions on Maryland Heights and in Pleasant Valley could prove disastrous. If Union troops intent on relieving Harpers Ferry got into Pleasant Valley before the garrison fell, McLaws could find himself between two hostile forces. Whatever solution Lee came up with had to provide those divisions with support or a viable escape route and opportunity to link up with the rest of the army. Lastly, Lee had to determine whether the Harpers Ferry mission could be completed in time for him to gather up his scattered army, mount a defense, and continue his campaign.

Options

With his Maryland operation now in danger of unraveling, Lee had three options to choose from. He could reinforce D. H. Hill at Boonsboro / South Mountain, fall back to a position west of South Mountain, or abandon the campaign and return to Virginia. From his headquarters near Hagerstown, Lee now had one more critical decision to make.

Option 1

If he determined that the main Federal attack would fall at Turner's Gap, Lee could order Longstreet's entire force to support D. H. Hill. Longstreet's two divisions were only seven miles away and a few hours' march from Hill and the gap. Hill would need all the support he could get because Turner's Gap was vulnerable to flanking movements via passes to its north and south, and he would be hard pressed to hold the position with his lone and undermanned division. Sending reinforcements to Hill would leave McLaws, Anderson, and Stuart to defend Crampton's Gap and hold Maryland Heights. This choice assumes that force was large enough to hold Crampton's on its own. In theory, this option could slow the Federals' advance long enough for the Harpers Ferry operation to finish, thus allowing Lee to reassemble his army someplace north of the Potomac.

Option 2

Lee might determine that his best course of action was the one supported by Longstreet. Perhaps buttressed with the gift of hindsight, Longstreet later wrote that he favored having both his and Hill's forces withdraw and take a stand west of Antietam Creek at Sharpsburg:

> He [Lee] sent for me, and I found him over his map. He told me of the reports and asked for my views. I thought it too late to march on the 14th and properly man the [position] at Turner's [Gap] and expressed preference for concentrating D. H. Hill's and my own force behind the Antietam at Sharpsburg where we could get together in season to make a strong defensive fight and at the same time check McClellan's March towards Harper's Ferry in case he thought to relieve the beleaguered garrison by that route, forcing him to first remove the obstacle on his flank.[105]

According to Longstreet, Lee listened respectfully to this opinion and weighed its merits. This was a viable option, but a question remained about whether it solved the dilemma of McLaws's vulnerable position or made it that much harder for him to get his division and Anderson's to the Confederate main body at Sharpsburg. Also, Lee had to speculate whether this plan provided enough resistance to the advancing Federal army at Turner's Gap.

<u>Option 3</u>

Lee could abandon his current campaign and reassemble his army in Virginia. The general might feel that he had extended his army too far, making its various parts vulnerable. If Lee did not sense that Hill or McLaws was strong enough to hold back the advancing Union forces, or if he thought that the Harpers Ferry operation was taking far too long, he could consider this his best option. Lee had to weigh the time he needed to reassemble his army versus the speed at which the Army of the Potomac could arrive west of the mountains. Given the current situation and the Rebel commander's predilection for aggressiveness, it is hard to see this genuine alternative as his first choice.

Decision

Opting for aggressiveness, Lee decided to support Hill and conduct a delaying action at Turner's and Fox's Gaps (Option 1). He left one brigade and the army's trains at Hagerstown while sending the rest of Longstreet's Command to Beaver Creek, located some three miles north of Boonsboro on the National Pike. From there, Longstreet would be in a position from which he could support Hill at either gap. Lee also sent messages to Jackson and McLaws urging them to capture Harpers Ferry as expeditiously as possible.

Based on this decision, we can make some assumptions about Lee's state of mind. The general must have felt optimistic or even sure about the inevitable capitulation of Harpers Ferry, and the ability of McLaws, Anderson, and Stuart to hold Crampton's Gap on their own. Lee must also have believed the Federals' main attack would fall at Turner's Gap and not Crampton's, as Stuart predicted. The combined Union force numbered over twelve thousand infantry and cavalry. Perhaps Lee did not know how imminent the threat to Crampton's was, or perhaps he did realize it but determined that the Turner's Gap position was the most critical. While time was becoming a factor, Lee must have believed that it was still on his side. No matter what action he took, he knew South Mountain's terrain would slow the Union army to a certain degree. It is also possible that the Confederate commander had more faith in McLaws's ability to hold his own than in D. H. Hill's, or maybe he simply felt that Hill lacked the numbers to cover all of the potential crossing points near Turner's Gap. Whatever the case, Lee needed time to allow the Harpers Ferry mission to succeed. The high-stakes poker game continued as McClellan had unexpectedly raised the bet, and Lee went all in to play the only move he felt was open to him. Robert E. Lee chose to bluff and raise.[106]

Results/Impact

With this decision, Lee guaranteed a major battle at South Mountain on September 14, and not just a continued delaying action by a single division. His choice also allowed the siege at Harpers Ferry to continue unabated. Most significantly, while his forces were eventually forced to fall back from all three of the South Mountain passes by September 14–15, Lee bought himself one more day and perhaps more. As mentioned regarding the last decision, it turned out to be a critical day. Those twenty-four hours proved essential to Lee's continuation of his Maryland Campaign, thus getting him one step closer to his operational objectives. Without that extra time, the Union army might have been in Pleasant Valley on the fourteenth, possibly splitting Lee's forces and creating a very different situation from the one we now know.

Alternative Decision/Scenario

Had Lee gone with Longstreet's suggestion (Option 2) and ordered his and Hill's forces to fall back and make a stand at some point west of Turner's Gap, any number of possible scenarios might have resulted.

Based on the terrain, Lee could have made a stand in several places west of South Mountain. He might have done so near Boonsboro, for example.[107] However, let us assume for a moment that Longstreet's version of events is correct, and Lee was convinced on the evening of the thirteenth that his best option was gathering his army at Sharpsburg. With Longstreet and D. H. Hill falling back, Lee would have been compelled to have McLaws and Anderson disengage as well and try to make their way to Sharpsburg via the Harpers Ferry Road or the Shepherdstown crossing. The general would also have had Jackson fall back to Shepherdstown. Walker might have had to retreat up the Shenandoah Valley or find another route around Harpers Ferry to join with the rest of the army. Suffice it to say, assuming all of the aforementioned movements could have been executed, the Harpers Ferry operation would have been canceled.

With the Confederates falling back and offering no significant resistance to the Union advance, McClellan could plausibly have gotten a sizable portion of the First and the Ninth Corps (including Jesse Reno) across South Moun-

Boonsboro, Maryland, near Turner's Gap, modern image. Author.

tain near Turner's Gap and into the valley beyond by the end of the day on September 14. With no force to block him, Franklin might have been able to get his entire wing over the mountain and into Pleasant Valley to link up with the Harpers Ferry garrison on the fourteenth. On the fifteenth, McClellan, faced with only a rearguard action, could have brought a more significant force for attacking Lee at Antietam. With the Harpers Ferry garrison or at least a portion of it at his disposal, McClellan could conceivably have had ninety to one hundred thousand men within his reach for a potential battle on September 15 or 16.

On the other side of the coin, without the surrender at Harpers Ferry to contend with, Lee might have had his entire army available to him as well, including A. P. Hill's division. Nor would Lee have had to cope with the South Mountain conflicts' added losses and severe straggling.[108] Conversely, McClellan might not have been able to overcome the authentic obstacle of assembling this massive force east of Antietam Creek on the few available roads in time to fight a battle before the seventeenth.

Exploring the endless possibilities brought about by Lee's decision is an interesting mental exercise. A battle at Antietam fought under these alternate conditions would indeed have been different, but we will never know exactly how different.

CHAPTER 2

SOUTH MOUNTAIN, HARPERS FERRY AND THE EVE OF ANTIETAM, SEPTEMBER 14–16, 1862

The Maryland Campaign and the Battle of Antietam cannot be understood in a vacuum. The days leading to September 17 were as critical to the campaign's outcome as the events that took place on that terrible Wednesday. As the clock counted down to the eventual struggle outside of Sharpsburg, events at South Mountain and Harpers Ferry became critical pieces of the larger situational puzzle. While much smaller in scale, South Mountain's engagements are often cited as one of the Union's great lost campaign opportunities.[1] Made during the Battles of South Mountain and Harpers Ferry and the eve of the Battle of Antietam, five critical decisions brought both armies closer to the banks of the Antietam Creek and America's bloodiest day.

Pleasonton Sends Willcox to Turner's Gap

Situation

By the time of the Battle of South Mountain, the thirty-seven-year-old Alfred Pleasonton had been in the army for eighteen years. Born in Washington, DC, he was the son of Stephen Pleasonton, who was famous for saving the Declaration of Independence and the US Constitution from the British

Brig. Gen. Alfred Pleasonton, Union Cavalry
Commander. Library of Congress.

during the War of 1812. The younger Pleasonton graduated from West Point
seventh in his class in 1844. His classmates included Simon Bolivar Buckner
and Winfield Scott Hancock. As a second lieutenant, Alfred Pleasonton
served with the Second US Dragoons. While with the Second, he fought
in the Mexican-American War and received a promotion to first lieutenant
for gallantry and then to captain on March 3, 1855. At the start of the Civil
War, Captain Pleasonton, who came from a posting in the West, steadily
rose through the ranks until President Lincoln formally appointed him to
the brigadier general grade in July 1862. On September 2, 1862, Pleasonton
assumed command of the Army of the Potomac's cavalry.[2]

As the Union army marched out from the nation's capital, Pleasonton and
his cavalry division formed the vanguard of McClellan's force.[3] The Federals had pressed their Confederate counterparts west for a week, and on the
morning of September 13, Pleasonton found himself west of Frederick in the
Middletown Valley engaged with J. E. B. Stuart and the Confederate cavalry
functioning as the rear guard for Lee. On that morning, McClellan directed
Pleasonton to make contact with the enemy to determine its strength and
whereabouts and open communication with Harpers Ferry. Conversely, the
Confederates received orders to conduct a delaying action and report the enemy's strength and position, but not to bring on a general engagement. Par-

tially due to the Confederate defenders' skill and partly due to the delay in infantry support, it took Pleasonton's men all of September 13 to push their opponents west of the Middletown Valley and back to Turner's Gap. The Ninth Corps of Burnside's wing was the first Union infantry corps to move west out of Frederick on the National Road. As a result, these men were in the best position to support Pleasonton's cavalry as they advanced through the Middletown Valley.[4]

On the morning of the fourteenth, Pleasonton and the Kanawha Division of the Ninth Corps, commanded by Brig. Gen. Jacob D. Cox, were the first to engage D. H. Hill's troops holding those mountain passes near the National Road. This principal element of the Union army was initially ordered to conduct a reconnaissance in force to determine the Rebel strength at South Mountain and to possess the gap (Turner's) controlling the National Road. It was supposed at the outset that the passes along the National Road were thinly held, but Pleasonton and Cox soon learned differently.[5]

At approximately 6:00 a.m., soldiers in the Kanawha Division, with Col. Eliakim P. Scammon's brigade of Ohioans in the lead, marched west on the National Road from their camp east of Middletown. Just west of town, Cox encountered Union colonel Augustus Moor, whom Wade Hampton's cavalry had captured east of Frederick only two days earlier. Cox described the revealing encounter in a *Battles and Leaders of the Civil War* article:

> I was myself on the road when Scammon marched out, and was riding forward with him to learn how Pleasonton intended to use the troops, when, just as we crossed Catoctin Creek, I was surprised to see Colonel Moor standing at the roadside. With astonishment, I rode to him and asked how he came there. He said he had been taken prisoner beyond the mountain, but had been paroled the evening before, and was now finding his way back to us on foot. "But where are you going?" said he. I answered that Scammon's brigade was going to support Pleasonton in a reconnaissance into the gap. Moor made an involuntary start, saying, "My God! be careful"; then, checking himself, said, "But I am paroled!" and turned away.[6]

Now convinced that there was a considerable enemy force in front of him, Cox requested support from Maj. Gen. Jesse Reno. Reno subsequently ordered Brig. Gen. Orlando B. Willcox's two-brigade division to his aid. Upon reaching the crossroads at Bolivar, Cox and Pleasonton agreed that the best strategy was to have Pleasonton's cavalry demonstrate against the position

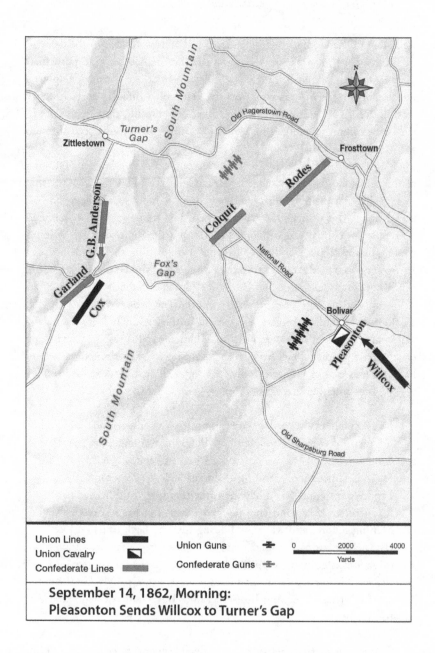

Union Lines
Union Cavalry
Confederate Lines
Union Guns
Confederate Guns

0   2000   4000
Yards

September 14, 1862, Morning:
Pleasonton Sends Willcox to Turner's Gap

at Turner's Gap on the right while Cox's infantry advanced on Fox's Gap on the left to outflank Turner's. Cox's two divisions (Scammon and Crook) were deployed east of Fox's Gap on the Old Sharpsburg Road and ordered to advance.

At 8:00 a.m., Willcox, located east of Middletown, had his men fed and on the march west. This move had the potential to pit two Union divisions numbering nearly seven thousand men against a Confederate position at Fox's Gap held by less than half that number of Rebels.

Meanwhile, D. H. Hill arrived at Turner's Gap before dawn. Now feeling his position was more tenuous than he had initially believed, Hill ordered up the brigade of Brig. Gen. G. B. Anderson from Boonsboro in support of the two brigades he already had in place at Turner's. Hill in turn ordered Brig. Gen. Samuel Garland to take his brigade and occupy Fox's Gap, which was almost a mile to the south and also threatened Hill's position. Once in place, Garland discovered that J. E. B. Stuart had left behind Col. Thomas Rosser's Fifth Virginia cavalry and a section of Capt. John Pelham's horse artillery before departing for Crampton's. Garland now had approximately 1,300 men and eight artillery pieces to hold the line here.[7]

Willcox sent forward an aide to find Cox and get directions to Fox's Gap. This aid mistakenly told Willcox to report to Pleasonton for orders. In fact, Willcox was only supposed to receive directions to Fox's Gap from Pleasonton. Following these erroneous instructions, Willcox sought out Pleasonton as his men approached South Mountain's eastern face.[8]

Options

Pleasonton could choose from three options: sending Willcox's division up the Old Sharpsburg Road, sending Willcox's men north of the National Road, or issuing no orders at all to Willcox, who was not his subordinate. With the morning phase of the battle approaching a critical juncture, Brig. Gen. Alfred Pleasonton had a critical decision to make.

Option 1

Pleasonton could decide to send Willcox's division up the Old Sharpsburg Road to Fox's Gap in the same direction as Cox. Earlier that morning, Colonel Scammon, who commanded the Kanawha Division's lead brigade, had been part of the discussion on the best way to assault the passes. The parties involved had agreed that the most desirable option would be to have Pleasonton occupy the Confederates' attention by demonstrating in front of Turner's Gap. Simultaneously, Scammon would attempt to flank the

Rebels by way of Fox's Gap, about a mile farther south. Pleasonton, Cox, and Scammon all deemed this a sound tactical decision. Based on this conversation, it is reasonable to assume that sending Willcox in the same direction would be the correct course of action. Cox could unquestionably use the support, and the First Corps was now on its way and could be deployed to assault Turner's Gap.

Option 2

Pleasonton could send Willcox north of Turner's Gap. He undoubtedly was somewhat mystified as to why he was being asked to direct the infantry, but Pleasonton was apparently more than happy to offer suggestions. The plan was not tactically unsound, and it might seem the correct thing for him to do at that moment. Additionally, he had no idea that Cox was waiting for these particular reinforcements at his position. Pleasonton did know that Confederate forces held Turner's Gap, and he might feel this was the best place for any newly arriving Union reinforcements.

Option 3

Pleasonton could send Willcox to someone more appropriate for orders. I can find no indication of any of the other infantry commanders on the field deferring to Pleasonton's authority. In some cases, it would be appropriate for the commander on the field who has the most knowledge about the situation and the ground to assume authority and direct men into the battle. At that moment, however, both Reno and Burnside were forward and leading the infantry. It would be entirely appropriate for Pleasonton to defer to one of these generals and send Willcox to that officer for orders.

Decision

Pleasonton sent Willcox and his division marching north of the National Road and Turner's Gap (Option 2). At some point, either Burnside or Reno spotted them and ordered a countermarch to the Old Sharpsburg Road and up toward Cox's position at Fox's Gap. By the time Willcox arrived on the field, both sides were fought out. Cox had gained the gap, but he did not believe he had the strength to continue. Willcox was not on the field until 2:00 p.m. as a result; he was just in time to meet the additional brigades of D. H. Hill and those of Hood sent to reinforce the position. The fight for Fox's Gap then went on until dark. While the Union held the ridge, the Confederates effectively blocked any further progress.[9]

Jacob Cox later recalled this decision:

Willcox's division reported to me about two o'clock, and would have been up earlier, but for a mistake in the delivery of a message to him. He had sent from Middletown to ask me where I desired him to come and finding that the messenger had no clear idea of the roads by which he had travelled, I directed him to say that General Pleasonton would point out the road I had followed, if inquired of. Willcox understood [from] the messenger that I wished him to inquire of Pleasonton where he had better put his division in, and on doing so, the latter suggested that he move against the crests on the north of the National Road. He was preparing to do this when Burnside and Reno came up and corrected the movement, recalling him from the north and sending him by the old Sharpsburg road to my position.[10]

Willcox corroborated the encounter in his after-action report:

In compliance with orders from General Reno, we left camp, 1 1/2 miles beyond Middletown, and marched to the base of South Mountain to support General Cox's division. Communicating with General Cox, he advised me to keep my command where it was, near the main pike or Cumberland road, and consult with General Pleasonton as to taking a position. Found General Pleasonton near his batteries on the left slope of the mountain. The general indicated an attack along the slope of the mountain on the right of the main pike, and, leaving Benjamin's battery with him, I marched my division to the front, and there formed, Welsh's brigade, the One hundredth Pennsylvania, under Lieutenant Colonel Leckey, leading as skirmishers, and was about to march Christ's brigade through the woods higher up the slope, when I was ordered by General Burnside to withdraw my division and march up by the Sharpsburg road, and take up a position near Cox. Found the latter to the left of the road some few hundred yards, skirmishing on the wooded slope with the enemy.[11]

Results/Impact

As with most battles, victory and defeat often concern crucial moments that seem insignificant on their face but result in far-reaching consequences when examined in detail. The fight for Fox's Gap was clearly one of these moments. The Confederates' main reason for defending the position was that Union control meant Turner's Gap could easily be outflanked. While several factors on both sides of the fighting influenced South Mountain's outcome, this one was perhaps the most essential. Due to a courier's confusion and Pleasonton's misdirection, as well as the countermarching, it took Orlando Willcox's division far longer to reach this crucial location than it should have. Willcox did not arrive on the field until well after 2:00 p.m. By that time, Brig. Gen. Thomas F. Drayton was up with his brigade of Georgians and South Carolinians. As a result, the Confederates were able to meet force with force and stop a potential Union assault with overwhelming numbers at this critical point during the battle. As it was, the Federals arrived just in time to meet the Confederate reinforcements.

The Ninth Corps held the gap when it was all over, but the fighting took the rest of the day, raging on until nightfall. Lee then ordered a general retreat under cover of darkness. McClellan's army did not cross over until the morning of September 15, thus allowing the Confederate commander to fall back to Sharpsburg relatively unmolested. Harpers Ferry subsequently surrendered, and Stonewall Jackson's message stating as much found Lee that morning near Sharpsburg. Lee was now convinced he had time to consolidate his army before McClellan could attack him. Indeed, it took the Union army all the next day to cross over the narrow South Mountain passes. These events were all possible because of Pleasonton's decision that guaranteed the Confederate position at Fox's Gap held out until dark, and Turner's Gap was subsequently not outflanked. Therefore, this decision was critical because it created a decisive Union delay in the battle, ensuring all the subsequent campaign events happened as we remember them.[12]

Alternative Decision/Scenario

Had Pleasonton had the proper clairvoyance, he might have known of the significant opportunity presented at Fox's Gap. Alternatively, had he simply made another guess about where to send Willcox, the battle might have ended much differently than it did. It is not unreasonable to assume that Willcox's 3,600-man division could have profoundly impacted the contest had it arrived at the gap before noon. At that moment, the morning phase of the engagement was winding down. Cox's Ohioans had battled the Confederate brigades of Samuel Garland and G. B. Anderson for three hours and all but decimated them. Cox's two brigades were also exhausted and low on ammunition. Now, the troops on each side were literally racing who see who could get reinforcements to the battlefield first. A fresh Union division at Fox's Gap before noon might have tipped the scales in the Federals' favor, as no significant Confederate forces were present to stop the enemy soldiers.

Longstreet's column was still several hours away and in no position to support Hill. Had the Union combatants been able to reinforce first, they might well have overrun the position at Fox's Gap, forcing Hill's men to retreat. As a result, the Federals would then have had an opportunity to flank the Confederate position north at Turner's. This flanking maneuver, combined with the First Corps attack, might have caused the entire Confederate position to collapse that afternoon.[13]

A breakthrough at Fox's Gap on the afternoon of September 14 instead of the following morning would have significantly altered the campaign's outcome. Had the Union been able to drive through the gaps at South Mountain on the afternoon of the fourteenth rather than the morning of the fifteenth, it is sensible to assume that Lee's response would have changed. We know he did not learn of Harpers Ferry's fall until the morning of the fifteenth because Jackson did not send him word until 8:00 p.m. on the fourteenth. We also know that Lee had ordered a general retreat from Turner's and Fox's Gaps on the evening of the fourteenth. Had the Rebel general been forced to evacuate South Mountain much sooner, he might not have paused east of Sharpsburg long enough to receive Jackson's dispatch and then decide to eventually fight a battle there.

The continuation of Lee's campaign now depended on three critical circumstances: Jackson capturing Harpers Ferry that day, Lee finding a position north of the Potomac where the army could reassemble, and McClellan giving the Confederates time to execute both of those objectives. The Union

Fox's Gap. *Battles and Leaders of the Civil War.*

army in force on the west side of South Mountain on the afternoon and evening of September 14 did much to prevent these events from happening the way history records.

Franklin Delays at Crampton's Gap

Situation

William B. Franklin was born in Pennsylvania into a family that apparently did very well for itself. His grandfather was an officer in the Continental Army, his father was a judge and attorney general of Pennsylvania, and his brother retired as a rear admiral in the US Navy. William Franklin graduated first in his West Point class of 1843 and then joined the Corps of Topographical Engineers. After various assignments, he served during the Mexican War and received a brevet promotion to first lieutenant in 1848. After the war, Franklin taught briefly at West Point and worked on various civil engineering duties around Washington, advancing to the rank of captain in 1857. From 1859 to 1861, he was the engineer supervising the United States Capitol dome's construction and then the supervising architect for the new Treasury Building.

Soon after the beginning of the Civil War, Franklin was promoted to colonel in command of the Twelfth US Infantry. That summer, he was further promoted to brigadier general of volunteers. He commanded a brigade at First Bull Run and afterward became a division commander in the newly created Army of the Potomac. In March 1862, when the army was formed into corps, Franklin was appointed to command the Sixth Corps, which he then led during the Peninsula and Second Bull Run Campaigns. He earned the rank of major general of volunteers in July 1862.[14]

McClellan responded to Lee's invasion by deploying his army on three separate lines of advance. This course of action facilitated the march and provided cover for Washington, DC, and Baltimore. Franklin's corps, accompanied by the Fourth Corps division of Maj. Gen. Darius N. Couch, made up the left wing of this formation. Franklin was instructed to advance on a line that kept the Potomac River on his left flank. He did so, and the bulk of his corps was south of Frederick and just west of Buckeystown, Maryland, by September 13. Couch's division was posted some five miles further south, spread out along the Potomac and watching the fords.[15]

Once the relief of Harpers Ferry became a campaign objective for the Union army, McClellan intended Franklin's corps to come to the garrison's aid. He also used the corps to placate Halleck. As soon as he learned the

Maj. Gen. William B. Franklin, Commander, Union Sixth Corps. Library of Congress.

Army of Northern Virginia had crossed the Potomac, Halleck believed the Confederates would draw the Union army out of the capital and then recross the Potomac to threaten Washington, DC. McClellan planned for the Sixth Corps to protect his left and be in a position to block Lee should he try to double back and fall on Washington. The Union commander made these arrangements even though he likely did not share the general-in-chief's concern over this threat to the capital. McClellan considered Franklin, whom he had temporarily rescued from a potential court-martial via Pope, a friend. Familiar with Franklin and his corps from the Peninsula Campaign, McClellan now trusted Franklin with a crucial part of his plans at South Mountain.

Reacting to the information in the Lost Dispatch, McClellan intended to use his army's main body, now at Frederick, to hold as many Confederates at the northern gaps as he could. This would allow Franklin and his corps to break through Crampton's Gap and relieve Harpers Ferry. On September 14, as the Union First and Ninth Corps assaulted Turner's and Fox's Gaps, respectively, Franklin was ordered to attack and move his corps through Crampton's to Rohrersville and possibly as far as Boonsboro. Any serious and expeditious penetration into these gaps would pose a real menace to Lee's plans. However, because of its proximity to the Confederates' rear on and adjacent to Maryland Heights, the Sixth Corps was best positioned to pressure those enemy units (McLaws and R. H. Anderson).[16]

On September 13, McClellan was aware that Harpers Ferry had not yet fallen. Furthermore, he noted signs that the divisions Lee had sent to capture the garrison were still more or less in the positions outlined in Special Orders 191. Like the Confederate commander, McClellan recognized that any sizable Union force in Pleasant Valley would essentially cut the Rebel forces in half by blocking the most direct route the Harpers Ferry troops could use to move north to rejoin the rest of the Confederate army.[17]

William B. Franklin received his orders on the evening of the thirteenth. In this order, McClellan gave Franklin an overview of Special Orders 191, a situational report, and a summary of what the commanding general expected of him and his corps. McClellan ordered Franklin to move at first light with or without Couch's division to destroy McLaws's forces and relieve Harpers Ferry. He then directed Franklin's, Miles's, and Couch's forces—combined, these units were more than half the size of Lee's entire army—to drive a wedge between the two halves of Lee's army. If Franklin could somehow pull off this feat, he would put approximately thirty thousand Union men amid Lee's Confederate forces.[18]

While Franklin did not know it, the Confederate troops defending Crampton's Gap were merely a fraction of the entire Confederate force under McLaws. The soldiers protecting the gap consisted of one battery of artillery, four regiments of infantry under Col. William A. Parham, four regiments under Brig. Gen. Howell Cobb, and a small cavalry detachment under Col. Thomas T. Munford. The Confederates could count at most 2,100 men to conduct the defense. On the other hand, Franklin had between 11,000 and 12,000 men in his corps alone.

McClellan finished his dispatch with the following request: "I ask of you, at this important moment, all your intellect and the utmost activity that a general can exercise."[19]

Options

Franklin had two options: move immediately on the night of September 13 or wait until dawn on September 14.

Option 1

Franklin could act aggressively and put his corps on the road immediately. His force would then be better positioned to launch its attack on Crampton's Gap at dawn on the fourteenth. McClellan's order indicated that he expected Franklin to move at first light, but McClellan also told Franklin he could adjust his directives as he saw fit provided the overall intent was carried

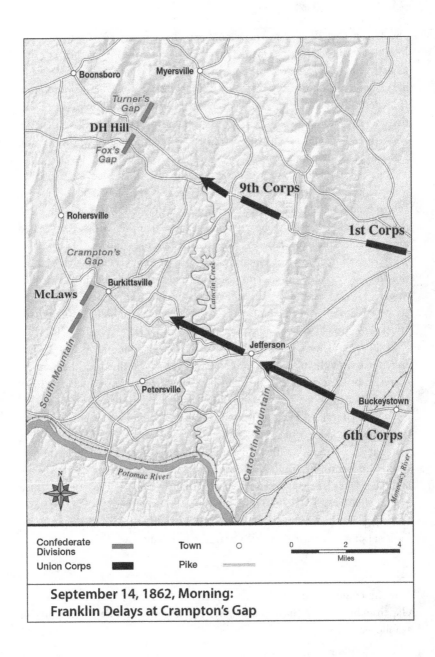

Boonsboro
Myersville
Turner's Gap
DH Hill
Fox's Gap
9th Corps
1st Corps
Rohersville
Crampton's Gap
Burkittsville
McLaws
Catoctin Creek
Jefferson
South Mountain
Petersville
Catoctin Mountain
Buckeystown
6th Corps
Potomac River
Monocacy River
N

Confederate Divisions
Union Corps
Town
Pike
0   2   4
Miles

September 14, 1862, Morning:
Franklin Delays at Crampton's Gap

out. Given that Buckeystown was almost fifteen miles from Burkittsville, Franklin could attempt to move as much of his corps as possible nearer to his objective. He could march once he received McClellan's order on September 13, or he could set out in the hours well before daybreak on the fourteenth. If he desired to launch his attack at dawn (5:49 a.m.), Franklin had to know that at least four and a half hours of marching must precede this offensive. Night marches while rare, were not without precedent during the war for Federals or Confederates.[20]

One additional complication for Franklin was that McClellan's orders were somewhat unclear. He instructed the Sixth Corps to move at daybreak and commence his attack thirty minutes after sounds of battle could be heard from Turner's Gap. These instructions suggest that McClellan anticipated Franklin's presence at Crampton's Gap near the same time as the attack on Turner's Gap opened. This circumstance then prompts the question of what timeline of events the commanding general envisioned. Did he think Franklin would arrive at Crampton's sooner than he eventually did, or did he expect the attack at Turner's to start later than it did? McClellan also ordered Franklin to attack with Couch's division, but not to delay his movement by doing so.

It is unclear how conscious Franklin was of the strength of the Confederate force directly in front of him on the night of the thirteenth. However, there can be little doubt that he knew how much was at stake. Even a cursory glance at a map of the area reveals how vulnerable the Rebels in Pleasant Valley and on Maryland Heights were. Additionally, Franklin's men alone were given the task of rescuing their comrades now under siege at Harpers Ferry, and that garrison could only hold out for so long. Based on McClellan's order of the thirteenth, Franklin knew that any window of opportunity was limited. That fact alone should convince him that time was of the essence. If we assume that it would take roughly three hours to overpower the Confederates at the gap on the fourteenth, a dawn attack would put Franklin in Pleasant Valley at 9:00 a.m. or 10:00 a.m. versus the following day.

Option 2

Franklin could wait until dawn on September 14 to move toward Crampton's Gap from his camp at Buckeystown. McClellan communicated with Franklin as follows:

> Without waiting for the whole of that division [Couch] to join, you will move at daybreak in the morning, by Jefferson and Burkittsville, upon the road to Rohrersville. I have reliable information that the mountain pass by this road is practicable for artillery and wag-

ons. If this pass is not occupied by the enemy in force, seize it as soon as practicable, and debouch upon Rohrersville, in order to cut off the retreat of or destroy McLaws' command.[21]

Nothing explicitly stated in this order told Franklin to attack at daybreak. He was only ordered to "move at daybreak." McClellan sent clear directions as to what he wanted, but he left some discretion to his lieutenant. Franklin had a rough idea of the Confederates' position holding the gap, but like McClellan, he did not know the exact size of the force defending it or what lay just beyond in Pleasant Valley. Franklin might believe that rushing in too fast could land him in a nasty spot. We know he held an almost ten-to-one superiority in numbers. However, at this moment, Franklin could only guess the size of the enemy force he might be facing, and he didn't know how many men were beyond the gap in Pleasant Valley. In his September 13 dispatch, McClellan told Franklin, "McLaws, with his own command and the division of R. H. Anderson, was to move by Boonsborough and Rohrersville to carry the Maryland Heights."[22] But Franklin had no more insight as to what constituted a command within the Confederate army than McClellan had.

Additionally, Franklin might assume that the Harpers Ferry garrison would hold out longer than it did. At that moment, he had no idea that Miles would capitulate so quickly; perhaps he felt time was on his side. General Franklin also felt most comfortable when every regiment was in place, every gun was accounted for, and the enemy's position and strength were absolutely known. In his mind, the risk of failure was far higher than the promise of reward for aggressiveness. Because of the looming charges brought by Pope, Franklin might be more risk-averse than usual.

Though unconfirmed, the possibility remains that Franklin believed that moving his force closer to his objective might alert the Confederates, prompting them to send a more significant force to defend the gap. It's also possible that Franklin believed McClellan had a compelling reason for indicating a morning march.[23]

Decision

Franklin decided to wait and begin his advance toward Crampton's Gap at dawn on September 14 (Option 2). He began marching at first light as instructed, putting the lead division of Maj. Gen. Henry Slocum on the road to Burkittsville between 5:30 and 6:00 a.m. Maj. Gen. William F. Smith's division was right behind this force. At about 10:00 a.m., the Sixth Corps halted at Jefferson, allowing Couch's division to join them. After waiting an hour, the corps continued on to Burkittsville at the eastern foot of Crampton's. Slocum's

Second Brigade under Col. Joseph Bartlett entered the eastern outskirts of the town at noon. Franklin seemed in no real hurry, and he spent the next several hours clearing the town, reconnoitering the Confederate position, placing his incoming units, and then enjoying lunch and cigars.

After positioning his brigade, Bartlett was ordered to report to corps headquarters. There he found a number of the corps's generals debating the best way to attack the Confederates.

> I found [them] grouped there, resting on the ground, in as comfortable positions as each one could assume after lunch, smoking cigars. . . .
>
> After a little preliminary conversation, not touching upon the battle before us, Gen. Slocum suddenly asked me on which side of the road leading through (Burkittsville) and over the Pass I would attack. Without a moment's hesitation, I replied, "On the right."
>
> "Well, gentlemen, that settles it," said Gen. Franklin. "Settles what general," I exclaimed. "The point of attack."[24]

Told he was to break the tie and decide how to open the battle, a somewhat indignant Bartlett returned to his brigade and led the opening attack on the gap. At 4:30 p.m., ten hours after the Sixth Corps had left camp that morning, the battle for Crampton's Gap began.

Results/Impact

Extending half a mile north of Burkittsville, Franklin's line overwhelmed and pushed the thin Confederate line up the mountain's steep eastern face. A last stand on the ridge by Confederate brigadier general Howell Cobbs's brigade and an artillery battery proved to be too little, too late. The Sixth Corps drove the Confederates from their positions at dusk. Some two and a half hours after the battle started, darkness finally ended the Union advance. The next day, September 15, Franklin got his whole force into Pleasant Valley only to stop again, believing he was outnumbered.[25]

For several reasons, Franklin's advancing to Crampton's Gap at dawn on September 14 was a critical decision. First, because Miles saw no real sign that a relief force was near at hand, this choice advanced his decision to surrender the next day. Second, the timing of Franklin's advance allowed Stonewall Jackson and those Confederate forces with him to complete the capture of the Harpers Ferry garrison on the morning of the fifteenth and be available to Lee on the sixteenth and seventeenth. Jackson was so sure of the garrison's fall that he sent Lee a message to that effect on the night of the fourteenth, twelve full hours before the surrender actually occurred. This communication was mostly responsible for Robert E. Lee's decision to concentrate at Sharpsburg and eventually offer McClellan battle. Last, Franklin's forward progress on September 14 allowed the Confederate divisions of McLaws and R. H. Anderson on Maryland Heights and Pleasant Valley to get away with minimal damage. The troops were then able to move on to Sharpsburg and play critical roles in the battle on September 17.[26]

Alternative Decision/Scenario

Had Franklin been more aggressive during those crucial hours and moved his corps closer before dawn on September 14, he might have significantly transformed the campaign. A window of some thirty-six hours existed from the time Franklin received his orders until Harpers Ferry's surrender. While he did not know precisely how long the garrison could hold out, he surely knew that it would not hold out forever. Had Franklin been only slightly more assertive in pushing the significantly smaller Confederate force off Crampton's Gap and somehow relieving the Harpers Ferry garrison, Lee might have had no choice but to abandon his campaign and return to Virginia. Indeed, this had been Lee's plan before he received Jackson's dispatch early on the morning of the fifteenth. We can only speculate what Franklin's, Miles's, and Couch's combined forces could or would have done to change history. In fact, they might not have had to do anything at all. Knowing over thirty thousand Union soldiers loose in Pleasant Valley alone would undoubtedly have profoundly affected Lee's decision-making. We might be talking about a completely different outcome, as the likelihood of a battle along the banks of Antietam Creek would have significantly diminished.

In addition, had Franklin decided to launch a more aggressive attack on the fifteenth, it could still have been too late to help the men trapped in Harpers Ferry, but his actions might have had a real effect on the clash of the seventeenth. It is reasonable to assume that a more forceful assault on September 14 and 15 might have held McLaws and Anderson in place for several more hours to avoid being overrun. As it was, these divisions did not arrive at Sharpsburg until very early in the morning on the seventeenth. Had they indeed been held in place to fend off a more aggressive attack by Franklin, McLaws might not have been available to launch the flank attack on Sumner in the West Woods. Also, Anderson's men might not have been available to reinforce the Sunken Road. Both of these actions were critical in their own right on the seventeenth.

Furthermore, Lee was now under a great deal of pressure because his

The Battle of Crampton's Gap. *Harpers Weekly.*

calculated risk could completely unravel. He recognized how vulnerable his whole army was and what a very precarious position McLaws was in on Maryland Heights. The Confederate commander was hoping his defense at South Mountain would buy him the time he needed to keep his campaign alive. Even if he had no idea how critical his attack was, had Franklin been able to get his entire force in Pleasant Valley on the afternoon of September 14 instead of the next day, then interposed himself between the separate parts of the Confederate army, he might have forced Lee to respond. That response could well have been a full-scale retreat from Maryland.[27]

Miles Surrenders Harpers Ferry

Situation

Born in Baltimore, Maryland, Dixon Stansbury Miles graduated from the United States Military Academy in 1824. Commissioned as a brevet second lieutenant in the Fourth US Infantry Regiment after graduation, Miles immediately transferred to the Seventh US Infantry, in which he served until 1847. He then served on the western frontier and became adjutant of the Seventh US. In 1836 he was elevated to the rank of captain. Miles subsequently fought in the Seminole Wars and then in Mexico, receiving both a brevet promotion to major and a brevet to lieutenant colonel. He spent the years before the Civil War on the frontier in New Mexico and Kansas. In 1859 Miles was promoted to colonel and commander of the Second US Infantry, stationed at Fort Leavenworth, Kansas.

When the Civil War began, Col. Dixon S. Miles briefly commanded a brigade in the division of Maj. Gen. Robert Patterson before being transferred to command a division in the army of Brig. Gen. Irvin McDowell. During the First Battle of Bull Run, Brig. Gen. Israel B. Richardson accused Miles of drunkenness. A court of inquiry validated this accusation, and after an eight-month leave of absence, Miles was reassigned to what should have been a quiet, out-of-the-way post. In March 1862, at the age of fifty-eight, Miles was given command of a brigade to defend the Baltimore and Ohio Railroad. He subsequently assumed command of the US arsenal at Harpers Ferry, and a garrison mainly made up of second-line and inexperienced troops. Little did Dixon Miles know he was about to play a pivotal role in one of the war's most significant chains of events. He obviously had no idea that by September 16 he would be dead, his legacy forever defined by the final act of his final command.[28]

By September 15, Lee's overdue operation to capture the garrison at Harpers Ferry and open his communications was finally reaching a climax.

Col. Dixon S. Miles, Commander, Union Harpers Ferry Garrison. Library of Congress.

This position was now at the center of the campaign. Lee assumed it would be abandoned as soon as he outflanked it. However, it was not, and he was forced to deal with it. On this pivotal day, one-third of the Confederate commander's army had fallen back from South Mountain toward the Potomac, and the other two-thirds under Stonewall Jackson had closed the trap on Miles and his men.

Two days earlier, after a short but sharp battle, two of McLaws's brigades, commanded by Brig. Gen. J. B. Kershaw and Brig. Gen. William Barksdale pushed a mixed bag of Union defenders commanded by Col. Thomas Ford from Maryland Heights and back into the town. That same day, Brig. Gen. John G. Walker's two-brigade division occupied Loudoun Heights to the south. The three divisions under Stonewall Jackson were now advancing east from Charles Town and would be in position by September 14. By the afternoon of the fourteenth, twenty-five thousand Confederates had surrounded the garrison's fourteen thousand Union soldiers.[29]

On the morning of September 14, the majority of the garrison was positioned on excellent high ground known as Bolivar Heights. These soldiers faced the combined divisions of Brig. Gen. Alexander R. Lawton, Brig. Gen. John R. Jones, and Maj. Gen. A. P. Hill. The day before, Miles's men had been given a preview of what was in store for them—a demoralizing four-hour cannonade had rained down on the Federals from three sides. Once the sun went down, they were granted a respite. Frustrated with the garrison's nonsurrender, Jackson staged a false frontal assault on the heights after dark. The plan worked as Miles pulled troops from other positions of his line to defend the Bolivar Heights position.

At first light on the fifteenth, the bombardment was renewed. Miles soon discovered that his own forces defending Bolivar Heights had been outflanked by A. P. Hill during the night. The Rebels were poised to attack Miles's now-vulnerable left. Confederate artillery fire once again saturated the Union positions from all sides, and Stonewall Jackson ordered the infantry attack to begin at 8:00 a.m.[30]

Decision

With the Confederate vise closing in on him from three sides, Col. Dixon S. Miles had three options: stand and fight, surrender, or attempt a breakout.

Option 1

Miles could stand and make a fight of it. From the moment Harpers Ferry was clearly under threat, Miles had been ordered to defend the installation. While its military significance is debatable, the general-in-chief and some Lincoln

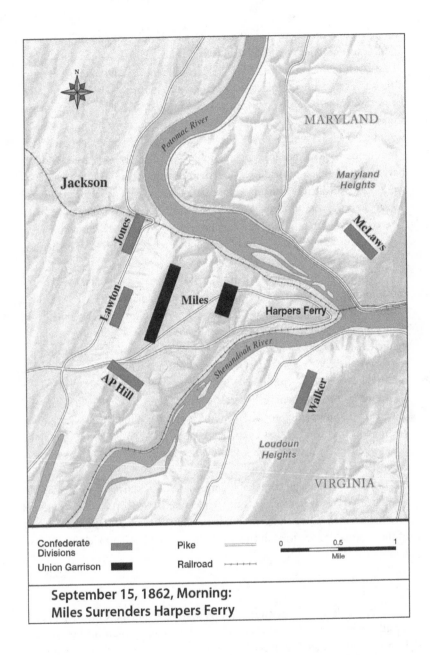

September 15, 1862, Morning:
Miles Surrenders Harpers Ferry

administration members evidently placed a high political and military value on this position. Henry Halleck had ordered the garrison to defend itself "until the latest moment" or until McClellan could relieve it. Despite the extreme difficulty of securing this place, Miles had sworn in turn, "[I] will do my best." Even though many of his regiments were untested, Miles had over fourteen thousand troops, and he also held the high ground on Bolivar Heights. It would be up to Jackson to attack the colonel to gain his objective and force a capitulation. By the morning of September 15, the garrison's surrender might have been a foregone conclusion, but there was merit in making the Rebels work for it. While it is difficult to speculate how long the garrison could hold out against the assault of Jackson's forces, many of the officers under Miles favored putting up a fight. They included Martinsburg garrison commander Brig. Gen. Julius White, who had abandoned that position days earlier and marched his men to Harpers Ferry.[31]

When you read about the difficulty the Union faced at Harpers Ferry, one common theme is that the place was nearly indefensible. However, this notion had been dispelled in late May 1862. A Union force of some seven thousand men and a naval battery of Dahlgren guns successfully defended against an attack led, coincidentally, by Stonewall Jackson. Jackson probed the garrison's position, but with rumors of two additional Union forces converging on him, he decided to withdraw. While Harpers Ferry's defenses were not put to the test, the approaching Federals demonstrated proper deployment and gave Jackson no opening to take advantage of. Brig. Gen. Rufus Saxton was the man in command of that Union force, and Dixon Miles was among those who served with him and witnessed his skillful handling of the Harpers Ferry defense.

Finally, even though the terrible cannonade demoralized the green Federals, it caused relatively few casualties. Union forces at Harpers Ferry suffered losses of only 44 killed and 173 wounded during the entire siege. The majority of these casualties occurred during the fighting for Maryland Heights on September 13.[32]

Option 2

Miles could decide to surrender and seek terms from the Confederates; after all, he had several good reasons to consider capitulation his best option. Experts and amateurs universally proclaim that Harpers Ferry was one of the most challenging locations to defend. The area is essentially a bowl surrounded on three sides by dominating heights, and it has few good positions for protection. In addition, several days had passed since Miles had heard anything from either McClellan or army headquarters. He had no idea whether anyone was coming to his relief or when such a force might arrive. Therefore, it is safe to assume he felt alone and abandoned by the rest of the Union army.

Moreover, as soldiers go, Miles's men were utterly outclassed by their more experienced Confederate counterparts. It is not a stretch to say the Harpers Ferry garrison was in no way the "varsity team" of the Union army. The men could put up a fight to be sure, but for how long and to what end? By this time, Miles had lost the key Maryland Heights position, so he was virtually surrounded. As Hill was now on his flank, prospects for successful defense dwindled by the moment. In addition, reports indicate that while the garrison soldiers had roughly fifty pieces of artillery at their disposal, the caissons were almost empty by September 14.[33]

<u>Option 3</u>

Miles could attempt a breakout as the 1,400 cavalry troopers had done the night before. Opinions differ as to the feasibility of the whole force leaving by the same route as the cavalry. Many felt this course of action was impossible, but it was indeed an option for Miles. Yet by 8:00 a.m. on the fifteenth, the opportunity had long since passed, if it had ever existed at all. Even if Miles believed he could not escape with the whole of his command, perhaps some of his soldiers could flee with Davis's troops. When Davis told Miles he was leaving, Miles cautioned him to keep the operation quiet to prevent general panic among the men left in the garrison. It is possible that the cavalry commanders were not the only Union officers seeking a way out of the trap.[34]

Decision

As it turns out, Miles decided to surrender the Harpers Ferry garrison to Jackson on the morning of September 15 (Option 2). However, a Rebel artillery shell struck him down before he could formally meet with the Confederate commander. He died of his wounds the next day. Before he was hit, Miles said to an aide, "We have done our duty, but where can McClellan be?"[35]

Results/Impact

By surrendering, Miles unwittingly provided Lee and the Army of Northern Virginia more time that would not have been available to them otherwise. As stated before, time was essential as events proceeded closer to the fighting at Antietam. The surrender of the Harpers Ferry garrison allowed the Confederates to reassemble their scattered forces at Sharpsburg and make a stand against McClellan and the Army of the Potomac. This critical decision allowed all the Confederate forces in Harpers Ferry to disengage when they did and move north to Sharpsburg, thereby providing Robert E. Lee additional essential manpower at crucial moments on September 17. Miles's surrender also continued the unbroken chain of events that would lead to the Battle of Antietam.

In late September 1862, the War Department convened a commission to investigate the events surrounding the garrison's surrender. In response to a question about Miles's actions and possible failure to follow orders, General Wool responded, "Colonel Miles appeared to be extremely zealous and extremely anxious, and I thought he would make a good defense. . . . Colonel Miles, himself, never seemed to doubt his ability to defend the place. His last dispatch to me was that he was ready for the enemy."[36] The commission ultimately found that Miles was primarily to blame and could have made a more vigorous defense of the garrison. The verdict also states that Lee had ninety-seven thousand troops in Maryland! Therefore, appropriate consideration should be given to this ruling.[37]

While Northerners almost universally vilified Miles for the Harpers Ferry surrender, many of the Southern officers who wrote about the situation, like fellow Marylander Henry Kyd Douglas, seemed more sympathetic to the Union colonel and his seemingly impossible task: "The memory of Colonel Miles has been harshly dealt with by his own people. He has been charged with cowardice and treachery at Harper's Ferry. He died with his face to the foe and he should not be called a coward."[38]

Alternative Decision/Scenario

Had Miles made a stand and forced Jackson to fight for the position, there is an excellent chance that circumstances might have been altered. Let us assume for a moment that Miles could defend his position for five additional hours, and that the garrison did not surrender until after 1:00 p.m. When Jackson sent Lee the dispatch on September 14, he stated that he expected Harpers Ferry to fall the next day. He never indicated what time the surrender would occur, so it is conceivable that Lee might still have decided to make a stand at Sharpsburg. It is also reasonable to assume that McClellan could not or would not attack on the fifteenth or the sixteenth. Even if the Harpers Ferry force had been delayed by a mere five hours, most of those troops would have had a better-than-zero chance of arriving on the field before the opening shots were fired on the morning of the seventeenth.

However, in the event of a delay by the Harpers Ferry troops, Jackson's men would not have been the same unscathed force that won the garrison without a protracted infantry engagement. Jackson and his lieutenants expected heavy losses while taking the Bolivar Heights, and these casualties

Union Artillery on Bolivar Heights, modern image. Author.

would have affected their ability to fight on Lee's imperiled left flank on the morning of the seventeenth. The losses might have significantly delayed or changed how Lee used McLaws's and Anderson's Divisions. Collectively, these units did not arrive at Sharpsburg until 4:00 a.m. on the seventeenth. If their departure had been postponed for five or more hours, they might not have been available to Lee as a general reserve. Consequently, there would have been no significant force to hit Sedgwick's division in the flank at the West Woods or to reinforce the Sunken Road.

Perhaps more significant is the fact that Franklin might have pressed harder had he known Miles was still holding out. On the fifteenth, Franklin sent a message to McClellan stating that he assumed Harpers Ferry had surrendered because the sound of cannon fire from that direction had ceased. It is possible that the sound of continued fighting from Harpers Ferry might have inspired Franklin to press his attack harder. This, in turn, might have forced McLaws to continue the difficult task of fighting on two fronts and delaying his eventual departure for Sharpsburg.[39]

Lee Offers Battle at Sharpsburg

Situation

From the moment Robert E. Lee decided to divide his army on September 9, his window of opportunity began to close. The general's force could only stay divided for a finite amount of time. Six days later, his calculated risk was starting to come apart, and very little had gone according to plan.

Lee faced a daunting situation on the evening of September 14. The garrison at Harpers Ferry had not evacuated in response to his incursion into the North, and the operation to eliminate this obstacle was now two days behind schedule. McClellan had suddenly and inexplicably taken a more aggressive posture in Lee's direct front at South Mountain. The Confederate general's ability to gain and maintain the initiative had given him the freedom to control the campaign's tenor, and up until now, he had done so very effectively. By the evening of September 14, however, the military scales had tipped in favor of the Union. McClellan's aggressiveness at South Mountain suddenly gave Lee pause. According to the Rebel commander, McClellan was now advancing "more rapidly than was convenient."[40]

The fighting at South Mountain resulted in a Union victory, and the setting sun was the only thing that prevented a more decisive one. After a meeting with his lieutenants, Lee determined that Longstreet's and D. H. Hill's men could not hold Turner's Gap once dawn came, and that the position was to be abandoned during the night. Additionally, the Confederate forces defending Crampton's Gap fell back into Pleasant Valley. Although Lee was unaware of the full extent of the Crampton's Gap defeat, he knew McLaws's and Anderson's combined force at Maryland Heights was the most vulnerable.

The geography of Pleasant Valley provided a genuine obstacle to the Confederate army. If the Union could get a sizable force into the valley, McLaws and R. H. Anderson would have no direct line back to the main Confederate force now north of the Potomac. Their only viable option would be to cross the river and fall back through Harpers Ferry. This could not happen if Harpers Ferry was still held by the Union. If the men in McLaws's Command were forced to remain north of the Potomac, they might find themselves between the proverbial rock of the Union Sixth Corps and the hard place of the Harpers Ferry garrison.

On the evening of September 14, Lee sent dispatches to his widely scattered commands: "The day has gone against us, and this army will go by Sharpsburg and cross the river." The divisions of Jones, Hood, D. H. Hill and Evans' brigade were to withdraw silently from South Mountain and fall back in Sharpsburg's direction. Brig. Gen. William N. Pendleton, Lee's chief of artillery, was ordered to position batteries west of Boonsboro and send the remainder of the reserve artillery to a position on Boteler's/Blackburn's Ford. Supported by infantry, this artillery would defend the critical Potomac crossing should the army need to continue to retreat. Cavalry under Brig. Gen.

Sharpsburg, Maryland, circa 1862. Library of Congress.

Fitzhugh Lee's and Brig. Gen. John B. Hood's divisions, with the aforementioned artillery, were ordered to act as the rear guard during the withdrawal. Lee also sent a dispatch to Jackson asking for an estimated completion time for the Harpers Ferry operation.[41]

Later that night, as the situation became more desperate, Lee sent two telling messages. The first ordered Jackson to abandon the Harpers Ferry operation, fall back to Shepherdstown, and cover the army's retreat. The second directed McLaws and his troops to abandon Maryland Heights and, with Anderson's Division, make their way back to Virginia's relative safety in any way they could. Robert E. Lee's great invasion into the North was about to come to a sudden and inglorious end. To General McLaws, Lee would write the following:

> The day has gone against us and this army will go by Sharpsburg and cross the river. It is necessary for you to abandon your position to-night. Send your trains not required on the road to cross the river. Your troops you must have well in hand to unite with this command, which will retire by Sharpsburg. Send forward officers to explore the way, ascertain the best crossing of the Potomac, and if you can find any between you and Shepherdstown leave Shepherdstown Ford for this command.[42]

After sending his dispatch to McLaws, Lee learned of the disaster at Crampton's Gap. Determining McClellan's forces were still firmly positioned in his front, the Confederate commander set his sights on the town of Keedysville as a dual-function position. He could use it to stand against the Federals in his front and threaten any Union forces' flank in Pleasant Valley.[43]

The scales of war tipped back in Lee's favor just a few hours later. Early on Monday, September 15, the general was scanning the countryside from a high meadow just east of the village of Sharpsburg. Pondering his next move, he absorbed the landscape's details with his military engineer's eye. While initially wanting to consolidate his force at Keedysville, Lee changed his mind upon seeing a better defensive position farther west, beyond Antietam Creek.

Lee was partial to the terrain west of Antietam Creek for several reasons. He needed favorable ground to conduct a new delaying action should McClellan continue his aggressive movements. The Confederate general also wanted an advantageous position to concentrate his army north of the Potomac River should he have the opportunity to continue the campaign north. Additionally, because Franklin's corps was now in between McLaws's and Anderson's Divisions and the main body of Lee's army, Lee needed to be west of Elk Ridge to give the Rebel units a feasible route to rejoin him. Finally, the Antietam Creek also provided a natural barrier for the general to position his army behind. The terrain west of the Antietam at Sharpsburg filled all of these requirements. Its only drawback was its proximity to the Potomac River, which provided limited maneuvering space and a single crossing point for a retreat.

Lee was here at 8:00 a.m., enjoying a hot cup of coffee gifted to him by a local citizen, when he received the dispatch Stonewall Jackson had sent him the night before.[44] The message from Jackson read in part, "Through God's blessing, the advance, which commenced this evening, has been successful thus far, and I look to Him for complete success to-morrow. The advance has been directed to be resumed at dawn to-morrow morning."[45]

Options

With Harpers Ferry's capitulation now imminent and this dispatch in hand, Lee had three options: continue his retreat to Virginia, reunite his army and fight at Sharpsburg, or unify his army and maneuver toward Hagerstown.

Option 1

Lee could continue with his current mind-set, end the campaign, and make for Virginia via the Potomac Ford at Shepherdstown. He had sound reasons to believe this was his best option. Despite Jackson's message, Lee had no

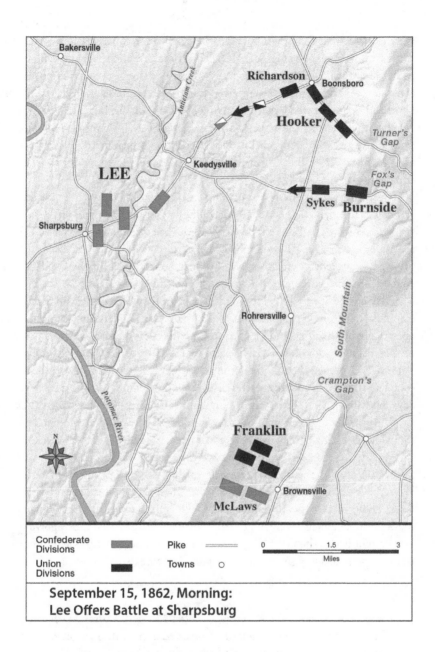

September 15, 1862, Morning:
Lee Offers Battle at Sharpsburg

real guarantee that the situation was turning in his favor. While the general trusted his lieutenant's judgment, Jackson's communication was more than twelve hours old, and there might be good cause to doubt the predictions it contained. At the moment Lee received the dispatch from Jackson, Harpers Ferry had not yet surrendered. The Army of Northern Virginia was still divided and vulnerable. On that morning, Lee had perhaps twelve thousand combat effectives to defend his line at Sharpsburg. Twenty-five of his thirty-nine brigades were still at or near Harpers Ferry, some fifteen miles and several hours' march away.[46]

Meanwhile, McClellan's army would soon be pouring through Fox's and Turner's Gaps, if it was not already. Nothing but a small delaying force was available to slow the Federal advance. While Lee was doubtless unsure of the Union troop strength, he probably believed he was outnumbered. With fifty thousand Federal effectives within a few hours' march of the Confederates' thinly held line, Lee would find himself in a very tight spot should McClellan continue to press him hard. Although the Rebel commander was consolidating a strong position west of Antietam Creek, it left him with only one avenue of retreat should he need it. Only Boteler's Ford downstream of Shepherdstown presented a viable place where Lee's army could cross the Potomac. Also, even though the Potomac was close, Lee had too few men to completely anchor his flanks on the river. At various times over the next few days, both flanks were thinly held only by cavalry forces, if they were held at all. Moreover, conventional military wisdom dictates that a commander should never fight a battle with a significant obstacle at his back.

Finally, Lee had to consider whether the benefits he had envisioned at the beginning of the campaign were still worth the risks his army now faced. Were the high stakes for the invasion worth the possible destruction of his force? Should Lee decide to fall back, he could still regroup and reorganize south of the Potomac, then look to cross the river again should the opportunity present itself. The Confederate commander still needed a battle, but he was not compelled to fight at this exact place and time.[47]

Option 2

Lee could attempt to reunite his army and offer McClellan battle at Sharpsburg. The Confederate commander had invested a great deal to get to this point in the campaign, and ending it here without accomplishing any of his operational objectives would be a bitter pill to swallow. If Lee did fall back across the Potomac to Virginia, he had no guarantee that the Army of the Potomac would allow him to recross the river later. The position his forces would soon occupy at Sharpsburg had many advantages for defense. The rolling terrain provided a good field of observation and fire. A predominant ridge along the Hagerstown Turnpike offered an ideal defensive position. Moreover, Antietam Creek created a tremendous natural obstacle in Lee's front that was just deep and wide enough to hamper any concerted effort to cross it, except in a few places.

Lee could defend the Middle and Lower Bridges with his limited forces and allow the enemy only the Upper Bridge as a means to move troops over the creek. The ridge running along the Hagerstown Turnpike just north of the town provided an optimal position to defend his left. The Confederate commander held interior lines, and he could exploit the area's good network of roads to concentrate his army and move infantry and artillery from point to point with relative ease. As the ground rose from Antietam Creek, it undulated in deep swales and gullies that would enable Lee to conceal or display his forces to the enemy as it suited him. While McClellan had been uncharacteristically aggressive at South Mountain, once he pushed the Rebels back, his forces were bottlenecked by the roads and the narrow mountain passes as Lee hoped they would be.

When given a choice, Lee always sought to be aggressive—so much so that this quality seemed his second nature. By keeping his campaign alive, he would reclaim the advantage he had fought so hard to gain.

Lastly, Lee's overarching operational objective was to force a decisive confrontation with the Army of the Potomac. As an opportunist, the general might have assumed that this location offered the best place to accomplish that goal at that particular moment.[48]

Option 3

Lee could try to reunite his army and proceed toward Hagerstown. While the Sharpsburg position was a strong one, and Lee was committed to no real destination once he crossed the Potomac River, traveling farther north would serve his overall operational goals. The Confederate commander looked for opportunities to threaten several points in the North, including Harrisburg directly and Baltimore and Philadelphia indirectly. Lee also could use Hagerstown as his jumping-off point for an invasion of Pennsylvania should he choose to do so. While we do not know for sure whether Lee really intended to move as far north as Harrisburg, it is reasonable to assume he would do so if it served his overall objectives. He might also believe that another position farther north could offer more room for maneuver.

Additionally, the farther north of the Potomac Lee moved, the more he would cause difficulties not only for the Union army but also for the Lincoln administration. He could gain additional military and political capital by spreading further panic in Maryland and Pennsylvania towns and cities. Lee contemplated this course of action while he was in Frederick, but the Harpers Ferry operation interrupted his plans. In fact, up until the moment the Union First Corps crossed over Antietam Creek on the afternoon of September 16, the general still considered a move north by way of the Hagerstown Turnpike a viable option.[49]

Decision

Lee decided to make a stand at Sharpsburg almost instantly upon receiving Jackson's message (Option 2). He at once sent orders for all of his forces to converge on the town. Lee counted on South Mountain's bottleneck to slow the Union army's advance for several days, thus giving him the time he needed. He outlined this thinking in a letter to Davis on the sixteenth: "Learning later in the evening that Crampton's Gap on the direct road from Frederick-town to Sharpsburg had been forced, and McLaws' rear thus threatened and believing from a report from Genl Jackson that Harper's Ferry would fall next morning, I determined to withdraw Longstreet and D. H. Hill from their positions and retire to the vicinity of Sharpsburg, where the army could be more readily united."[50]

Based on some accounts and the previous statement, you could argue that Lee initially intended Sharpsburg to be used only as a concentration point for his army to continue his campaign north into Pennsylvania (Option 3). Some historians indicate Lee sent a force to reconnoiter a route north late on September 16. This patrol reported that a large Union force (Hooker) had crossed the creek and now blocked the way. Only after receiving this news did Lee decide to stand and fight (Option 2). However, even if Lee had initially selected Option 3, current circumstances dictated that he would fight here regardless.

Lee also believed he had time before McClellan would attack him. However, assuming that McClellan would loiter east of Antietam for several days and not send forces across Antietam Creek to engage him seems to underestimate an enemy that had shown unpredictable aggressiveness for days. Additionally, even if Lee contemplated a turning movement on the Union right, he could not execute it while his army was still divided. McLaws and Anderson would not be on the field until the early morning of the seventeenth, and A. P. Hill would not arrive until later in the afternoon. The Rebel commander had to wait for these units to join the main body. Otherwise, the whole reason for standing at Sharpsburg would become pointless. For all intents and purposes, once Lee told his men, "We will make our stand on these hills," he committed himself to battle at Antietam whether he realized it or not.[51]

Results/Impact

Lee's decision was critical for the following reasons: Making a stand at Sharpsburg helped determine the upcoming engagement's location and proved the next step in bringing it on. Additionally, Lee's choice ensured the continuation of the Maryland Campaign and guaranteed that the Antietam battle would take place.

Converging for a clash at Sharpsburg had one other effect on events. Faced with a Rebel army turning to meet him, McClellan now paused to wonder why. On September 15 and 16, Lee's aggressive stance on the west bank of Antietam Creek was almost entirely a bluff. However, it was a good enough bluff to make McClellan contemplate what his enemy was up to and why his opponents were choosing to stand and fight here and now. Lee's defiance seemed to be a sign that, just as the Union commander had suspected since the outset of the campaign, the Confederates indeed possessed vast numbers of men.[52]

Alternative Decision/Scenario

Had Lee decided to abandon his campaign at this point, events might have unfolded quite differently. We might have still seen a battle at Sharpsburg, but it would have occurred several days later. We might have seen an engagement at Williamsport or even Shepherdstown as Lee attempted to recross

Sharpsburg, Maryland, view looking west along main street, modern image. Matt Brant.

the Potomac, or we might have seen no fighting at all. Once Lee retreated over the Potomac on September 18 after fighting along Antietam Creek, McClellan considered his campaign a success and did not engage in a vigorous pursuit. There is an excellent chance that McClellan, feeling he had accomplished his objective of driving Lee from Northern soil, might have simply have let the Confederate general go at this time as well.[53]

McClellan Launches His Attack

Situation

To understand the Maryland Campaign's story in its fullest sense is to recognize that many conspicuous themes surround it. One of the most famous or infamous of these is that despite his vastly superior numbers on September 15 and 16, an overly cautious or even cowardly McClellan decided not to attack, giving Lee valuable time to consolidate his army. Scholars' views on this particular subject vary. Stephen Sears implies that McClellan squandered those critical hours and missed an opportunity to attack due to his own incompetence and caution. Ethan Rafuse tells of a McClellan who wanted to attack but was let down by his corps commanders and by pure bad luck. Writing more recently, Steven Stotelmyer points out that the Union commander had compelling military reasons not to attack on the fifteenth—the fact that it was far too late to attack by the time McClellan had sufficient forces on the east bank was not the least of them. Stotelmyer argues that the battle had essentially begun once McClellan ordered Hooker to cross the Antietam on the sixteenth. Whatever version of McClellan the reader believes commanded the Army of the Potomac during these critical hours is not nearly as important as the alternatives the general had before him.[54]

At dawn on September 15, it became evident to the Union troops advancing on the now-abandoned Confederate positions at South Mountain that they had struck the campaign's critical first blow. McClellan possessed Lee's operational plans and had used them to drive the enemy forces from the South Mountain passes. Initial reports indicated that the Rebels were falling back, possibly as far as the Potomac. For the briefest of moments, McClellan had stolen the initiative from his opponent, and what he did next would determine how long he could hold it. The next two days proved essential to the course of the campaign and the impending battle.

From his headquarters at Bolivar, George McClellan sensed an opportunity to follow up on the successes from the night before and continue to pressure the retreating Confederate army. It is safe to say that the general was

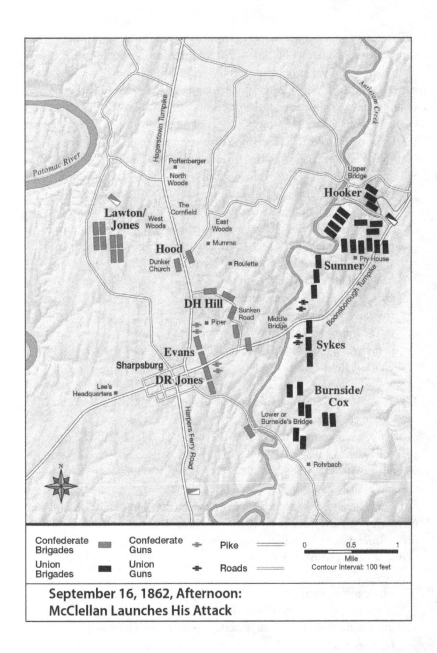

Potomac River

Hagerstown Turnpike

Poffenberger
North
Woods

The
Cornfield

Lawton/
Jones
West
Woods

East
Woods

Mumma

Hood

Dunker
Church

Roulette

DH Hill

Sunken
Road

Piper

Middle
Bridge

Evans

Sharpsburg

DR Jones

Lee's
Headquarters

Harpers Ferry Road

Antietam Creek

Upper
Bridge

Hooker

Pry House

Sumner

Boonsborough Turnpike

Sykes

Burnside/
Cox

Lower or
Burnside's Bridge

Rohrbach

N

Confederate	Confederate	Pike	0	0.5	1
Brigades	Guns				
Union	Union	Roads		Mile	
Brigades	Guns			Contour Interval: 100 feet	

**September 16, 1862, Afternoon:
McClellan Launches His Attack**

still in the dark about the number of enemy troops in his front. But in those early morning hours, he did know that a significant portion of the Confederate army remained at Harpers Ferry. McClellan would not learn about the surrender of the Harpers Ferry garrison until later on the fifteenth, and that information quickly changed the dynamics of the situation. Lee still had a chance to consolidate his army. Yet the odds were still in McClellan's favor for the moment, as this action would take some time for Lee to complete.[55]

McClellan sent the following to Halleck on the evening of September 14:

> After a very severe engagement, the corps of Hooker and Reno have carried the heights commanding the Hagerstown road. The troops behaved magnificently. They never fought better. Franklin has been hotly engaged on the extreme left. I do not yet know the result, except that the firing indicated progress on his part. The action continued until after dark, and terminated leaving us in possession of the entire crest. It has been a glorious victory. I cannot yet tell whether the enemy will retreat during the night or appear in increased force in the morning. I am hurrying up everything from the rear, to be prepared for any eventuality. I regret to add that the gallant and able General Reno is killed. [56]

Like most of McClellan's military career, controversy surrounds the decision outlined in the above letter.

By 8:00 a.m. on the morning of the fifteenth, McClellan and his staff, perhaps believing that Lee was falling back as far as the Potomac, shot off several dispatches to his commands indicating that his army would pursue and attack. Even before that, at 7:00 a.m., Hooker ordered Maj. Gen. Israel B. Richardson's Second Corps division, temporarily attached to his own corps, to move out and chase the retreating enemy. McClellan then fired off two somewhat premature messages to Halleck seeming to combine rumor and speculation with a few facts:

> I have just learned from General Hooker, in the advance, who states that the information is perfectly reliable that the enemy is making for Shepherdstown in a perfect panic; and General Lee last night stated publicly that he must admit they had been shockingly whipped. I am hurling everything forward to endeavor to press their retreat to the utmost. [57]

Later that morning, McClellan sent another dispatch:

There are already about 700 rebel prisoners at Frederick, under very insufficient guard, and I shall probably send in a larger number to-day. It would be well to have them either paroled or otherwise disposed of, as Frederick is an inconvenient place for them. Information this moment received completely confirms the rout and demoralization of the rebel army. General Lee is reported wounded and Garland killed. Hooker alone has over 1,000 more prisoners. It is stated that Lee gives his loss as 15,000. We are following as rapidly as the men can move.[58]

Alfred Pleasonton's cavalry, also on the move at first light, was ordered to pursue the fleeing Rebels. The balance of the Union infantry corps was ordered to follow Hooker and Pleasonton. Learning of Franklin's success at Crampton's, McClellan ordered him to advance as well.

After that, very little went right for the Union army commander. Burnside delayed getting the Ninth Corps moving from Fox's Gap, shoddy staff work congested all the roads, and McClellan himself did not cross over South Mountain until noon. To add to McClellan's bad luck, he received two messages from Franklin as he moved west into Pleasant Valley. The first, arriving at 11:00 a.m., indicated that Franklin's advance on Maryland Heights had stalled, and the second, arriving at 3:15 p.m., stated that Harpers Ferry had fallen to the Confederates.[59]

Just after noon, Richardson, accompanied by Col. John F. Farnsworth's cavalry brigade, reached the east bank of Antietam Creek. They soon discovered that the Confederate army was not, in fact, retreating but turning to make a stand. Richardson was joined by Hooker at 2:00 p.m. and by Sumner an hour later. The generals determined they lacked the manpower to immediately assault the Confederate position. Hooker speculated that the enemy might have as many as fifty thousand men. Rather than deploying straightaway, the Union generals then halted the advance. The resulting traffic jam clogged the roads all the way back to Turner's Gap. McClellan arrived at approximately 4:00 p.m., also declaring it impossible to attack that day.

At this moment, the Union high command had only the vaguest idea of what the ground was like on the other side of the creek, and the size of the forces opposing them was anybody's guess. Additionally, the rest of the Army of the Potomac was spread out in a nine-mile-long column from Keedysville back to Turner's and Fox's Gaps. As darkness fell, McClellan ordered the army deployed but did not issue any orders to prepare for an attack the next day.[60]

On September 16, McClellan's manpower situation improved slightly. By that morning, all his forces except Franklin's corps, Couch's division, and Humphreys's Third Division of the Fifth Corps were stationed within a few miles of McClellan's forward headquarters at the Pry House. Although he did not know it, the Union commander held the advantage in troop strength over his enemy. As the nine thousand or so soldiers that made up Jackson's Command arrived from Harpers Ferry, this soon changed.

When McClellan awoke, he discovered a dense fog in the valley that completely shrouded his view of Antietam Creek and the foe beyond. Once it lifted, at about 10:00 a.m., McClellan began to develop his plan. He also spent the next several hours assigning bivouacs, placing batteries, and riding his positions on the creek's east side to ascertain the Confederate dispositions.[61]

Options

With the situation changing by the moment, McClellan could either attack or wait. With his foe standing defiantly in front of him, he had a critical decision to make.

Option 1

McClellan could send his army across Antietam Creek and launch an attack on Lee, continuing to press his initiative and falling on the Confederate

The Battle of Antietam. *Harpers Weekly*.

commander before he was prepared. If McClellan acted quickly, he might descend on the enemy troops and defeat them in detail. Part of his mission was to drive the invaders from Maryland, and by that morning, it might seem to him that the Rebels had no intention of leaving on their own. Lee would probably have retreated by now had he wanted to. McClellan might conclude that if the Confederates were to be extricated from Maryland, they would have to be attacked and driven out by force. In addition, perceived delays on the part of the army could create more political pressure on McClellan. With each passing day, it would become more difficult for him to justify a passive stance.

Additionally, while he was still unsure of his opponent's strength, McClellan might think that the longer he waited, the longer his odds would be. As each hour passed, inevitably, those forces at Harpers Ferry would continue to make their way to Lee. The Union commander now had roughly fifty thousand men of all arms assembled east of the creek. Still flush with victory after the encounter at South Mountain, his men's morale was as high as he could desire. This is what Abraham Lincoln and the War Department were hoping would happen. After the news of the victory at South Mountain reached him, the president sent an enthusiastic and somewhat prodding telegram to McClellan: "God bless you and all with you. Destroy the rebel army if possible."[62]

Option 2

McClellan could wait and see what, if anything, Lee would do. McClellan might deem waiting for Lee to either continue his retreat or attempt to attack first his best option. Despite his best efforts, the Federal commander had only the vaguest idea of the Confederate position across the river. In his memoirs, McClellan bemoaned the advantages of Lee's location: "On all favorable points the enemy's artillery was posted, and their reserves, hidden from view by the hills on which their line of battle was formed, could manoeuvre unobserved by our army, and from the shortness of their line could rapidly reinforce any point threatened by our attack. Their position, stretching across the angle formed by the Potomac and Antietam, their flanks and rear protected by these streams, was one of the strongest to be found in this region of country, which is well adapted to defensive warfare." The general's assessment of his opponent's position was correct.[63]

Even though McClellan had the bulk of his army with him, it was not in the best shape. While the Army of the Potomac's situation was not as acute as Lee's, the force had its own challenges combating straggling and feeding its men. Disorganization caused commissary wagons to be too far from the men they were supposed to feed. Hungry Ninth Corps men reportedly searched the haversacks of dead Rebels after South Mountain. Furthermore, in battling the Confederates for South Mountain, McClellan's army suffered over 2,300 casualties. The exhausted First and Ninth Corps men not only marched and fought from dawn until dusk on September 14, but they also slept in the cold on their arms that night. They then were awakened to pursue their foe that next morning. To add to McClellan's misfortune, Ninth Corps commander Jesse Reno had been mortally wounded, and new Twelfth Corps leader Maj. Gen. Joseph K. Mansfield possessed sparse combat command experience. Mansfield arrived on September 15 to take command of the Twelfth.[64]

Additionally, this dramatically reorganized Army of the Potomac had only existed in its current state for perhaps a week. McClellan was still getting to know his command, which was not the army he had led on the Virginia Peninsula. Under ideal conditions, these soldiers were closer to an unwieldy mob than to a professional army. Thus, it was a genuine challenge for McClellan to bend this immature force to his will. Many of the regiments he commanded were new and untested in battle, and the army was often being assembled as it marched. Caution was not uncalled for—even at this relatively early stage of the war, Robert E. Lee had established a reputation for doing the unexpected in combat.

Decision

McClellan chose to attack (Option 1). At 2:00 p.m. on the sixteenth, he ordered Hooker and his First Corps to advance across the Antietam. Decoding McClellan's ultimate plan for the battle is challenging to be sure, as he seems to have contradicted himself in accounts made after the fact. In his after-action report dated October 15, 1862, he stated, "The design was to make the main attack upon the enemy's left—at least to create a diversion in favor of the main attack, with the hope of something more by assailing the enemy's right—and, as soon as one or both of the flank movements were fully successful, to attack their center with any reserve I might then have on hand."[65]

We can argue that there were unnecessary delays and that McClellan might have been able to attack on September 15 or 16. However, he did make the ultimate decision to attack, perhaps despite some lingering doubts he had about his chances for success.

Results/Impact

The most obvious and direct result of McClellan's decision was that it inaugurated the Battle of Antietam by forcing Robert E. Lee to fight. Secondarily, it ensured that the battle occurred at the location and on the day history now records. The Union general's choice also allowed Lee to participate in a defensive engagement on ground of his own choosing possessing good interior lines. One other impact of note is that McClellan's decision prevented Lee from moving his army north to continue his campaign of maneuver, perhaps making the determination to fight here somewhat quixotic. As mentioned in the discussion of the last critical decision, Lee likely never planned to linger for very long in the vicinity of Sharpsburg. Instead, he wanted to move north beyond McClellan's right flank. McClellan effectively blocked Lee from executing this movement by deciding to attack and sending Hooker's corps across the creek. Modern scholars like Dennis Frye argue that this is precisely what McClellan had planned all along. Lastly, the Federal commander's course of action was the next step in a series of decisions that led to combat at Antietam and ensured the continuation of the ever-evolving Maryland Campaign.[66]

Alternative Decision/Scenario

Any number of scenarios could have resulted had McClellan waited to see what Lee would do. The most likely outcome is that we might have seen the Battle of Antietam occur on September 18, September 19, or even later. The fighting would very likely have happened someplace else farther north.

The Pry House, McClellan's Forward H.Q., modern image. Matt Brant.

If McClellan had given him time, the Confederate commander would have taken full advantage of it. With an opportunity to rest, feed, and, most importantly, concentrate his army, Lee would have made his men stronger. After the battle, hundreds and perhaps thousands of stragglers would rejoin his army at Sharpsburg. Any fighting beyond the seventeenth would have involved Lee's former stragglers, who were then up and with him. More significantly, after A. P. Hill joined Lee's force at Sharpsburg on the afternoon of the seventeenth, Lee accomplished his goal of reuniting his army, and he was free to march his entire force north on the Hagerstown Turnpike to continue his campaign into Pennsylvania.

The next day, September 17, 1862, was known as the bloodiest day in American history. For twelve almost continual hours, the two armies went at each other hammer and tongs. When the sun set on that day, nearly twenty-four thousand casualties were the result of this dreadful battle. Refer to my previous book, *Decisions at Antietam* for a detailed review of the critical decisions related to the Battle of Antietam.

CHAPTER 3

THE AFTERMATH OF ANTIETAM, SEPTEMBER 18–20, 1862

After a struggle that lasted from dawn until dusk, the fighting finally died as darkness covered the battlefield. On September 18, Col. David Hunter Strother on McClellan's staff recorded his impressions of the day in his diary.

Saw General McClellan ride to the front and was called to accompany him. We rode to Sumner's post on the right where the General remained for some time in consultation. We then rode to the point of woods where there had been hard fighting. Generals Franklin, Smith, and Slocum with staff officers lay on some straw in the field behind the wood. Near them was the spot where General Mansfield fell, the trees scarred with bullets and broken with cannon shot. In every direction around men were digging graves and burying the dead. Ten or twelve bodies lay at the different pits and had already become offensive. In front of this wood was the bloody cornfield where lay two or three hundred festering bodies, nearly all of Rebels, the most hideous exhibition I had yet seen. Many were black as Negroes, heads and faces hideously swelled, covered with dust until they looked like clods. Killed during the charge and flight, their attitudes were wild and frightful. One hung upon a fence killed as he was climbing it. One lay with hands wildly clasped as if in prayer.

From among these loathsome earth-soiled vestiges of humanity, the soldiers were still picking out some that had life left and carrying them in on stretchers to our surgeons. All the time some picket firing was going on from the wood on the Hagerstown turnpike near the white church.[1]

Two critical decisions drove the direction of the campaign after September 17, 1862.

McClellan Does Not Attack

Situation

On September 18, 1862, the cool and foggy dawn broke on the fields and farms around Sharpsburg, Maryland. The mist slowly cleared, revealing the death and devastation the previous day's struggle had brought.

On the Confederate side of the line, Robert E. Lee and his battered Army of Northern Virginia braced themselves for renewed fighting. On the Union side, McClellan and his army spent that morning waiting for reinforcements to arrive. In the meantime, McClellan busied himself by sending telegrams to the War Department and letters to his wife, Mary Ellen. While the general's communication with Halleck was somewhat reserved, the message to his wife took a decidedly different tone, extolling his performance of the day before.[2]

To Halleck, McClellan wrote as follows: "The battle of yesterday continued for fourteen hours, and until after dark. We held all we gained, except a portion of the extreme left; that was obliged to abandon a part of what it had gained. Our losses very heavy, especially in general officers. The battle will probably be renewed to-day. Send all the troops you can by the most expeditious route."[3] In contrast, he sent this message to Mary Ellen:

We fought yesterday a terrible battle against the entire rebel Army. The battle continued 14 hours & was terrific—the fighting on both sides was superb. The general result was in our favor, that is to say we gained a great deal of ground & held it. It was a success, but whether a decided victory depends on what occurs today. I hope that God has given us a great success. It is all in his hands, where I am content to leave it. The spectacle yesterday was the grandest I could conceive of; nothing could be more sublime. Those in whose judgement I rely on tell me I fought the battle splendidly & and that it was a masterpiece of art.[4]

Federal buried, Confederate unburied, where they fell at the Battle of Antietam, circa 1862.
Library of Congress.

Both sides began the onerous task of caring for the almost twenty thousand wounded men scattered across the field. The recovery and care of injured
combatants was made more difficult by the fact that no official truce had
been called, and stretcher-bearers risked their lives collecting the fallen. Every structure in the immediate area capable of harboring men now became a
hospital; many other soldiers awaiting treatment lay in makeshift shelters.

George McClellan's view across the lines told him that the Confederates
were still there but more concentrated than the day before. Meanwhile, the
soldiers in the Army of the Potomac anxiously awaited a battle they, too,
presumed would very soon recommence. The Union commander could only
speculate about the damage he had inflicted on his opponent, but he was no
doubt getting preliminary returns on the losses his own forces had suffered.
In twelve hours of fighting, over twelve thousand Union men became casualties, or just over 21 percent of those engaged. Among McClellan's corps and
division commanders, losses were around 30 percent.[5]

By that morning, McClellan had the whole of his army on the west side
of Antietam Creek save the reserve artillery, the cavalry, and some units of
the Fifth Corps. On the right, the Federal line now started at a point about
half a mile north of Joseph Poffenberger's farm and a few hundred yards east
of the Hagerstown Pike. The formation then meandered southward toward

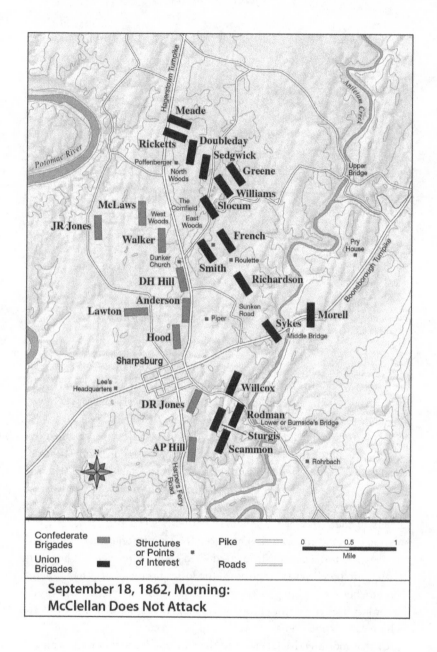

Meade

Ricketts

Doubleday

Sedgwick

Greene

Poffenberger

North
Woods

Williams

McLaws

The
Cornfield

West
Woods

East
Woods

Slocum

JR Jones

Walker

French

Dunker
Church

Roulette

Smith

Richardson

DH Hill

Anderson

Sunken
Road

Morell

Lawton

Piper

Sykes

Hood

Middle Bridge

Sharpsburg

Lee's
Headquarters

Willcox

DR Jones

Rodman

Lower or Burnside's Bridge

Sturgis

AP Hill

Scammon

Rohrbach

Potomac River

Hagerstown Turnpike

Antietam Creek

Upper
Bridge

Pry
House

Boonsborough Turnpike

Harpers Ferry Road

N

Confederate
Brigades

Union
Brigades

Structures
or Points
of Interest

Pike

Roads

0   0.5   1
Mile

September 18, 1862, Morning:
McClellan Does Not Attack

the Mumma Farm, along the Sunken Road to a point just east of and below the Lower Bridge.[6]

By noon that day, McClellan received what amounted to a brand-new corps. An additional twelve thousand men now reinforced the Union army, including Brig. Gen. Darius Couch's Fourth Corps division attached to Franklin's Sixth Corps and Brig. Gen. Andrew A. Humphreys's Fifth Corps division. These forces almost entirely replaced the Federal losses from the previous day's fighting. McClellan now had somewhere between fifty thousand and sixty thousand men of all arms with whom he could renew the attack if he so desired.[7]

Across the field, the injured Rebel army stood defiantly. Robert E. Lee's contracted line started on his left, just west of the Hagerstown Pike at the north end of the West Woods. It followed the pike into the town and along the heights of the Harpers Ferry Road south of Sharpsburg. It ended at roughly the same point the Union army's line did, only several hundred yards farther west. J. E. B. Stuart's cavalry still held positions on each flank. Over the next several days, Lee's force managed to gather up roughly six thousand stragglers to add to his various commands. In so doing, he covered nearly half of his losses from the battle on September 17. While it is unclear how many of the stragglers arrived on the eighteenth, Lee could now field an army with an estimated strength of between twenty-five thousand and thirty thousand men. However, it is safe to say that these stragglers were probably not in prime fighting condition. Lee's troops as a whole were exhausted and worn out. While the aforementioned details were significant, McClellan and his staff were no doubt unaware of the actual state of Lee's army.[8]

Options

In his 1863 after-action report, McClellan stated, "The night, however, brought with it grave responsibilities. Whether to renew the attack on the 18th or to defer it, even with the risk of the enemy's retirement, was the question before me."[9] With the specter of the previous day's carnage hanging over him, the general could attack immediately or wait. Choosing either option would be a critical decision.

Option 1

McClellan could renew the attacks from the day before. Several factors indicated that this option might be his best one. The general now had thousands of fresh troops to make use of, including the Sixth and Fifth Corps, which had been only lightly engaged the day before. These units were augmented by the divisions of Couch and Humphreys. By some estimates, then, McClellan now had thirty thousand fresh infantrymen at his disposal. This number constituted only one-third fewer men than the entire force he had committed to battle the day before. While he presumably did not realize it, McClellan now outnumbered his opponent by two to one. Even if McClellan believed the corps that were the most heavily engaged and used up from the previous day's fighting were not fit for offensive action, he could surely count on them to at least hold the ground already gained.

Although we don't know precisely what his perception of Lee's army was on September 18, McClellan needed only to look at the casualties on the field to know his enemy had taken a real beating at the hands of his own men. There was a good chance the Confederates were in no shape to defend themselves. The fact that Lee's anticipated counterattack never materialized might also be a telling clue as to the state of the Confederate army.[10]

Furthermore, the Union commander had most of his forces west of Antietam Creek, and he held all the critical crossing points. As a result, Lee could no longer count on the creek posing a significant obstacle to the Union army. It seems that some of McClellan's corps and division commanders favored continuing the offensive. William B. Franklin, for example, was still eager to lead his Sixth Corps back into the fray, or so he later wrote:

> Later in the day General McClellan came again to my headquarters, and there was pointed out to him a hill on the right, commanding the wood, and it was proposed that the hill should be occupied by our artillery early the next morning, and that after shelling the wood, the attack should be made by the whole corps from the position then held by it. He assented to this, and it was understood that the attack was to be made. During the night, however, the order was countermanded. I met him about 9 o'clock on the morning of the 18th. He informed me that he countermanded the order because fifteen thousand Pennsylvania troops would soon arrive, and that upon their arrival the attack would be ordered.[11]

Additionally, the Army of Northern Virginia was still north of the Potomac at this moment. One of McClellan's campaign objectives was to drive the Rebels from the state of Maryland; so long as Lee remained in the North, that part of the operational objective was not realized. With no guarantee that Lee would retreat on his own, an additional assault might be required to persuade him.[12]

Option 2

McClellan could wait and see what, if anything, his opponent might do first. While it is easy to criticize McClellan's inaction, he had good reasons to be cautious. In the fight for the ground at Antietam, over 21 percent of the Army of the Potomac became casualties. This is not an insignificant figure. Two of McClellan's six corps commanders had been wounded or killed, and that total increased to three if counting Reno's death at South Mountain. McClellan had also lost five of sixteen division commanders. However, most devastating of all was the Union command's loss of 52 of the 165 brigade and regimental leaders—an almost 32 percent casualty rate—along with an untold number of company-grade and noncommissioned officers. Casualties in the officer and noncommissioned officer ranks dramatically compromised McClellan's ability to exercise authority. Nineteenth-century armies relied heavily on the experience and knowledge of the brigade- and regimental-level commissioned and noncommissioned officers to effectively maneuver and deploy their forces in combat.[13]

While the Federal commander indeed had some fresh infantry, the four corps that had been most heavily engaged the day before were in deplorable shape. While some reports contradict, indications are that the First Corps had suffered 2,590 total casualties, or 27 percent of its men; the Second Corps 5,138 total losses, or 32 percent; the Ninth Corps 2,349 total casualties, or 19 percent; and the Twelfth Corps 1,746 total losses, or 23 percent. Though McClellan had also expected Brig. Gen. John Reynolds coming from Pennsylvania with 15,000 militiamen, those troops refused to cross the border into Maryland.

It should also be noted that Humphreys's division of Pennsylvanians of the Fifth Corps, arriving before noon, consisted entirely of green regiments. On September 18, Humphreys had marched his division from Washington, DC, for four straight days to reach Antietam Creek, and McClellan believed the troops were fatigued. While Humphreys disputed this claim, he could not deny these men's glaring lack of combat experience. Many of the rookie regiments that had fought on the seventeenth suffered immeasurably due to their inexperience.

The Union combatants were also reaching the end of their endurance. The previous day, McClellan's army had fought continuously from dawn until dusk. Collectively, the Army of the Potomac had been marching and fighting since leaving the defenses of Washington, DC, thirteen days before. Many units, like the First Corps, had fought on both September 17 and September 14. On the fourteenth, the corps had been heavily engaged in the struggle for South Mountain, a significant battle in its own right.[14]

Furthermore, while damaged and somewhat disorganized, most of the Union army's artillery had enough ammunition for another engagement. Yet the long-range twenty-pound Parrott rifles, so essential to counter–battery fire the day before, had mostly empty caissons. The promised ammunition was miles away, and replenishment would take some time.[15]

Based on the evidence, McClellan had good reason to believe that Robert E. Lee still outnumbered him and that the long-expected Confederate counterattack was inevitable. If McClellan overexposed himself, he might be playing right into the Rebel commander's hands. In any case, it appears that Lee expected another day of battle and was waiting for it, as illustrated by his unwillingness to retreat after the fighting on the seventeenth.[16]

On a personal level, and adding to McClellan's tactical and logistical dilemmas, dysentery afflicting him since his time in Mexico flared up yet again. The Union general was ill for the next several days.[17]

Decision

McClellan wrote on September 18, "After a night of anxious deliberation and a full and careful survey of the situation and condition of our army, the strength and position of the enemy, I concluded that the success of an attack on the 18th was not certain."[18] The Union commander decided not to renew the attack on the eighteenth (Option 2). He outlined his reasoning in his 1863 after-action report:

> The troops were greatly overcome by the fatigue and exhaustion attendant upon the long continued and severely contested battle of the 17th, together with the long day and night marches to which they had been subjected during the previous three days. The supply trains were in the rear, and many of the troops had suffered from hunger. They required rest and refreshment. One division of Sumner's and all of Hooker's corps on the right had, after fighting most valiantly for several hours, been overpowered by numbers, driven back in great disorder, and much scattered, so that they were for the time somewhat demoralized. In Hooker's corps, according to the return made by General Meade, commanding, there were but 6,729 men present on the 18th, whereas on the morning of the 22nd there were 13,093 men present for duty in the same corps, showing that previous to and during the battle 6,364 men were separated from their command.[19]

McClellan did give orders that night to prepare for an assault on the nineteenth, but when the Federals advanced the following morning, they discovered the Confederates were gone.

Results/Impact

While circumspect, this critical decision concluded the Battle of Antietam and ensured that no additional Union assaults would be made at Sharpsburg. Soldiers on both sides observed one another warily as September 18 came and went. The battle was technically over, but the decision was not absolute. The end of the engagement and the overall campaign now hinged on the outcome of the next and final decision facing Robert E. Lee.

Alternate Decision/Scenario

Had McClellan decided that he was indeed in an excellent position to launch one more attack, the history of the Battle of Antietam would undoubtedly be different. There is certainly no guarantee that any attacks on the eighteenth would have been more successful than those on the seventeenth. Yet based on the results from the day before, Lee would likely have had to retreat to save his army. As we will see in the discussion of the next decision, the Rebel general did so despite any new offensive; however, withdrawing your force under cover of darkness and doing so while under attack are two very different things.

Lee had nearly no more reserves to commit to a renewed fight other than the unknown number of stragglers that joined the army. His men were desperately tired and just as worn down as their opponents, if not more so. This fact alone, however, would not have made a more decisive victory by McClellan a certainty. Nor would it have guaranteed the destruction of Lee's army. Additionally, both forces would inevitably have suffered more casualties in fighting on September 18, and recovery from this action would have taken more time than it did.

After the war, James Longstreet summed up the Confederate position this way: "We were so badly crushed that at the close of the day ten thousand fresh troops could have come in and taken Lee's army and everything it had."[20] We will never know whether he was correct in this assessment or merely adding to a narrative.

Lee Withdraws to Virginia

Situation

As George McClellan struggled with the decisions and challenges the previous day had laid before him, Robert E. Lee faced an abundance of his own

View from Capt. Hugh Garden's (Palmetto) South Carolina Battery at the National Cemetery, modern image. Matt Brant.

dilemmas. Dawn on September 18 revealed the substantial damage the Confederate commander's army had suffered. John Bell Hood witnessed the sight and described his recollections of the dreadful aftermath of the battle: "The following morning I arose before dawn and rode to the front where, just after daybreak, General Jackson came pacing up on his horse, and instantly asked, 'Hood, have they gone?' When I answered in the negative, he replied, 'I hoped they had,' and then passed on to look after his brave but much-exhausted command."[21]

Confederate stragglers scattered all over the Maryland and Virginia countryside slowly began to rejoin the Army of Northern Virginia. In small numbers, they continued to trickle in for the next week and beyond. Lee ordered the commissary and ammunition trains brought up, and he was able to feed his men and replenish their ammunition. Lee also concentrated his lines, bracing for a new attack.[22]

Although still ready to fight, the Confederate army had suffered immeasurably. An estimated 25,000 to 30,000 Rebels were prepared for a new battle, although these numbers might be wildly optimistic. Lee's total casualties from the day before amounted to between 25 and 28 percent of his forces. While his overall losses were devastating, those among his leadership ranks were more catastrophic—death or wounding claimed 3 of Lee's 9 division commanders, 19 of his 39 brigade commanders, and 86 of his 173 regimental commanders. This is a casualty rate of nearly 50 percent at the command level.

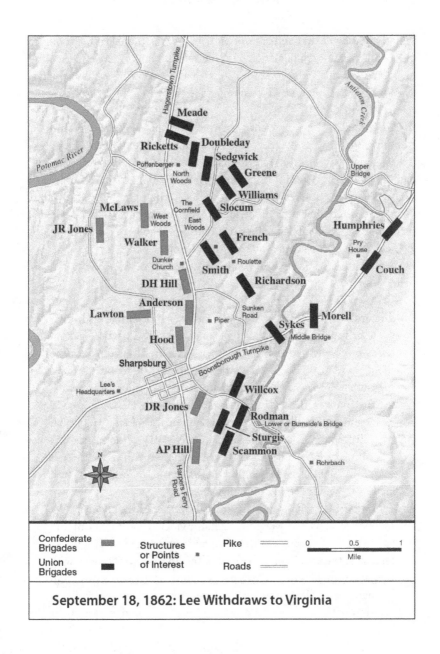

September 18, 1862: Lee Withdraws to Virginia

Maintaining command and control on Civil War battlefields was trying on the best days, but such depletion of the leadership ranks increased the difficulty exponentially. It is hard to imagine an army suffering such destruction of its core leadership and still retaining the same level of control as it had before the battle.

Additionally, Lee's army had to overcome the significant problem of gathering the dead and caring for the wounded. Henry Kyd Douglas of Jackson's staff gave a grim description of the Army of Northern Virginia's state following Antietam: "The night after the battle of Sharpsburg was a fearful one. Not a soldier, I venture to say, slept half an hour. Nearly all of them were wandering over the field, looking for their wounded comrades, and some of them, doubtless, plundering the dead bodies of the enemy left on the field. Half of Lee's army were hunting the other half."[23]

In his after-action report, Lee spoke at length of the condition of his army:

> The arduous service in which our troops had been engaged, their great privations of rest and food, and the long marches without shoes over mountain roads, had greatly reduced our ranks before the action began. These causes had compelled thousands of brave men to absent themselves, and many more had done so from unworthy motives. This great battle was fought by less than 40,000 men on our side, all of whom had undergone the greatest labors and hardships in the field and on the march. Nothing could surpass the determined valor with which they met the large army of the enemy, fully supplied and equipped, and the result reflects the highest credit on the officers and men engaged.
>
> Our artillery, though much inferior to that of the enemy in the number of guns and weight of metal, rendered most efficient and gallant service throughout the day, and contributed greatly to the repulse of the attacks on every part of the line. General Stuart, with the cavalry and horse artillery, performed the duty entrusted to him of guarding our left wing with great energy and courage, and rendered valuable assistance in defeating the attack on that part of our line.
>
> On the 18th we occupied the position of the preceding day, except in the center, where our line was drawn in about 200 yards. Our ranks were increased by the arrival of a number of troops, who had not been engaged the day before, and, though still too weak to assume the offensive, we awaited without apprehension the renewal of

the attack. The day passed without any demonstration on the part of the enemy, who, from the reports received, was expecting the arrival of re-enforcements.[24]

It is not an overstatement to say that even the unflappable Robert E. Lee now had cause for concern. In his treatment of the campaign, historian Joseph Harsh deftly and accurately describes the state of affairs the morning after the fighting at Antietam: "The Confederate soldiers awoke fully expecting another battle. Their brief war experience taught them that when unentrenched armies remained within several hundred yards of one another, the fighting was irresistibly renewed. Along the Chickahominy and at Second Manassas, the two forces had clawed at each other day after day until one had yielded and reached safe haven. But Antietam had been a different kind of battle. Its concentrated fury knocked the wind from both armies."[25]

Perhaps Lee was finally realizing that the opportunity he sought with the calculated risk of invading the North had slipped from his fingers and was drifting farther and farther from his grasp.

Options

With the fate of his campaign and possibly that of the Army of Northern Virginia hanging in the balance, Lee had three options to choose from and one last critical decision to make. He could stand on the defensive, attack, or withdraw.

Confederate dead near the Hagerstown Turnpike, circa 1862. Library of Congress.

Option 1

Lee could continue on the defensive and wait for McClellan to attack again. The Rebel general's plan upon entering Maryland had been relatively basic. From the outset of the campaign, Lee wanted to advance into Maryland or possibly Pennsylvania, turn the Federals out of their Washington defenses, and compel the Union army to pursue him far from its base of supply and support. On ground of his choosing, he would then deliver the enemy a critical blow. Other than the mission to capture Harpers Ferry, Lee had followed this script for two weeks, endeavoring to keep his campaign on course.

Given that the Confederate commander envisioned his campaign in this manner, it could reasonably be assumed that he would continue to do so on September 18. The casualties he suffered doubtless gave him pause. But Lee evidently considered allowing the Federals to continue their assaults his best tactical option. While his army had given up a significant swath of ground during the previous day's fighting, Union soldiers had gained that ground at a substantial cost. The Army of Northern Virginia was wounded but still able to fight. Several questions remained: How badly had the Army of the Potomac itself been wounded? Would it attack again? Could the Confederates prevail in another battle similar to the one fought the day before?

Option 2

Lee could decide to attack. If one thing can be accurately stated of Robert E. Lee, it is that he favored aggressive action. And while it might be unlikely to succeed, Lee did have the option of an offensive. He still desired to deliver that counterpunch that we know he desired. The Rebel general had wanted to launch a counterattack at the Federals on two separate occasions. On the afternoon of the seventeenth and again on the eighteenth, Lee had ordered his commanders to evaluate a counteroffensive's viability on the Union right. Reconnaissance on McClellan's right determined that both endeavors would be futile. Finally, because Lee had invested so much into the campaign up until this point, he likely hoped that his army was still capable of some kind of aggressive action to salvage that investment.[26]

Option 3

Lee could determine that withdrawal was his best option and pull his army back to the Virginia side of the Potomac. The general perhaps realized that his soldiers were in no condition to continue the fight. As the day unfolded, he continued receiving more and more casualty reports from the day before, but it is unknown whether Lee realized how badly his army was wounded.

Only the brigades of Brig. Gen. William D. Pender and Col. John M. Brockenbrough (Field's) of A. P. Hill's Light Division had not been heavily engaged the day before, and most of the men collected in the rear had been stragglers from the forced marches from Harpers Ferry. Every one of Lee's nine divisions had been engaged on September 17. All of these divisions, save A. P. Hill's and D. R. Jones's, had a casualty rate of over 28 percent. Lafayette McLaws's and D. H. Hill's divisions had casualty rates approaching 40 percent, and Hood's Division was the most devastated, suffering an overall casualty rate of more than 44 percent of those engaged. Twenty of the 173 infantry regiments in Lee's army had suffered losses exceeding 50 percent. Twenty of the thirty-nine infantry brigades now had fewer than four hundred men to fill their ranks.

Insomuch as the 25 percent overall Confederate casualty rate was overwhelming, the price paid by the army's leadership was devastating to contemplate. Only twenty-two of the 173 regiments Lee brought to Maryland were now headed by colonels. Twenty-two of his thirty-eight brigades did not have a single regiment led by a colonel, and five of these had captains commanding. Moreover, Lee had only twenty-seven general officers on hand to lead this ravaged force that day. In a perfect scenario, his army would have had seventy-two generals. As was the case nine months later in Pennsylvania, the Rebel commander also had thousands of severely wounded men to care for. His choice was to either leave them on Northern soil or figure out how to transport this multitude back to Virginia.[27]

From a purely tactical perspective, Lee's position was precarious at best. While he could still fight, his only escape route on the Potomac was now more vulnerable. One more determined push from McClellan might very well cut off the Confederates' only line of retreat. Saving his army to fight another day might have been a prudent choice but a bitter pill for Lee to swallow. Following this course of action would absolutely relinquish the strategic initiative the general and his ragged army had fought so hard to gain.

Decision

Brig. Gen. John Walker later recalled, "We had fought an indecisive battle, and although we were, perhaps, in as good a condition to renew the struggle as the enemy were, General Lee recognized the fact that his ulterior plans had been thwarted by this premature engagement, and after a consultation with his corps commanders he determined to withdraw from Maryland."[28]

Lee selected Option 3, withdrawing his army on the evening of September 18. Under cover of darkness, the Confederate force slipped out of line and began to fall back to the Potomac crossing at Shepherdstown to Virginia.[29]

Results/Impact

The final battle of the campaign, Shepherdstown, began the next day, September 19. McClellan wired Halleck this proclamation: "I have the honor to report that Maryland is entirely freed from the presence of the enemy, who have been driven across the Potomac. No fears need now be entertained for the safety of Pennsylvania. I shall at once occupy Harper's Ferry."[30] Conversely, Lee sent the following in a dispatch to Davis: "During the night of the 18th the army was accordingly withdrawn to the south side of the Potomac, crossing near Shepherdstown, without loss or molestation."[31]

One could certainly argue that the Maryland Campaign was not concluded at this point, but only the Battle of Antietam. As Lee departed Sharpsburg on the evening of the eighteenth, he intended to cross back over the Potomac at Williamsport and continue on to Pennsylvania. In fact, the general was moving his army in that direction when his rear guard at Boteler's Ford was attacked and subsequently collapsed on the evening of the nineteenth. Lee was forced to turn his army around to address this threat.

However, once Lee traversed the Potomac on the evening of the eighteenth, the campaign was over for all intents and purposes. Even if Lee himself did not come to this realization until five days later, there was no coming back once his army crossed the river. The Confederate commander ended the

Antietam National Cemetery, modern image. Matt Brant.

first great campaign into the North having achieved none of his operational objectives except for gaining a few supplies and some artillery, wagons, and small arms. Lee's final critical decision ended the battle and effectively ended the Maryland Campaign.[32]

Alternate Decision/Scenario

Had Lee decided to stand and fight one more day, history would indeed have been irrevocably altered. McClellan would still have been under pressure to attack had the Confederates remained on September 19. So long as Lee's army was on Union soil, the Federal commander was obligated to take some kind of action. By now, McClellan's reinforcements were up and with him, and all indications pointed to his decision to launch some sort of attack. While we can only speculate about how that attack might have manifested or what the outcome of new fighting on September 19 would have been, several things are certain. The carnage from the seventeenth surely portended thousands more names on the rolls of Union and Confederate killed, wounded, and missing.

Further blows by McClellan would have had only adverse effects. The Battle of Shepherdstown would have been different, perhaps even culminating in a fighting retreat all the way to the Potomac. In the end, one thing is sure: the Battle of Antietam would not now be known as the bloodiest single day in American history. It might instead have earned some other unfortunate cognomen that history would record.

CONCLUSION

On the morning of September 19, 1862, as the head of the withdrawing Army of Northern Virginia was several miles southwest of the Potomac, its tail was crossing the river at Boteler's (Packhorse) Ford back into Virginia. This column was spotted by Brig. Gen. Alfred Pleasonton's Union cavalry, who were themselves advancing from Sharpsburg. A Confederate force commanded by Brig. Gen. William Pendleton was shielding the Potomac crossing. Posted here by Lee on September 15, this rear guard now consisted of forty-four guns from the reserve artillery and two understrength infantry brigades totaling about six hundred men. The infantry consisted of Lawton's Brigade under Col. John H. Lamar, Armistead's Brigade under Col. James G. Hodges, and Col. Thomas Munford's cavalry brigade. Pleasonton's Union troopers lacked the strength to do anything but watch the Rebels go and report the same to McClellan.[1]

To support Pleasonton, McClellan ordered a reconnaissance in force directed at the area near Shepherdstown and the retreating Confederate army. Elements of Maj. Gen. Fitz John Porter's Fifth Corps, supported by artillery, advanced from Sharpsburg to the banks of the Potomac River at Boteler's Ford, a mile downstream of Shepherdstown. The Twelfth Corps was ordered to seize Maryland Heights to prevent the Confederates' reoccupation of Harpers Ferry. Meanwhile, Darius Couch's Fourth Corps division was sent to Williamsport to deal with a Rebel force reported to be there. These troops were J. E. B. Stuart's Confederate cavalry, and they were securing a point by

Capt. Joseph M. Knap's Union Battery, circa 1862. Library of Congress.

which the Rebels could recross the Potomac back into Maryland. Robert E. Lee's exhausted army was now on the Virginia side of the Potomac and headed upstream toward Williamsport in an effort to somehow salvage his campaign.[2]

Porter's Union infantry, four regiments under Col. Gouverneur K. Warren's command, pushed across the ford later that afternoon. As darkness fell, the Federals chased off the small contingent of Rebel infantrymen and artillerymen, captured several guns, and established a bridgehead. Pendleton fell back once his position was overrun. Riding to catch up with the rest of the army, he went from one Confederate camp to another in a desperate attempt to find Robert E. Lee or any Rebel commander who would come to his aid. At around 1:00 a.m., Pendleton finally found Lee asleep in his tent. Once the general was awakened, Pendleton informed him that all of the reserve artillery was captured. "All?" asked a somewhat stunned Lee. "Yes, General, I fear all," replied Pendleton. In response, Lee issued orders for Jackson's Command to return to Boteler's Ford at first light.[3]

The next morning, September 20, McClellan ordered Porter to press the enemy south of the river. Porter sent four brigades from his First and Second Divisions across the Potomac to strengthen his position at Boteler's. By 9:00 a.m., twelve Union regiments/battalions supported by five artillery batteries held a line almost a mile wide on the Potomac's south side. Advanced pickets soon informed the Union command that a large Confederate force was bearing down on them from the south.

At just after 8:00 a.m., two Confederate divisions under Jubal Early and A. P. Hill attacked the Union force moving up from the Potomac. Jackson's counterattack stopped the Federals in their tracks, driving them back across the Potomac. The 118th Pennsylvania, on the extreme left of the Union line, got the worst of the fighting. This green regiment was hit in its front and flank, suffering 38 percent casualties and losing its commander in the process. To compound the humiliation of defeat, the Pennsylvanians complained that fully half of their Enfield rifles malfunctioned, making them completely useless.

By noon the fight was over—the Confederates' aggressive stand discouraged any further large-scale Federal pursuit. This final and somewhat anticlimactic act of the Maryland Campaign ended in a Union defeat. The Battle of Shepherdstown resulted in an additional seven hundred names on the combined list of casualties, equal to 3 percent of the total losses from the fight three days earlier.[4] Thus, with renewed confidence and perhaps breathing a sigh of relief, McClellan sent the following to Halleck on September 19: "We may safely claim a complete victory. Pleasonton is driving the enemy across the river. Our victory was complete. The enemy is driven back into Virginia. Maryland and Pennsylvania are now safe."[5]

Once Lee turned his army back to the Potomac to protect his rear at Shepherdstown, the Confederates remained in the vicinity for six more days. During this time, the general contemplated continuing his campaign by recrossing the Potomac at Williamsport and moving on Hagerstown. However, as the days passed, Robert E. Lee realized that his force was in no physical shape to continue the operation.

On September 26, orders were issued from Lee's headquarters to have the troops begin moving to the Shenandoah Valley's relative safety near Winchester. There Lee would rest, refit, and reinforce until mid-November, when the Army of the Potomac, then commanded by Ambrose Burnside, began advancing toward the Rappahannock River and Fredericksburg.[6] George McClellan paused as well once it became clear that Maryland was fully liberated from the Confederate menace. The Federal general remained north of the Potomac until October 26, 1862.

Here is but one more example of the numerous controversial themes surrounding this campaign. A traditional version of events states that McClellan considered his operational objectives fulfilled once Lee had withdrawn to Virginia. He therefore saw no need to pursue the Rebels into the state. However, more recent scholarship describes a McClellan severely handicapped by lack of food, general supplies, and severe straggling—not to mention the twelve thousand casualties resulting from the Antietam battle. Author and Antietam guide Steven Stotelmyer goes so far as to speculate that McClellan's enemies in Washington, DC, conspired to keep supplies from his army to hasten his downfall.[7]

While the true nature of the logistics and the politics at play during this time may never be fully known, the evidence does support some conclusions. The first is that McClellan spent the next several weeks corresponding with the administration and the War Department about the general state of military affairs and the Army of the Potomac's next moves. Secondly, McClellan was reluctant to pursue the Rebel army and argued day after day as to why this was impossible. The Union commander communicated that he needed time to rest, refit, and reorganize his own army that had suffered significantly from the recent campaign. McClellan and his generals constantly complained about shortages of provisions ranging from shoes and clothing to horses and food. Lastly, the commander feared that recent rains would make the Potomac Fords impassable, and that more pontoon bridges were needed to secure his lines of communication once he moved south.

Lincoln, on the other hand, believed McClellan's concerns were just excuses. He wanted his commanding general to advance at once and finish off the wounded Army of Northern Virginia. The president began to see McClellan as a political liability and was increasingly frustrated, perhaps feeling pressure from the Republican Party's most radical element. He attempted to prod the officer into action but to no avail.[8]

On October 1, Abraham Lincoln took matters into his own hands and traveled to McClellan's headquarters near Sharpsburg to assess the army's state and meet with its commander. Despite giving what Lincoln considered a promise to advance at once, McClellan resumed arguing against this move as soon as the president returned to Washington, DC. On October 6, Henry Halleck sent a dispatch to McClellan indicating that the president was directing him to cross the Potomac, move south, and battle the enemy.

On October 13, the president sent McClellan a letter that seemed to continue their long-running disagreement over the Army of the Potomac's capabilities. In a stinging rebuke, Lincoln pushed back on the argument that lack of supplies made the Union army unable to move into Virginia:

> You remember my speaking to you of what I called your overcautiousness. Are you not overcautious when you assume that you cannot do what the enemy is constantly doing? Should you not claim to be at least his equal in prowess, and act upon the claim? As I understand, you telegraphed General Halleck that you cannot subsist your army at Winchester unless the railroad from Harper's Ferry to

Lt. Rufus King, Lt. Alonzo Cushing, Lt. Evan Thomas, and three other artillery officers in front of tent, Sharpsburg, Maryland, circa 1862. Library of Congress.

that point be put in working order. But the enemy does now subsist his army at Winchester, at a distance nearly twice as great from railroad transportation as you would have to do, without the railroad last named. He now wagons from Culpeper Court-House, which is just about twice as far as you would have to do from Harper's Ferry. He is certainly not more than half as well provided with wagons as you are.[9]

On October 26, 1862, forty days after the Battle of Antietam had ended, and after continual urging by the Lincoln administration, McClellan finally sent his army across the Potomac River in force. After twelve days, the Army of the Potomac progressed just over forty miles to Warrenton, Virginia, although no significant engagement resulted from this advance.[10]

Lee moved Longstreet's Corps more quickly than McClellan's men, and it interposed itself between the Army of the Potomac and Richmond. An increasingly frustrated Lincoln was once again under a great deal of pressure to make a change. According to John Hay, Lincoln's private secretary, the president told him, "Delaying on little pretexts of wanting this and that, I began to fear that he was playing false—that he did not want to hurt the enemy." Lincoln also described what he would do if McClellan delayed again, giving

Lee the advantage: "I determined to . . . remove him [McClellan]. He did so & I relieved him."[11]

On November 5, 1862, he ordered Halleck to relieve McClellan of command of the Army of the Potomac for good. For the third time, Lincoln turned to the affable Maj. Gen. Ambrose E. Burnside with an offer of command. This time Burnside reluctantly accepted. He and Brig. Gen. Catharinus P. Buckingham visited McClellan and informed him of the change in leadership: "On receipt of the order of the President, sent herewith, you will immediately turn over your command to Major-General Burnside, and repair to Trenton, N.J., reporting, on your arrival at that place, by telegraph, for further orders."[12]

By no coincidence, McClellan's dismissal came one day after the 1862 midterm elections in which the Republican Party saw a fifty-seat swing to the Democrats in the House of Representatives. Despite this result, Lincoln's party still held a plurality in the House and increased its majority in the Senate. Just over two months had passed since Robert E. Lee and the Army of Northern Virginia had splashed across the Potomac in the first great invasion of the North.[13]

In his memoirs, McClellan provided valuable insight into what he considered his objective in the campaign, and perhaps into his rationale for not pursuing Robert E. Lee and the wounded Army of Northern Virginia:

> The movement from Washington into Maryland, which culminated in the battles of South Mountain and Antietam, was not a part of an offensive campaign, with the object of the invasion of the enemy's territory and an attack upon his capital, but was defensive in its purposes, although offensive in its character, and would be technically called a "defensive-offensive campaign." It was undertaken at a time when our army had experienced severe defeats, and its object was to preserve the national capital and Baltimore, to protect Pennsylvania from invasion, and to drive the enemy out of Maryland. These purposes were fully and finally accomplished by the battle of Antietam, which brought the Army of the Potomac into what might be termed an accidental position on the upper Potomac. Having gained the immediate object of the campaign, the first thing to be done was to insure Maryland from a return of the enemy; the second, to prepare our own army—exhausted by a series of severe battles, destitute to a great extent of supplies, and very deficient in artillery and cavalry horses—for a definite offensive movement, and to determine upon the line of operations for a further advance. At the time of the battle of Antietam the Potomac was very low, and presented a

comparatively weak line of defense unless watched by large masses of troops. The reoccupation of Harper's Ferry and the disposition of troops above that point rendered the line of the Potomac secure against everything except cavalry raids. No time was lost in placing the army in proper condition for an advance, and the circumstances which caused the delay after the battle of Antietam have been fully enumerated.[14]

The sum total of all Union and Confederate casualties during the Maryland Campaign was around forty-one thousand men. This number includes the losses incurred in the five major battles that made up the campaign, as well as the twelve thousand Union men captured at Harpers Ferry.[15] What this figure does not include, however, is the untold number of soldiers both armies lost due to straggling. While it is safe to assume many of these men eventually rejoined their respective units, noncombat losses due to straggling had an enormous and lasting effect on both armies' fighting ability during the campaign. Yet it cannot be overstated that Lee felt this negative effect more keenly and found that it severely hampered his ability to conduct his campaign. On September 23, 1862, the Confederate commander sent a message to President Davis in which he opined on his army's condition and laid the blame for his retreat and inability to continue the operation on this fact alone:[16]

Joseph Poffenberger Farm, Antietam National Battlefield, modern image. Matt Brant.

The subject of recruiting this army is also one of paramount importance. The usual casualties of battle have diminished its ranks, but its numbers have been greatly decreased by desertion and straggling. This was the main cause of its retiring from Maryland, as it was unable to cope with advantage with the numerous host of the enemy.[17]

Recent estimates place Lee's total noncombat losses for the entire Maryland Campaign at forty-five percent, or just shy of forty-four thousand men. If this number is correct, it is hard to underestimate its negative impact on Lee's ability to conduct his campaign. The degree to which it did so can only be speculated.[18]

On September 22, 1862, in direct response to the Union victory at Antietam, Abraham Lincoln issued the Preliminary Emancipation Proclamation. He stated therein that the proclamation would take effect on January 1, 1863, forever altering the nature of the Civil War and the trajectory of our nation's history.[19]

Nine months after the Maryland Campaign, no doubt having learned from the events of 1862, Robert E. Lee led his army onto Northern soil once again. In early July 1863, this campaign culminated in the small Pennsylvania town of Gettysburg.

APPENDIX I

BATTLEFIELD GUIDE TO THE CRITICAL DECISIONS OF THE MARYLAND CAMPAIGN

This portion of the book is a guide to the critical decisions of the Maryland Campaign. As the campaign encompassed such a large geographical area, this tour may take some time, cover some distance, and require a reliable vehicle. A navigation device or smartphone will come in handy to help find the stops quickly and efficiently. I recommend using a compass or a compass mobile app to better orient yourself at the various points of interest. Part of the tour will involve some light hiking, so plan accordingly.

The tour will begin in Virginia and make stops in both Maryland and West Virginia. Depending on how much time you spend at each destination, the journey could take up to two days. The total distance you will cover is 122 miles. With each stop, an address is included if one exists, as well as GPS co-ordinates. For example: 11919 Leesburg Pike, Herndon, Virginia (39.008419, -77.360867).

Each decision will be recapped, not necessarily in order or in the exact location where it occurred. Finally, this tour is not a detailed, blow-by-blow account of the Maryland Campaign; instead, its destinations align with the critical decisions covered in this book. A basic understanding of the operation's events is essential to comprehending this work and the Maryland Campaign

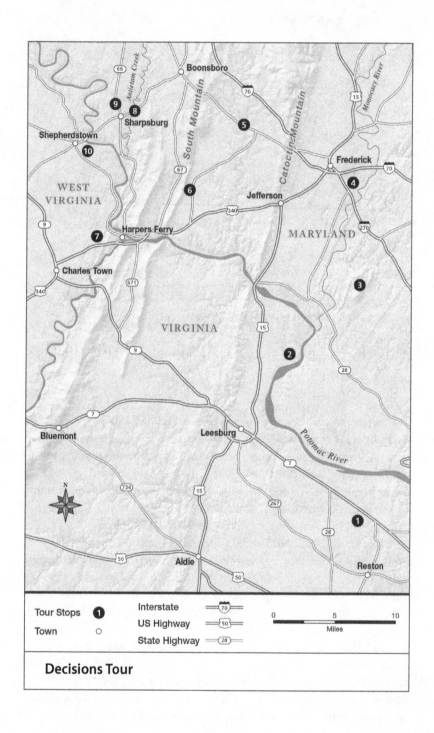

Decisions Tour

tour. Please note that the critical decisions specific to the Battle of Antietam are not covered here. For details on those, please refer to my book *Decisions at Antietam*. You may also enter or exit the tour at any appropriate point.

An essential part of the critical decision process is recognizing how location frequently influenced decision-makers. Knowing what these individuals saw or could not see often provides context that may not otherwise be apparent. Before starting your journey, I recommend reviewing a map of the area to enhance your understanding of the ground to be covered.

Notable changes in the past 150 years have impacted the ground this tour will cover. Yet the terrain is unaltered enough to provide a sense of the challenges each army faced. While we will be traveling on modern roads and visiting modern cities and towns, preservationists have retained the essence of their appearance in 1862.

Stop 1—Old Dranesville Tavern

11919 Leesburg Pike, Herndon, Virginia 20170 (39.008362, -77.360865)

Decision—Lee Invades the North

The tour begins at the **Old Dranesville Tavern** about one mile west of the intersection of the Leesburg (VA SR 7) and Georgetown Pikes (VA SR 193), or five hundred feet east of the junction of Leesburg Pike and Fairfax Parkway (VA SR 286). Depending on what direction you approach from, you will turn either left or right at Dranesville Manor Drive, and then you will be going south. Make an immediate right at the **Dranesville Tavern Historic Site** sign, then follow the driveway to the parking lot. You will see an informational placard for the Battle of Dranesville that was fought nearby on December 20, 1861. In 1862 Dranesville was little more than a wide spot in the road. Drane's Tavern opened in 1810 as a stage stop, was here during the war, and is now part of the township of Herndon, Virginia, in Fairfax County.

If you stand on the tavern's front porch and face the Leesburg Pike, you will be looking north. The Potomac River is 3.75 miles in that direction, with Frederick, Maryland, about 25.0 miles beyond that. If you follow Leesburg Pike to the northwest—on your left—you will arrive at Leesburg, Virginia, 13.5 miles from this spot. If you take Leesburg Pike to the southeast—on your right—you will reach Washington, DC, after about 25.0 miles. Behind you, the Chantilly Battlefield is located approximately 10.0 miles to the south, with the Bull Run Battlefield located 9.0 miles southwest of it. Had you been here on September 3, 1862, you might have seen columns of Confederate

Dranesville Tavern, modern image. Author.

soldiers marching along this road to Leesburg, a staging area for the invasion of Maryland.

While records leave Lee's exact location on September 3 unclear, his correspondence to Confederate president Jefferson Davis on that date was written from "Headquarters—Alexandria and Leesburg Road, Near Dranesville." Thus we can safely assume he was very near this place on the road to Leesburg.

Decision—Lee Invades the North

In September 1862, Lee chose to invade the North partly because he understood, perhaps better than any other general in the war, the advantages of gaining the strategic initiative and the ways of maintaining it. He had worked hard to seize the upper hand from McClellan and Pope, and he was not about to give it back. When and where Lee determined to conduct an "expedition into Maryland," as he called it, can be debated. He could have been contemplating this move well before the Battle of Second Bull Run began. However, it is clear that if not before, then very soon after the Battle of Chantilly (September 1, 1862), Lee had decided to get his army closer to the Potomac and a potential crossing point into Maryland at the very least. It is safe to assume the general contemplated the invasion before issuing the order to his army.

Orders for the march were delivered on September 2, and by the fourth, the lead elements of his force had reached Leesburg and begun probing the Potomac River for potential crossing points. Additionally, it served Lee's plans to keep his army moving north to maintain pressure on Washington, DC.[1]

The Confederate commander sent Jefferson Davis a dispatch announcing his intentions.

Communication to Jefferson Davis from Robert E. Lee, September 3, 1862

The present seems to be the most propitious time since the commencement of the war of the Confederate Army to enter Maryland. The two grand armies of the United States that have been operating in Virginia, though now united, are much weakened and demoralized. Their new levies, of which I understand 60,000 men have already been posted in Washington, are not yet organized, and will take some time to prepare for the field. If it is ever desired to give material aid to Maryland and afford her an opportunity of throwing off the oppression to which she is now subject, this would seem the most favorable.

After the enemy had disappeared from the vicinity of Fairfax Court-House, and taken the road to Alexandria, and Washington, I did not think it would be advantageous to follow him farther. I had no intention of attacking him in his fortifications and am not prepared to invest them. If I possessed the necessary munitions, I should be unable to supply provisions for the troops. I therefore determined, while threatening the approaches to Washington, to draw the troops into Loudoun, where forage and some provisions can be obtained, menace their possession of the Shenandoah Valley, and, if found practicable to cross into Maryland. The purpose, if discovered will have the effect of carrying the enemy north of the Potomac, and, if prevented, will not result in much evil.

The army is not properly equipped for an invasion of an enemy's territory. It lacks much of the material of war, is feeble in transportation, the animals being much reduced, and the men are poorly provided with clothes, and in thousands of instances are destitute of shoes. Still, we cannot afford to be idle, and though weaker than our opponents in men and military equipments, must endeavor to harass if we cannot destroy them. I am aware that the movement is attended with much risk, yet I do not consider success impossible, and shall endeavor to guard it from loss. As long as the army of the enemy are employed on this frontier I have no fears for the safety to Richmond, yet I earnestly recommend that advantage be taken of this period of comparative safety to place its defense, both by land and water, in the most perfect condition. A respectable force can be collected to defend its approaches by land, and the steamer Richmond, I hope, is now ready to clear the river of hostile vessels.

Should General Bragg find it impracticable to operate to advantage on his present frontier, his army, after leaving sufficient garrisons, could be advantageously employed in opposing the overwhelming numbers which it seems to be the intention of the enemy now to concentrate in Virginia.

I have already been told by prisoners that some of Buell's cavalry have been joined to General Pope's army, and have reason to believe that the whole of McClellan's, the larger portion of Burnside's and Cox's, and a portion of Hunter's, are united to it.

What occasions me most concern is the fear of getting out of ammunition. I beg you will instruct the Ordnance Department to spare no pains in manufacturing a sufficient amount of the best kind, and to be particular, in preparing that for the artillery, to provide three times as much of the long-range ammunition as of that for smooth-bore or short-range guns. The points to which I desire the ammunition to be forwarded will be made known to the Department in time. If the Quartermaster's Department can furnish any shoes, it would be the greatest relief. We have entered upon September, and the nights are becoming cool. [2]

Lee began to move his army closer to the Potomac and crossed it into Maryland well before Jefferson Davis officially authorized him to do so. This action suggests Lee's confidence that the Confederate president would support his decision. Alternatively, it could be that the two had discussed this plan beforehand. Joseph Harsh indicates that the general was merely sure of Davis's approval. Although Davis and Lee possibly considered an incursion into the North should the opportunity present itself, it seems evident that Davis trusted Lee throughout the war and almost to a fault. As their relationship was based primarily on this trust, it is not implausible that Lee foresaw Davis's approval.[3]

In an additional message to President Davis, Lee indicated he was more convinced of his decision to invade the North.

Communication to Jefferson Davis
from Robert E. Lee, September 4, 1862

Since my last communication to you, with reference to the movements which I propose to make with this army, I am more fully persuaded of the benefit that will result from an expedition into Maryland, and I shall proceed to make the movement at once, unless you should signify your disapprobation.[4]

That same day, Lee issued General Orders 102. The directive provided his commanders with details about what he expected during the campaign.

General Orders 102 Issued by Robert E. Lee,
September 4, 1862

I. It is ordered and earnestly enjoined upon all commanders to reduce their transportation to a mere sufficiency to transport cooking utensils and the absolute necessaries of a regiment. All animals not actually employed for artillery, cavalry, or draught purposes will be left in charge of Lieutenant-Colonel Corley, chief quartermaster Army of Northern Virginia, to be recruited, the use of public animals, captured or otherwise, except for this service, being positively prohibited. Division, brigade, and regimental commanders, and officers in charge of artillery battalions, will give special attention to this matter. Batteries will select the best horses for use, turning over all others. Those batteries with horses too much reduced for service will be, men and horses, temporarily transferred by General Pendleton to other batteries, the guns and unserviceable horses being sent to the rear, the ammunition being turned in to reserve ordnance train. All cannoneers are positively prohibited from riding on the ammunition chests or guns.

II. This army is about to engage in most important operations, where any excesses committed will exasperate the people, lead to disastrous results, and enlist the populace on the side of the Federal forces in hostility to our own. Quartermasters and commissaries will make all arrangements for purchase of supplies needed by our army, to be issued to the respective commands upon proper requisitions, thereby removing all excuse for depredations.

III. A provost guard, under direction of Brigadier General L. A. Armistead, will follow in rear of the army, arrest stragglers, and punish summarily all depredators, and keep the men with their commands. Commanders of brigades will cause rear guards to be placed under charge of efficient officers in rear of their brigades, to prevent the men from leaving the ranks, right, left, front, or rear, this officer being held by brigade commanders to a strict accountability for proper performance of this duty.

IV. Stragglers are usually those who desert their comrades in peril. Such characters are better absent from the army on such momentous occasions as those about to be entered upon. They will, as bringing discredit upon our cause, as useless members of the service and as especially deserving odium, come under the special attention of the provost-marshal, and be considered as unworthily members of an army which has immortalized itself in the recent glorious and successful engagements against the enemy, and will be brought before a military commission to receive the punishment due to their misconduct. The gallant soldiers who have so nobly sustained our cause by heroism in battle will assist the commanding general in securing success by aiding their officers in checking the desire for straggling among their comrades.[5]

On September 4, the seventy thousand men who now made up the Army of Northern Virginia began to cross the Potomac near Leesburg. Lee's decision, the first and most critical one, inaugurated the Maryland Campaign.

Henry Kyd Douglas, "Stonewall Jackson in Maryland"
Battles and Leaders of the Civil War

On the 3d of September, 1862, the Federal army under General Pope having been confounded, General Lee turned his columns toward the Potomac, with Stonewall Jackson in front. On the 5th of September Jackson crossed the Potomac at White's Ford, a few miles beyond Leesburg. The passage of the river by the troops marching in

Lieut. Henry Kyd Douglas, CSA. National Park Service.

fours, well closed up, the laughing, shouting, and singing, as a brass band in front played "Maryland, my Maryland," was a memorable experience. The Marylanders in the corps imparted much of their enthusiasm to the other troops' but we were not long in finding out that if General Lee had hopes that the decimated regiments of his army would be filled by the sons of Maryland he was doomed to a speedy and unqualified disappointment.[6]

Stop 2—White's Ford Regional Park, White's Ford

43646 Hibler Road, Leesburg, Virginia 20176 (39.187440, -77.483337)

Decision—McClellan Takes Command

From the Dranesville Tavern, turn left on the Leesburg Pike (VA SR 7). Drive northwest for 12.0 miles, and exit onto the Leesburg Bypass (US-15) heading north. Drive for 4.8 miles, and turn right at Limestone School Road (VA SR 661). After 2.0 miles, turn right at Hilber Road (VA SR 656). After 1.1 miles, make a right, follow the road to the parking lot, get out of your car, and walk to the river landing. You are now at **White's Ford Regional Park**, where a significant portion of the Rebel army crossed the Potomac.

White's Ford, modern image. Author.

Several information plaques give details on the site. As you face the river, you are looking east. Frederick, Maryland, is 15.0 miles to the north on your left. Harpers Ferry is about 20.0 miles upstream by river (behind you), and Sharpsburg is about 25.0 miles northwest of you (behind you and to the left). Lincoln was obviously not here when he made his decision, but this is an excellent spot to review it.

Decision—McClellan Takes Command

In the late summer of 1862, Abraham Lincoln faced what amounted to an existential crisis. In just over a year of war, his administration had become almost exclusively defined by the conflict, and his emotional state alternatively rose and fell with the Union military's fortunes. In early September 1862, affairs were looking bleak.

The president's two principal eastern armies were in shambles, and the war effort as a whole was now bordering on chaos. Brimming with confidence and swagger, the seemingly unstoppable Confederate army was now poised to cross the Potomac into Maryland. The war effort that had begun the year with such promise and hope had quite literally gone south for the Union. Abraham Lincoln was facing some of the darkest days of his presidency.

Lincoln endured a firestorm of criticism and second-guessing on both the military and political fronts, and the mood of the country after the long list of defeats was understandably gloomy. On August 27, 1862, lawyer George Templeton Strong seemed to tap into Northern sentiments of the day.

George Templeton Strong, Diary Entry for August 27, 1862

It is almost time for another great disaster. It will occur in Western Virginia, probably. Can any disaster and disgrace arouse us fully? Perhaps we are destined to defeat and fit only for subjugation. Perhaps the oligarchs of the South are our born rulers. Northern communities may be too weak, corrupt, gelatinous, and unwarlike to resist Jefferson Davis and his confederates. It is possible that New York and New England and the Free West may be unable to cope with the South. If so, let the fact be ascertained and established as soon as possible, and let us recognize our masters.[7]

Lincoln reluctantly placed McClellan back in command of the reorganized Army of the Potomac. "We must use the tools we have," the president famously stated of his decision.[8]

On September 7, McClellan left Washington, DC, in pursuit of Lee. Two days before, McClellan had regaled his wife with the news of his recent success.

Letter to Mary Ellen from McClellan, September 5, 1862

Again I have been called upon to save the country—the case is desperate, but with God's help I will try unselfishly to do my best & if he wills it accomplish the salvation of the nation. My men are true & will stand by me to the last. I still hope for success & will leave nothing undone to gain it. . . .

How weary I am of this struggle against adversity. But one thing sustains me—& that is my trust in God—I know that the interests at stake are so great as to justify his interference—not for me, but for the innocent thousands, millions rather, who have been plunged in misery by no fault of theirs. It is probable that our communications will be cut off in a day or two—but don't be worried. You may rest assured that I am doing all I can for my country & that no shame shall rest upon you willfully brought upon you by me. . . .

My hands are full, so is my heart. . . .

4 pm . . . It makes my heart bleed to see the poor shattered remnants of my noble Army of the Potomac, poor fellows! And to see how they love me even now. I hear them calling out to me as I ride among them—"George—don't leave us again!" "They shan't take you away from us again" etc etc. I can hardly restrain myself when I see how fearfully they are reduced in numbers & realize how many of them lie unburied on the field of battle where their lives were uselessly sacrificed. It is the most terrible trial I ever experienced— Truly God is trying me in the fire.[9]

Lincoln's decision to place McClellan in command was critical because he and his leadership style drove the campaign's course and the coming battles. Subsequent events were influenced in large part by the choices the commanding general did or did not make.

President Abraham Lincoln, circa 1863.
Library of Congress.

Sugar Loaf Mountain, Maryland, view looking south. Matt Brant.

Stop 3—Sugar Loaf Mountain, East View Parking Lot

Sugar Loaf Mountain East View Parking Lot, Sugar Loaf Mountain Drive, Dickerson, Maryland 20842 (39.260422, -77.390085)

Decision—Sugar Loaf Mountain Is Occupied

From White's Ford, turn left at Hilber Road (VA 656). Drive 1.1 miles, turn left at Limestone School Road (VA 661), drive 2.0 miles, and turn right on US Highway 15/501. You will stay on US Highway 15/501 for about 6.0 miles heading toward Maryland. Then you will cross the Potomac River at Point of Rocks. Immediately after crossing the Potomac, exit on the right at MD RT 28, or Clay Street. Stay on MD RT 28 for 7.6 miles. Turn right at Mouth of Monocacy Road. After 0.4 mile, turn right at Mount Ephraim Road. At the 2.0-mile mark, continue northeast on Sugarloaf Mountain Road. After 2.3 miles, you will come to the intersection of Sugarloaf Mountain Road and Comus Road. On your left, you will see the entrance to **Sugarloaf Mountain**. Follow the signs on Sugarloaf Mountain Drive for 1.4 miles to the **East View** parking lot. Park here, and walk to the east end of the parking lot to the overlook. The battle to retake the mountain took place near the park entrance, but this is the most visually stunning location to review our next decision. It also illustrates why the position was so valuable to both sides.

If you stand with the parking lot directly at your back, you are looking more or less east, and on a clear day you can see the outskirts of Baltimore, some thirty miles away. Frederick is roughly ten miles to the north (on your left). The suburbs of Washington, DC, are twenty-two miles to the southeast (on your right). Just over four miles behind you is the confluence of the Potomac and Monocacy Rivers.

Decision—Sugar Loaf Mountain Is Occupied

McClellan tasked Pleasonton and his cavalry with the task of retaking Sugar Loaf Mountain. On Tuesday, September 9, attacks by Farnsworth's brigade and a section of horse artillery drove a small contingent of Munford's Confederate troopers from the vicinity of Barnesville back to the base of Sugar Loaf. On September 10, Union cavalry tried again to dislodge the Confederates holding the mountain, but the enemy force fighting dismounted made fair use of the terrain and held the Federals off once again for the balance of the day. Calling for infantry support, William Franklin's Sixth Corps reinforced Pleasanton's cavalry, but Franklin decided it was too late in the day to assault the position.

On September 11, the Sixth Corps and a much larger contingent of Union cavalry made ready to attack Sugar Loaf. Witnessing the advancing Federal infantry, the Confederate troopers decided that the position at Sugar Loaf had been held long enough. The Confederates withdrew, having held up the Union recapture of the mountain by almost three full days. [10]

Abner Hard, the surgeon for the Eighth Illinois Cavalry that was part of Farnsworth's brigade, described the action in his postwar memoirs.

Postwar Account of Dr. Abner Hard, MD

In sight of Barnesville, and only a few miles distant, stands Sugar Loaf Mountain towering high in the air, from whose summit the country can be seen from a great distance in all directions. On the top of this mountain was a rebel signal station, where their signal flag could be seen waving all day and their signal fires swinging to and fro at night. September 10th, the Sixth United States Regular Cavalry attempted to take this mountain and capture the signal station, but were unsuccessful. One or two companies of the Eighth Illinois were ordered to support them, but when the rebel artillery opened their fire, the Sixth Cavalry beat a hasty retreat, leaving our men in a very critical and dangerous position. They however extricated themselves without loss, while the Sixth Cavalry lost a number [of] killed and wounded.

Other detachments of the regiment were sent in various directions; one toward the mouth of the Monocacy, where it drove in the rebel pickets and had a lively skirmish.

On the 11th, another expedition was planned to capture the mountain. Our regiment was to take a round-about route and encircle the east side. Other cavalry [,] some [the] other side[']s, while General Franklin's infantry, which was just arriving, was to defend the west; but the enemy probably discovered our movements from their elevated position, so that after a hard day's march we actually took the mountain, though not until they had made good their escape. A party of our regiment advanced to the summit and fired a volley therefrom. [11]

Sugar Loaf Mountain, Maryland, view looking northwest.
Matt Brant.

Because the mountain remained in Confederate hands for several vital days, there were no Union eyes on top of Sugar Loaf to clarify the morass of confusing intelligence reports McClellan was receiving. He lost a real opportunity to bring the operational situation into focus during those crucial few days as his army approached Frederick.

As you descend Sugar Loaf, additional pullouts, parking lots, and trails allow you to take advantage of views west and south.

Stop 4—Lee's Headquarters, Best Farm, Frederick, Maryland

Monocacy National Battlefield, Frederick, Maryland 21703 (39.370546, -77.398804)

Decisions—Lee Divides His Army
and McClellan Responds to Special Orders 191

Follow the one-way Sugar Loaf Mountain Drive to descend the mountain. After 1.5 miles take a left on Comus Road, proceed for 0.2 mile, and make a left on Sugarloaf Mountain Road. Continue on Sugarloaf Mountain Road for 2.5 miles, and then take a left on Thurston Road. Drive on Thurston Road for 4.0 miles. At this point, you will come to the intersection of Thurston Road and MD RT 80. Follow signs for MD RT 80 W (Fingerboard Road). Continue on MD RT 80 for 1.3 miles, then turn right at Park Mills Road. Proceed on Park Mils Road for 1.0 mile until you reach the Urbana Pike (MD RT 355). Turn left here and drive 2.6 miles. Just before the Monocacy Battlefield site entrance, you will see the entrance to the **Best Farm**. Turn left here, follow the driveway for just over 600 yards, and park at the wayside markers near the Best Farmhouse.

As you face north (opposite the farmhouse), you will see a line of trees about five hundred yards away. The town of Frederick and the Old National Pike (US 40) lies approximately 3.0 miles north of you. Both armies used the pike extensively in 1862 during the campaign. If you follow that road northwest through Frederick, it will eventually take you through the Middletown Valley and then on to Turner's and Fox's Gaps, about 15.0 miles from this location. Harpers Ferry is about 17.0 miles southwest (on your left). Baltimore, Maryland, is roughly 42.0 miles east of you (on your right). The Potomac River is located about 10.5 miles south of here, behind you and slightly to your left.

The spot where Lee's headquarters tent was located on September 9, 1862, when he issued the now infamous Special Orders 191, lies someplace between you and the line of trees. It is believed that the grove of trees was much larger

Lee's H.Q. Near Frederick, Maryland, September 6–10, modern image. Michael Doyle.

in 1862. Lee's orders primarily outlined his operational plans for the capture of the Union garrison at Harpers Ferry. You are standing on what is part of the Monocacy National Battlefield site. The Battle of Monocacy was fought here on July 9, 1864, and was part of Jubal Early's 1864 campaign.

The **Best Farm** comprises the southern 274 acres of what was a 748-acre plantation. Because of its proximity to the Georgetown Pike and Monocacy Junction, portions of both the Union and Confederate armies camped there throughout the Civil War.[12]

Decision—Lee Divides His Army

Shortly after arriving in Frederick, Lee realized that the Union garrisons in the lower Shenandoah had not evacuated in response to his invasion as he believed they would. He now felt compelled to change his plans, divide his army, and remove this threat to his rear and lines of communication. The bulk of the Confederate commander's force was camped around Frederick, where he hoped to rest and resupply before moving on with the next stage of his campaign. Although the Union army was by now advancing out of Washington and Federal cavalrymen were a few miles west of Urbana (about five miles to the southeast), Lee still believed that time was on his side.

James Longstreet described the scene and his apprehensions as he first learned of Lee's change in his operation plan:

James Longstreet, From Manassas to Appomattox

Riding together before we reached Frederick, the sound of artillery fire came from the direction of Point of Rocks and Harper's Ferry, from which General Lee inferred that the enemy was concentrating his forces from the Valley, for defense at Harper's Ferry, and proposed to me to organize forces to surround and capture the works and the garrison. I thought it a venture not worth the game, and suggested, as we were in the enemy's country and presence, that he would be advised of any move that we made in a few hours after it was set on foot; that the Union army, though beaten, was not disorganized; that we knew a number of their officers who could put it in order and march against us, if they found us exposed, and make serious trouble before the capture could be accomplished; that our men were worn by very severe and protracted service, and in need of repose; that as long as we had them in hand we were masters of the situation, but dispersed into many fragments, our strength must be greatly reduced. As the subject was not continued, I supposed that it was a mere expression of passing thought, until, the day after we reached Frederick, upon going over to head-quarters, I found the front of the general's tent closed and tied. Upon inquiring of a member of the staff, I was told that he was inside with General Jackson. As I had not been called, I turned to go away, when General Lee, recognizing my voice, called me in. The plan had been arranged. Jackson, with his three divisions, was to recross the Potomac by the fords above Harper's Ferry, march via Martinsburg to Bolivar Heights; McLaws's division by Crampton's Gap to Maryland Heights; J. G. Walker's division to recross at Cheek's Ford and occupy Loudoun Heights, these heights overlooking the positions of the garrison of Harper's Ferry; D. H. Hill's division to march by the National road over South Mountain at Turner's Gap, and halt at the western base, to guard trains, intercept fugitives from Harper's Ferry, and support the cavalry, if needed; the cavalry to face the enemy and embarrass his movements. I was to march over the mountain by Turner's Gap to Hagerstown. As their minds were settled firmly upon the enterprise, I offered no opposition further than to ask that the order be so modified as to allow me to send R. H. Anderson's division with McLaws and to halt my own column near the point designated for bivouac of General D. H. Hill's command. These suggestions were accepted, and the order so framed was issued.

It may be well to digress from my narrative for a moment just here to remark that General Lee's confidence in the strength of his army, the situation of affairs, and the value of the moral effect upon the country, North and South, was made fully manifest by the nature of the campaign he had just entered upon, especially that portion of it directed against Harper's Ferry, which, as events were soon to prove, weakened the effectiveness of his army in the main issue, which happened to be Antietam.[13]

True to form, Lee's aggressive nature compelled him to take another calculated risk and divide his army.

Special Orders, No. 191—September 9, 1862
Hdqrs. Army of Northern Virginia

I. The citizens of Fredericktown being unwilling, while overrun by members of this army, to open their stores, in order to give them

Maj. Gen. James Longstreet, CSA,
circa 1860–1870. Library of Congress.

confidence, and to secure to officers and men purchasing supplies for benefit of this command, all officers and men of this army are strictly prohibited from visiting Fredericktown except on business, in which case they will bear evidence of this in writing from division commanders. The provost-marshal in Fredericktown will see that his guard rigidly enforces this order.

II. Major Taylor will proceed to Leesburg, Va., and arrange for transportation of the sick and those unable to walk to Winchester, securing the transportation of the country for this purpose. The route between this and Culpeper Court-House east of the mountains being unsafe will no longer be traveled. Those on the way to this army already across the river will move up promptly; all others will proceed to Winchester collectively and under command of officers, at which point, being the general depot of this army, its movements will be known and instructions given by commanding officer regulating further movements.

III. The army will resume its march to-morrow, taking the Hagerstown road. General Jackson's command will form the advance, and, after passing Middletown, with such portion as he may select, take the route toward Sharpsburg, cross the Potomac at the most convenient point, and by Friday morning take possession of the Baltimore and Ohio Railroad, capture such of them as may be at Martinsburg, and intercept such as may attempt to escape from Harper's Ferry.

IV. General Longstreet's command will pursue the main road as far as Boonsborough, where it will halt, with reserve, supply, and baggage trains of the army.

V. General McLaws, with his own division and that of General R. H. Anderson, will follow General Longstreet. On reaching Middletown they will take the route to Harper's Ferry, and by Friday morning possess himself of the Maryland Heights and endeavor to capture the enemy at Harper's Ferry and vicinity.

VI. General Walker, with his division, after accomplishing the object in which he is now engaged, will cross the Potomac at Cheek's Ford, ascend its right bank to Lovettsville, take possession of Loudoun Heights, if practicable, by Friday morning, Keys' Ford on his left, and the road between the end of the mountain and the Potomac on his right. He will, as far as practicable, co-operate with Generals McLaws and Jackson, and intercept retreat of the enemy.

VII. General D. H. Hill's division will form the rear guard of the army, pursing the road taken by the main body. The reserve artillery, ordnance, and supply trains, camp, will precede General Hill.

VIII. General Stuart will detach a squadron of cavalry to accompany the commands of Generals Longstreet, Jackson, and McLaws, and, with the main body of the cavalry, will cover the route of the army, bringing up all stragglers that may have been left behind.

IX. The commands of Generals Jackson, McLaws, and Walker, after accomplishing the objects for which they have been detached, will join the main body of the army at Boonsborough or Hagerstown.

X. Each regiment on the march will habitually carry its axes in the regimental ordnance wagons, for use of the men at their encampments, to procure wood, &c. [14]

A copy of Lee's order was somehow lost, and it ultimately found its way into McClellan's hands and changed the campaign's course. The directive revealed the Confederate operational plans, confirming much of what McClellan already knew. Armed with this knowledge, the Federal general made a critical decision of his own. We believe McClellan's headquarters was actually located someplace west of Frederick.

Decision—McClellan Responds to Special Orders 191

By Saturday, September 13, McClellan had advanced his army along a front as much as twenty miles wide. This action shielded Washington and Baltimore as he progressed. Despite a deluge of intelligence, the Union commander acknowledged, at least for the moment, that he had only the haziest notion of the Army of Northern Virginia's disposition and course.

Learning that the Rebels were now mainly west of the Catoctin and South Mountain ranges and divided into several parts, McClellan began concentrating his forces at Frederick from the south and the east.[15]

Communication Sent to Halleck from McClellan, September 12, 1862

10:00 a.m.

My columns are pushing on rapidly to Frederick. I feel perfectly confident that the enemy has abandoned Frederick, moving in two directions, viz, on the Hagerstown and Harper's Ferry roads. Fitz. Lee, with four regiments of cavalry and six pieces of artillery, left New Market yesterday for Liberty. They are being followed by Burnside's cavalry.

Communication Sent to Halleck from McClellan, September 12, 1862
5:30 p.m.

I have just learned, by signal from Sugar Loaf Mountain, that our troops are entering Frederick. The remainder of Burnside's troops are between Frederick and New Market. Sumner is near Urbana, with our advance guard thrown out to the Monocacy; Williams on his right; Franklin on his left; Couch at Barnesville. Cavalry has been sent toward point of Rocks to ascertain whether there is any force of the enemy in that direction. Burnside has cavalry in pursuit of Fitzhugh Lee, toward Westminster. Should the enemy go toward Pennsylvania I shall follow him. Should he attempt to recross the Potomac I shall endeavor to cut off his retreat. Movements tomorrow will be dependent upon information to be received during the night. The troops have marched to-day as far as it was possible and proper for them to move.[16]

On September 13, Union two soldiers found a copy of Special Orders 191 southeast of Frederick. The order was recognized for what it was, and it eventually made its way up the chain of command to McClellan.[17] The Federal general considered the dispatch genuine and made plans to attack his divided opponent. Spread out over an area of roughly 240 square miles, the Army of Northern Virginia was somewhat vulnerable—six of its nine divisions were concentrated near Harpers Ferry, two were at Hagerstown, and one was at Boonsboro. McClellan's First, Second, and Twelfth Corps, plus one division of the Fifth Corps, were themselves concentrated near Frederick, Maryland. The Union Ninth Corps was situated west and south of Frederick in support of the cavalry operations. In addition, the Sixth Corps was south of Frederick at Buckeystown, and Couch's Fourth Corps division was south of the Sixth on the Potomac.[18]

Meanwhile, in Washington, Lincoln, desperate for good tidings and no repeat of the previous campaign, prodded his general along:

Maj. Gen. George B. McClellan and
Mary Ellen Marcy McClellan, circa
1860–1865. Library of Congress.

Communication to McClellan from Lincoln,
September 12, 1862
4:00 a.m.

How does it look now?

Communication to McClellan from Lincoln,
September 12, 1862
5:45 p.m.

Governor Curtin telegraphs me:

I have advices that Jackson is crossing the Potomac at Williamsport, and probably the whole rebel army will be drawn from
Maryland.

Receiving nothing from Harper's Ferry or Martinsburg to-day,
and positive information from Wheeling that the line is cut, corrob-
orates the idea that the enemy is recrossing the Potomac. Please do
not let him get off without being hurt.[19]

Responding to Lincoln on the thirteenth, McClellan seemed self-assured in the face of this opportunity and optimistic about future events:

Communication to Lincoln from McClellan, September 13, 1862
Midnight

I have the whole rebel force in front of me, but am confident, and no time shall be lost. I have a difficult task to perform, but with God's blessing will accomplish it. I think Lee has made a gross mistake, and that he will be severely punished for it. The army is in motion as rapidly as possible. I hope for a great success if the plans of the rebels remain unchanged. We have possession of Catoctin. I have all the plans of the rebels, and will catch them in their own trap if my men are equal to the emergency. I now feel that I can count on them as of old. All forces of Pennsylvania should be placed to co-operate at Chambersburg. My respects to Mrs. Lincoln. Received most enthusiastically by the ladies. Will send you trophies. All well, and with God's blessing will accomplish it.[20]

Union forces marching through Middletown, Maryland. *Harpers Weekly.*

On September 14, 1862, armed with the knowledge the Lost Order gave him, McClellan advanced the army at the Confederate units holding the South Mountain passes. After an all-day struggle, the Rebels were forced to fall back from the gaps during the night, and the Union army marched through them the next day. McClellan described his actions and the finding of the Lost Dispatch as follows:

1863 After-Action Report
by Maj. Gen. George B. McClellan, USA
Commanding Army of the Potomac

On the 13th the main bodies of the right wing and center passed through Frederick. It was soon ascertained that the main body of the enemy's forces had marched out of the city on the two previous days, taking the roads to Boonsborough and Harper's Ferry, thereby rendering it necessary to force the passes through the Catoctin and South Mountain ridges and gain possession of Boonsborough and Rohrersville before any relief could be extended to Colonel Miles at Harper's Ferry.

On the 13th an order fell into my hands, issued by General Lee, which fully disclosed his plans, and I immediately gave orders for a rapid and vigorous forward movement.[21]

McClellan's decision brought on the battles at South Mountain, the subsequent Confederate retreat, and the Union advance the next day, leading both armies to the clash at Antietam.

Stop 5—Middletown Valley, Maryland

Intersection of Bolivar Road and Old National Pike (39.466344, -77.59225)

Decision—Lee Stands at South Mountain
and Pleasonton Sends Willcox to Turner's Gap

From Lee's headquarters at Frederick, head northwest on the Urbana Pike (MD 355). After 1.6 miles, turn right onto MD 85 N. Go 0.4 mile farther, then left onto I-70 W / US 40 W. Continue to follow I-70 W for 4.5 miles, and take Exit 49 for US 40 Alternate toward Braddock Heights / Middletown. Proceed 0.2 mile to turn left onto US 40 Alternate, then drive 6.9 miles (through Middletown) before turning left onto Bolivar Road. Immediately on your left, you will see a historical marker with directions to the Reno Monument and a wide spot where you can pull over just beyond it.

The road you just left is the Old National Pike. From Frederick, it extends northwest to Turner's Gap and then on to Hagerstown, Maryland. Union forces used the pike to advance at Turner's and Fox's Gaps on September 13 and 14. You are now in the Middletown Valley.

From the edge of the road, stand with the marker at your back; you will be facing west and South Mountain. Depending on the time of year, you can just see the gaps from this location. By all accounts, far fewer trees were here in 1862, and the house in front of you was not here. You can walk about twenty yards west on the National Pike to the high ground to better view the gap, but be mindful of the traffic. The road you are on (Bolivar) connects to Reno Mountain Road (formally the Old Sharpsburg Road) less than a mile to the southwest. If you turn right on that road, you will find yourself at the summit of Fox's Gap in just over a mile. McClellan's headquarters on September 14 and 15 (now a private residence) is about nine hundred yards behind you. The left flank of the Union First Corps started here and extended a mile north on your right.

Robert E. Lee was actually near Hagerstown when he made his decision, but this position offers a good perspective to review it.

The intersection of Old National Road and Bolivar Road, modern image. Author.

Decision—Lee Stands at South Mountain

On September 13, Federal forces were now closing in from the east, Lee's Harpers Ferry operation was behind schedule, and time was beginning to run out. On September 11, Lee learned that a Union infantry force was near Hagerstown, Maryland. In response, he sent three divisions under Longstreet from Boonsboro. At that time, Lee still believed that the Union forces east of South Mountain posed no immediate hazard to his plans. However, the Rebel commander's perspective changed dramatically over the next several days.

By noon on September 12, Lee learned that the Union army was now just east of South Mountain and concentrating at Frederick. By contrast, the Rebel general's force was disassembled into four parts, with no one part in a position to immediately support the others. That left only D. H. Hill's single eight-thousand-man division and some cavalry standing between roughly forty-five thousand Federals in four infantry corps.[22]

Assigned to hold Turner's Gap, D. H. Hill outlined his dilemma:

After-Action Report of Maj. Gen. D. H. Hill, CSA
Commanding Hill's Division, Army of Northern Virginia

On the 13th, I was ordered by General Lee to dispose of my troops so as to prevent the escape of the Yankees from Harper's Ferry, then besieged, and also to guard the pass in the Blue Ridge near Boonsborough. Major-General Stuart reported to me that two brigades only of the Yankees were pursuing us, and that one brigade would be sufficient to hold the pass. I, however, sent the brigades of Garland and Colquitt, and ordered my other three brigades up to the neighborhood of Boonsborough.

An examination of the pass, very early on the morning of the 14th, satisfied me that it could only be held by a large force, and was wholly indefensible by a small one. I accordingly ordered up Anderson's brigade. A regiment of Ripley's brigade was sent to hold another pass, some 3 miles distant, on our left. I felt reluctant to order up Ripley and Rodes from the important positions they were holding until something definite was known of the strength and design of the Yankees.[23]

Maj. Gen. J. E. B. Stuart had been pushed out of the Middletown Valley by Pleasonton, and he believed he could not defend the gaps with only his two brigades of cavalry. After Hill's men came to his support, Stuart relocated his

The Battle of South Mountain. Library of Congress/National Archives.

two brigades minus one regiment and a battery of horse artillery, traveling south to support McLaws at Crampton's Gap. The major general outlined these movements:

After-Action Report of Maj. Gen. J. E. B. Stuart, CSA
Commanding Cavalry, Army of Northern Virginia

The enemy soon appeared in force crossing the mountain, and a spirited engagement took place, both of artillery and sharpshooters, the First North Carolina, Colonel Baker, holding the rear and acting with conspicuous gallantry. This lasted for some time, when, having held the enemy in check sufficiently long to accomplish my object, I withdrew slowly toward the gap in the South Mountain, having given General D. H. Hill ample time to occupy that gap with his troops, and still believing that the capture of Harper's Ferry had been affected. On reaching the vicinity of the gap near Boonsborough, finding General Hill's troops occupying the gap, I turned off General Hampton, with all his cavalry except the Jeff. Davis Legion, to re-enforce Munford, at Crampton's Gap, which was now the weakest point of the line. I remained myself at the gap near Boonsborough until night, but the enemy did not attack the position. This was obviously no place for cavalry operations, a single horseman passing from point to point on the mountain with difficulty. Leaving the Jeff. Davis Legion here, therefore, and directing Colonel Rosser, with a detachment of cavalry and the Stuart Horse Artillery, to occupy Braddock's Gap, I started on my way to join the main portion of my command at Crampton's Gap, stopping for the night near Boonsborough. I had not, up to this time, seen General D. H. Hill, but about midnight he sent General Ripley to me to get information concerning totals and gaps in a locality where General Hill had been lying for two days with his command. All the information I had was cheerfully given, and the situation of the gaps explained by map. I confidently hoped by this time to have received the information which was expected from Brig. Gen. Fitz. Lee. All the information I possessed or had the means of possessing had been laid before General D. H. Hill and the commanding general. His troops were duly notified of the advance of the enemy, and I saw them in line of battle awaiting his approach, and, myself, gave some general directions concerning the location of his lines during the afternoon, in his absence.[24]

On September 13, believing that the Federals were now advancing on South Mountain, Lee needed an aggressive action to hold them in check while allowing his Harpers Ferry operation to continue. He decided to support Hill's position and defend Turner's Gap by sending Longstreet's Command to his aid. Lee also sent messages to Jackson and McLaws urging them to complete Harpers Ferry's capture as precipitously as possible.

With this decision, Lee guaranteed a major battle at South Mountain on September 14, not just a minor delaying action. His choice also allowed the siege at Harpers Ferry to continue unabated. Most significantly, while his troops were eventually forced to fall back from all three South Mountain passes by the fifteenth, Lee bought himself one more day and perhaps more. Those hours proved essential to continuing the general's Maryland Campaign, thus getting him one step closer to his operational objectives.

Had you been standing here on September 14, 1862, you would have seen the Union First Corps advancing on Turner's Gap to the north (on your right), and the Ninth Corps moving on Fox's Gap to the south (on your left). While it is unclear exactly where Alfred Pleasonton made one of the campaign's most critical decisions, it was likely somewhere near this spot.

Brig. Gen. Orlando B. Willcox, USA,
circa 1855–1865. Library of Congress.

Decision—Pleasonton Sends Willcox to Turner's Gap

On September 13, Pleasonton found himself in the Middletown Valley engaged with Confederate cavalry acting as the rear guard for the Army of Northern Virginia. McClellan directed Pleasonton to open communication with Harpers Ferry and make contact with the enemy to determine its strength and whereabouts. It took Pleasonton's men all day to push the Confederate troopers out of the valley and back to Turner's Gap.

On the morning of September 14, the balance of the Army of the Potomac was moving west from Frederick. Pleasonton and the Kanawha Division of the Ninth Corps, commanded by Brig. Gen. Jacob D. Cox, were the first to engage the Rebels holding South Mountain. It was discovered that the Confederates were there in force, and they intended to make a stand.[25]

Confederate general D. H. Hill, who had arrived at Turner's Gap before dawn, reinforced his position at Turner's Gap and Fox's Gap. At approximately 7:00 a.m., the Kanawha Division of the Ninth Corps, with Col. Eliakim P. Scammon's brigade in the lead, was deployed east of Fox's Gap and ordered to advance. Cox almost immediately requested support for this attack from Maj. Gen. Jesse Reno. Reno responded by calling Brig. Gen. Orlando B. Willcox's division to Cox's aid. This move could pit two Union divisions of nearly 7,000 men against a Confederate position reinforced by G. B. Anderson's 2,500-man brigade. If successful, the Federals might outflank Turner's Gap and imperil the entire Rebel-held area.[26]

Pleasonton described the day's events in his after-action report:

After-Action Report of Brig. Gen. Alfred Pleasonton, USA Commanding Cavalry, Army of the Potomac

Being soon satisfied that the enemy would defend his position at Turner's Gap with a large force, I sent back to General Burnside for some infantry, and in the intermediate time I caused a force of dismounted cavalry to move up the mountain on the right of the turnpike, to examine the position on that side. This produced some skirmishing with the enemy, and induced him to mass a considerable force on that side during the night. I learned also that there were two roads, one on the right and the other to the left of the gap, both of which entered the turnpike beyond the gap, and would assist us materially in turning the enemy's position on both flanks. General Burnside's troops did not arrive in time to engage on the 13th, but on the morning of the 14th instant the general kindly sent me a brigade of infantry, under Colonel Scammon, and some heavy batteries. Scammon's brigade I directed to move up the mountain on the left hand road, gain the crest, and then move to the right to the turnpike in the enemy's rear. At the same time I placed Gibson's battery and the heavy batteries in position to the left, covering the road on that side, and obtaining a direct fire on the enemy's position in the gap.

Shortly after this, General Cox arrived with a second brigade of infantry, and upon my explaining the position to him, he moved to the support of Scammon, who was successful in his movement to gain the crest of the mountain.[27]

An aide sent forward to find Cox and get directions to Fox's Gap mistakenly told Willcox to report to Pleasonton for orders. In fact, Willcox was only supposed to receive Pleasonton's directions to the gap. Following these faulty instructions, Willcox sought out Pleasonton as his men approached South Mountain.

Pleasonton sent Willcox and his division north of the National Road and Turner's Gap. Either Burnside or Reno spotted the troops and ordered a countermarch to the Old Sharpsburg Road and up toward Cox's position at Fox's Gap. By the time Willcox arrived on the field, combatants on both sides were fought out. Cox had gained the gap, but he did not feel he had the strength to continue. As a result, Willcox was not on the field until 2:00 p.m., just in time to meet the additional brigades of D. H. Hill and those of Hood sent to reinforce the position. The fight for Fox's Gap dragged on until dark, and while the Union held the ridge, the Confederates effectively blocked any further progress.[28]

In his war memoir, Jacob Cox recalled this decision:

Jacob D. Cox, *Military Reminiscences of the Civil War*

Willcox's division reported to me about two o'clock, and would have been up earlier, but for a mistake in the delivery of a message to him. He had sent from Middletown to ask me where I desired him to come, and finding that the messenger had no clear idea of the roads by which he had travelled, I directed him to say that General Pleasonton would point out the road I had followed, if inquired of. Willcox understood the messenger that I wished him to inquire of Pleasonton where he had better put his division in, and on doing so, the latter suggested that he move against the crests on the north of the National road. He was preparing to do this when Burnside and Reno came up and corrected the movement, recalling him from the north and sending him by the old Sharpsburg road to my position.[29]

Willcox corroborated the encounter in his after-action report:

After-Action Report of Brig. Gen. Orlando B. Willcox, USA
Commanding First Division / Ninth Corps,
Army of the Potomac

Communicating with General Cox, he advised me to keep my command where it was, near the main pike or Cumberland road, and consult with General Pleasonton as to taking a position. Found General Pleasonton near his batteries on the left slope of the mountain. The general indicated an attack along the slope of the mountain on the right of the main pike, and, leaving Benjamin's battery with him, I marched my division to the front, and there formed, Welsh's brigade, the One hundredth Pennsylvania, under Lieutenant Colonel Leckey, leading as skirmishers, and was about to march Christ's brigade through the woods higher up the slope, when I was ordered by General Burnside to withdraw my division and march up by the Sharpsburg road, and take up a position near Cox. Found the latter to the left of the road some few hundred yards, skirmishing on the wooded slope with the enemy.[30]

Due to a confused courier, a misdirection by Pleasonton, and the counter-marching, Orlando Willcox's division took far longer to arrive at this crucial point than it should have. Willcox did not enter the battlefield until after 2:00 p.m. By that time, the Confederates were reinforced.

The Union army held the gaps once darkness fell, and the fighting ended. That night, Lee ordered a general retreat under cover of darkness. McClellan's army did not cross over until the morning of September 15, allowing Lee to fall back to Sharpsburg. Harpers Ferry surrendered, and Stonewall Jackson's message stating as much found Lee that morning near Sharpsburg. Lee was now convinced that he had time to consolidate his army before McClellan could attack him. It took the Union army all of the next day to traverse the South Mountain passes. All of the above circumstances were possible because of Pleasonton's decision, which ensured that the Confederate position at Fox's Gap held out until dark and prevented Turner's Gap from being outflanked.

Jesse Reno Monument, Fox's Gap, circa 1920. Fred Wilder Cross's South Mountain Photographs (Christen Collection).

Stop 6—Franklin's Headquarters, Burkittsville, Maryland

5500 Catholic Church Road, Burkittsville, Maryland 21755 (39.382150, -77.613512)

Decision—Franklin Delays at Crampton's Gap

Return to your car and turn right on the National Pike (US 40 Alternate). Drive 9.0 miles and then turn right on N. Church Street (MD RT 17) in Middletown. This will become the Burkittsville Road. After 3.5 miles, turn left on Broad Run Road (MD RT 383). After 1.3 miles, as you cross Picknick Woods Road, Broad Run Road becomes Catholic Church Road. After 1.2 more miles, you will see a yellow house on your left at the intersection with Gapland Road. You can park on the south side of the house, which was William B. Franklin's headquarters during the fight for Crampton's Gap. As of this book's publication, the **Martin Shafer Farmhouse** is vacant and owned by the Burkittsville Preservation Association. Efforts are underway to restore this historic structure.

From the western side of the yard, you can see Crampton's Gap as Franklin saw it on September 14, 1862. Looking northwest (in your front), Crampton's Gap is 2.2 miles in that direction. Turner's Gap is just over 7.0 miles to the north (in your front and right). Harpers Ferry is 7.5 miles to the southwest (on your left), and Frederick is just over 11.0 miles to the northeast (behind you and to the right). We will read about the next decision here.

Decision—Franklin Delays at Crampton's Gap

With his Sixth Corps accompanied by the Fourth Corps division of Maj. Gen. Darius N. Couch, Maj. Gen. William B. Franklin made up the left wing of McClellan's advance. Franklin was instructed to move on a line that kept the Potomac River on his left flank. By September 13, his corps was south of Frederick and just west of Buckeystown, Maryland, about ten miles southeast of your present location. Couch's division was situated some five miles south. Early on the morning of September 14, William B. Franklin departed his camp on his way to Crampton's Gap.

Once the relief of Harpers Ferry became a campaign objective for the Union army, McClellan intended Franklin's corps to be the garrison's relief force. Responding to the information contained in the Lost Order, McClellan planned to use the main body of his army, now at Frederick, to hold as many Confederates at the northern gaps as he could. Franklin and his corps would then be able to break through and relieve Harpers Ferry. The major general received orders to attack and move his corps through Crampton's Gap.[31]

View of Crampton's Gap from east of Burkittsville, Maryland, modern image. Matt Brant.

McClellan sent two dispatches to Franklin on September 13.

Communication to Franklin from McClellan, September 13, 1862 6:20 p.m.

I have now full information as to movements and intentions of the enemy. Jackson has crossed the Upper Potomac to capture the garrison at Martinsburg and cut off Miles' retreat toward the west. A division on the south side of the Potomac was to carry Loudoun Heights and cut off his retreat in that direction. McLaws, with his own command and the division of R. H. Anderson, was to move by Boonsborough and Rohrersville to carry the Maryland Heights. The signal officers inform me that he is now in Pleasant Valley. The firing shows that Miles still holds out. Longstreet was to move to Boonsborough and there halt with the reserve corps, D. H. Hill to form the rear guard, Stuart's cavalry to bring up stragglers, & camp. We have cleared out all the cavalry this side of the mountains and north of us.

The last I heard from Pleasonton he occupied Middletown, after several sharp skirmishes. A division of Burnside's command started several hours ago to support him. The whole of Burnside's command, including Hooker's corps, march this evening and early to-morrow morning, followed by the corps of Sumner and Banks and Sykes' division, upon Boonsborough, to carry that position. Couch has been ordered to concentrate his division and join you as rapidly as possible. Without waiting for the whole of that division to join, you will move at daybreak in the morning, by Jefferson and Burkittsville, upon the road to Rohrersville. I have reliable information that the mountain pass by this road is practicable for artillery and wagons. If this pass is not occupied by the enemy in force, seize it as soon as practicable, and debouch upon Rohrersville, in order to cut off the retreat of or destroy McLaws' command. If you find this pass held by the enemy in large force, make all your dispositions for the attack, and commence it about half an hour after you hear severe firing at the pass on the Hagerstown pike, where the main body will attack. Having gained the pass, your duty will be first to cut off, destroy, or capture McLaws' command and relieve Colonel Miles. If you effect this, you will order him to join you at once with all his disposable troops, first destroying the bridges over the Potomac, if not already done, and leaving a sufficient garrison to prevent the enemy from passing the ford, you will then return by Rohrersville on the direct road to Boonsborough if the main column has not succeeded in its attack. If it has succeeded, take the road by Rohrersville to Sharpsburg and Williamsport, in order either to cut off the retreat of Hill and Longstreet toward the Potomac, or prevent the repassage of Jackson. My general idea is to cut the enemy in two and beat him in detail. I believe I have sufficiently explained my intentions. I ask of you, at this important moment, all your intellect and the utmost activity that a general can exercise.

Communication to Franklin from McClellan,
September 13, 1862
6:20 p.m.

Knowing my views and intentions, you are fully authorized to change any of the details of this order as circumstances may change provided the purpose is carried out; that purpose being to attack the enemy in detail and beat him. General Smith's dispatch of 4 p.m. with your comments is received. If, with a full knowledge of all the circumstances, you consider it preferable to crush the enemy at Petersville before undertaking the movement I have directed, you are at liberty to do so, but you will readily perceive that no slight advantage should for a moment interfere with the decisive results I propose to gain. I cannot too strongly impress upon you the absolute necessity of informing me every hour during the day of your movements, and frequently during the night. Force your colonels to prevent straggling, and bring every available man into action. I think the force you have is, with good management, sufficient for the end in view. If you differ widely from me, and being on the spot you know better than I do the circumstances of the case, inform me at once, and I will do my best to re-enforce you. Inform me at the same time how many more troops you think you should have.[32]

If Franklin could defeat Crampton's Gap's defenders and relieve the garrison and combine it with his command, roughly thirty thousand men would stand between the two halves of Lee's army. This force was more than half the size of the Rebel commander's own.[33]

The Confederate force at the gap consisted of one battery of artillery, four regiments of infantry under Col. William A. Parham, four regiments under Brig. Gen. Howell Cobb, and a small cavalry detachment under Col. Thomas T. Munford. The Confederates could count at most 2,100 men to conduct the defense. On the other hand, Franklin had between 11,000 and 12,000 men in his corps alone.[34]

Franklin decided to wait and begin his march to Crampton's Gap at dawn on the fourteenth. After a journey that took the better part of the day and involved a number of delays, Franklin began his attack at 4:30 p.m. He eventually overwhelmed the enemy troops, pushing them up the mountain's steep eastern face. Brig. Gen. Howell Cobb's Confederate brigade and an artillery battery made a last stand on the ridge, but the Sixth Corps drove the Rebels from their positions at dusk. Some two and a half hours after the battle commenced, darkness finally ended the Union advance.

Cobb's after-action report illustrates the weakness of the Confederate position:

After-Action Report of Brig. Gen. Howell Cobb, CSA
Commanding Cobb's Brigade of Mclaws's Division,
Army of Northern Virginia

Thus impressed with the importance of the position, I went forward with the utmost dispatch. When I reached the top of the mountain, I found that the enemy had been repulsed and driven back in the center and had been pursued down the other side of the mountain by Mahone's brigade. I soon discovered, however, that the enemy, by their greatly superior numbers, were flanking us both upon the right and left. Two of my regiments were sent to the right and two to the left to meet these movements of the enemy. In this we were successful, until the center gave way, pressed by fresh troops of the enemy and increased numbers. Up to this time the troops had fought well, and maintained their ground against greatly superior forces. The Tenth Georgia Regiment, of General Semmes' brigade, had been ordered to the gap from their position at the foot of the mountain, and participated in the battle with great courage and energy. After the line were broken, all my efforts to rally the troops were unsuccessful. I was enabled to check their advance by momentary rallies, and, the night coming on, I made a successful stand near the foot of the mountain, which position we held during the night, and until a new position was taken about day-dawn the next morning, in the rear of Brownsville, which position was held until the surrender of Harper's Ferry. General Semmes' brigade and Wilcox's brigade, under the command of Colonel Cumming, of the Tenth Georgia Regiment, had been ordered, the former by General Semmes, the latter by yourself, to my support. They came up to the position I occupied during the night; they could not have reached me sooner. The whole number of troops engaged on our side did not exceed 2,200, whilst the force of the enemy was variously estimated from 10,000 to 20,000 men. It could not have been less than 10,000 and probably reached 15,000.[35]

Franklin described the situation in his own after-action report:

After-Action Report of Maj. Gen. William B. Franklin Commanding Sixth Corps, Army of the Potomac

In compliance with the instructions of the commanding general, the Corps advanced on the morning of the 14th instant from a point 3 miles east of Jefferson, in the direction of the Blue Ridge. At Jefferson a halt was ordered, to afford General Couch an opportunity of coming up. After a short delay, upon learning that this division was still some distance in the rear, I advanced to the vicinity of the village of Burkittsville. Upon ascertaining that the pass over the mountains at this point, which I was directed to secure and hold, was occupied by the enemy in force, I caused immediate preparations to be made for an attack. The enemy was strongly posted on both sides of the road, which made a steep ascent through a narrow defile, wooded on both sides, and offering great advantages of cover and position. Their advance was posted near the base of the mountain, in the rear of a stone wall, stretching to the right of the road at a point where the ascent was gradual, and for the most part over open fields. Eight guns had been stationed on the road, and at points on the sides and summit of the mountain to the left of the pass.

It was evident that the position could be carried only by infantry attack. Accordingly, I directed Major-General Slocum to advance his division through the village of Burkittsville, and commence the attack upon the right. Wolcott's First Maryland Battery was stationed on the left and to the rear of the village, and maintained a steady fire on the positions of the enemy until they were assailed and carried by our troops. Smith's division was placed in reserve on the east side of the village, and held in readiness to co-operate with General Slocum, or support his attack, as occasion might require. Captain Ayres' battery, of this division, was posted on commanding ground to the left of the reserves, and kept up an uninterrupted fire on the principal battery of the enemy until the latter was driven from its position.[36]

Franklin's advancing to Crampton's Gap at dawn on September 14 is a critical decision for several reasons. First, because Miles at Harpers Ferry saw no real sign that a relief force was near at hand, this choice furthered his decision to surrender the next day. Second, the timing of Franklin's advance allowed Stonewall Jackson and those Confederate forces with him to

View of Crampton's Gap from Martin Shafer Farmhouse, modern image. Matt Brant.

complete the capture of the Harpers Ferry garrison on the morning of the fifteenth. These troops were then available to Lee on the sixteenth and seventeenth. Last, the September 14 advance allowed the Confederate divisions of McLaws and R. H. Anderson on Maryland Heights and Pleasant Valley to get away with minimal damage.

Stop 7—Harpers Ferry, West Virginia, Bolivar Heights Scenic Overlook

Whitman Avenue, Bolivar, West Virginia 25425 (39.323754, -77.761072)

Decision—Henry Halleck Does Not Evacuate Harpers Ferry and Miles Surrenders Harpers Ferry

Return to your car and drive northwest on Gapland Road. Follow Gapland Road through Burkittsville, over the gap, and into Pleasant Valley. After 3.3 miles, turn left on Rohrersville Road (MD RT 67). After 5.0 miles, you will exit right onto US-340 W. Travel 4.5 miles, and then turn right onto ALT

Union Guns on Bolivar Heights, modern image. Author.

N/W Washington Street (US 340). You will reenter Virginia and immediately cross over into West Virginia. Drive 0.2 mile, turn left onto Whitman Avenue, and then drive another 0.2 mile to the parking lot of the Bolivar Heights Scenic Overlook.

Park your car here. You will see several informational placards on the Battle of Harpers Ferry and a large grove of trees directly behind them. If you face the placards and the trees, you are looking west at the position Jackson advanced from on Schoolhouse Ridge. The Union position was where you are standing. To your left, you will see several cannon that represent the line commanded by Union colonel Frederick D'Utassy on September 14 and 15, 1862. The town of Harpers Ferry is directly behind you, with Maryland Heights beyond that. Thirteen hundred yards north (to your right) is the Potomac River. Fifteen hundred yards to the south (behind you and to your left) is the Shenandoah River, which A. P. Hill held with Lawton in the center and J. R. Jones on the Confederate left. If you look through the gap in the tree line, you can see the Confederate position on the opposite ridge. We will review two decisions from this location.

Decision—Henry Halleck Does Not Evacuate Harpers Ferry

As Robert E. Lee began his advance into the North, he counted on the evacuation of the Union garrisons at Harpers Ferry and Martinsburg, Virginia, once their positions had been outflanked.

Once Lee's army entered Maryland, it served his overall plan to push west over the Catoctin and South Mountain ranges. The mountains provided a natural barrier between his soldiers and the Army of the Potomac. Moving west would also draw the Union forces farther away from the relative safety of the Washington defenses. Furthermore, Lee could use the Shenandoah Valley as his supply line and a possible line of retreat should he need it. The Confederate commander now saw the Federal garrisons at Harpers Ferry and Martinsburg as genuine obstacles to his plan, and he indicated as much in a dispatch to Davis:

Communication to Davis from Lee, September 12, 1862

Before crossing the Potomac I considered the advantages of entering Maryland east or west of the Blue Ridge. In either case it was my intention to march upon this town. By crossing east of the Blue Ridge, both Washington and Baltimore would be threatened, which I believed would ensure the withdrawal of the mass of the enemy's troops north of the Potomac. I think this has been accomplished. I had also supposed that as soon as it was known that the army had reached Fredericktown, the enemy's forces in the Valley of Virginia, which had retired to Harper's Ferry and Martinsburg, would retreat altogether from the State. In this I was disappointed."[37]

Since Col. Dixon Miles, the garrison commander at Harpers Ferry, was not directly under McClellan's command, he could not order him to evacuate the position without permission from the general-in-chief, Maj. Gen. Henry W. Halleck.

Communication to Halleck from McClellan, September 11, 1862

I believe this army fully appreciates the importance of a victory at this time, and will fight well; but the result of a general battle, with such odds as the enemy now appears to have against us, might, to

Maj. Gen. Henry W. Halleck, general
in chief, Union Army. Library of Con-
gress/National Archives.

say the least, be doubtful; and if we should be defeated the consequences to the country would be disastrous in the extreme. Under
these circumstances, I would recommend that one or two of the
three army corps now on the Potomac, opposite Washington, be at
once withdrawn and sent to re-enforce this army. I would also ad-
vise that the force of Colonel Miles, at Harper's Ferry, where it can
be of but little use, and is continually exposed to be cut off by the
enemy, be immediately ordered here. This would add about 25,000
old troops to our present force, and would greatly strengthen us.[38]

McClellan was factually correct in his assessment of the situation at Harpers
Ferry. Military doctrine indicates that once the enemy outflanks a position, it
should be evacuated or risk being cut off and captured.

Halleck told McClellan that he believed Washington was the real objective of the Rebel advance, and all else was a Confederate ruse.

Communication to McClellan from Halleck,
September 13, 1862

Yours of 5.30 p.m. yesterday is just received. General Banks cannot safely spare eight new regiments from here. You must remember that very few troops are now received from the North, nearly all being stopped to guard the railroad. Four regiments were ordered to General Dix to replace Peck's division. Porter yesterday took away over 20,000. Until you know more certainly the enemy's force south of the Potomac, you are wrong in thus uncovering the capital. I am of [the] opinion that the enemy will send a small column toward Pennsylvania, so as to draw your forces in that direction; then suddenly move on Washington with the forces south of the Potomac and those he may cross over. In your letter of the 10th, you attach too little importance to the capital. I assure you that you are wrong. The capture of this place will throw us back six months, if it should not destroy us. Beware of the evils I now point out to you. You saw them when here, but you seem to forget them in the distance. No more troops can be sent from here till we have fresh arrivals from the North. [39]

Halleck's decision not to evacuate Harpers Ferry forced Robert E. Lee to put his operation on hold to deal with the garrison. In the end, Halleck could not have imagined how far-reaching his choice would be.

After-Action Report of Maj. Gen. Henry W. Halleck, USA
General-in-Chief

As this campaign was to be carried on within the department commanded by Major-General Wool, I directed General McClellan to assume control of all troops within his reach, without regard to departmental lines. The garrisons of Winchester and Martinsburg had been withdrawn to Harper's Ferry, and the commanding officer of that post had been advised by my chief of staff to mainly confine his defense, in case he was attacked by superior forces to the position of Maryland heights, which could have been held a long time against overwhelming numbers. To withdraw him entirely from that position, with the great body of Lee's forces between him and our army, would not only expose the garrison to capture, but all the artillery and stores collected at that place must either be destroyed or left to the enemy. The only feasible plan was for him to hold his position until General McClellan could relieve him or open a communication so that he could evacuate it in safety. These views were communicated both to General McClellan and to Colonel Miles.[40]

Decision—Miles Surrenders Harpers Ferry

While it is likely that Colonel Miles was farther behind these lines on September 15, this is a great spot to get a perspective of the battlefield.

In March 1862, fifty-eight-year-old Col. Dixon Miles was given command of the US arsenal at Harpers Ferry, a garrison primarily staffed by second-line troops. Miles little knew what a pivotal role he was about to play in one of the most significant chains of events of the war.

On September 13, two of McLaws's brigades had pushed a mixed bag of Union defenders commanded by Col. Thomas Ford off Maryland Heights and into the town. That same day, Brig. Gen. John G. Walker's two-brigade division occupied Loudoun Heights to the south. The three divisions under Stonewall Jackson advanced on this position from the direction of Martinsburg, and the units were in place by September 14. By that afternoon, somewhere between

The confluence of the Potomac and Shenandoah Rivers at Harpers Ferry, modern image. Author.

twenty thousand and twenty-five thousand Confederates had surrounded the garrison's fourteen thousand Union defenders.[41]

Brig. Gen. Julius White described the garrison's dilemma.

After-Action Report of Brig. Gen. Julius White, USA
Commanding Martinsburg / Harpers Ferry

In the afternoon the enemy opened a battery from beyond the Charlestown turnpike, shelling our skirmishers thrown out to the front, in the woods. Late in the afternoon, a division of the enemy, under General A. P. Hill, made an assault upon the extreme left, advancing with great spirit.

Colonel Miles not being present, I took command for the time, and ordered the Ninth Vermont to support Colonel Downey, and subsequently re-enforced them with the Thirty-second Ohio and one section of Captain Rigby's battery. The attack continued until after dark, the firing being very sharp and the troops engaged behaving very handsomely, when the enemy was repulsed.

The fire now ceased, but during the night the enemy obtained a lodgment upon and beyond our extreme left. During the engagement I had placed the One hundred and twenty-fifth New York in the rear of the line as a reserve, with a section of Captain Pott's battery on the turnpike and another section on our left, as a support, if needed.

At daylight on the morning of the 15th the enemy opened from their batteries previously mentioned, and from the following, which he had planted during the night, viz: Two upon the plateau at the foot of Loudoun Heights, on the east side of the Shenandoah; one of the guns upon a knoll to the front of our extreme left, enfilading our works upon Bolivar Heights; one upon the Charlestown turnpike, in a belt of woods; one opposite the center of Bolivar Heights, and one upon our extreme right, near the Potomac; in all about fifty guns. Their fire was mostly concentrated upon Captain Rigby's battery, in the work on our left and upon Captain Potts' battery, near by, which I had ordered up and placed in position to reply to the batteries in front. Both of these sustained a heavy fire with the utmost gallantry, and replied rapidly and well. The preceding day a line of rifle-pits had been thrown up along the crest of Bolivar Heights, and the infantry were protected in them and the ravines to our left.

The long-range ammunition had now almost entirely failed, and it became evident that, from the great preponderance of the enemy's artillery and his ability to keep up a fire at long range to which we were no longer able to reply, our ability to hold the position became a mere question of time, and that our defense could only be continued at a great sacrifice of life without any corresponding advantage.

Colonel Miles, at about 9 o'clock a.m., called a council of the officers commanding brigades, and conferred with them upon the propriety of surrendering without further resistance. It was the unanimous opinion of the officers present that it was useless to attempt to hold the position long, and that, if reasonable terms could be obtained, it was best to surrender at once. By order of Colonel Miles, the white flag was accordingly displayed along our lines, and I was requested by him to arrange the terms of capitulation, which duty I accepted. I met Maj. General A. P. Hill, who was appointed by Major-General Jackson to arrange the terms of capitulation with me, and agreed with him upon the terms of surrender, the original of which agreement is herewith submitted.[42]

Harpers Ferry, Virginia/West Virginia, circa 1862. Library of Congress.

Miles surrendered on the morning of September 15. However, before he could formally meet with Jackson, he was struck down by a Confederate artillery shell. Miles died of his wounds the next day. His decision to yield the garrison was critical because it allowed all the Confederate forces in Harpers Ferry to disengage when they did. The Rebels then moved north to Sharpsburg, providing Robert E. Lee manpower at crucial moments on September 17.

In September 1862, the War Department convened a commission to investigate the events surrounding the Harpers Ferry garrison's surrender. In response to a question about Miles's actions and whether Wool thought he had failed to follow orders, Wool responded,

> Colonel Miles appeared to be extremely zealous and extremely anxious, and I thought he would make a good defense. . . . Colonel Miles, himself, never seemed to doubt his ability to defend the place. His last dispatch to me was that he was ready for the enemy.[43]

The tour now shifts to the edge of the **Antietam National Battlefield.**

Stop 8—*Pry House Field Hospital Museum*

18906 Shepherdstown Pike, Keedysville, Maryland 21756 (39.475900, -77.714034)

Decision—Lee Offers Battle at Sharpsburg and McClellan Launches His Attack

The route you will take to Sharpsburg is a bit circuitous, but it will acquaint you with an interesting aspect of the siege of Harpers Ferry, your starting point. On the night of September 14, 1,400 cavalry troopers ostensibly commanded by Col. Benjamin Franklin "Grimes" Davis managed to break out of the besieged town and find their way north. Along the way, they were able to capture General Longstreet's reserve ordnance train. We will follow the route along the Harpers Ferry Road to Sharpsburg these Federals took that night. This improvised command eventually made its way to Greencastle, Pennsylvania.[44]

From Bolivar Heights, drive back down Whitman Avenue and turn right at Washington Street. Go east on (US 340 N). You will travel back to Virginia and then into Maryland. After 3.4 miles, take the Keep Tryst Road exit.

Pry House, McClellan's forward H.Q., modern image. Matt Brant.

Continue on Keep Tryst Road for 0.2 mile, then turn right onto Sandy Hook Road. After 1.6 miles on Sandy Hook Road, turn slightly right, and the road will become Harpers Ferry Road. Go 1.3 miles farther, and take a slight left to stay on Harpers Ferry Road. After 1.0 mile, take a slight right to remain on Harpers Ferry Road. After traveling 8.8 miles and entering the town of Sharpsburg, you will see the Harpers Ferry Road become South Mechanic Street. Drive a farther 0.2 mile, and turn right onto East Main Street, which eventually becomes the Shepherdstown Pike (MD 34 E). In 1862 this road was more commonly referred to as the Boonsboro Pike. Go east 3.9 miles, and your destination **(Pry House Field Hospital Museum)** will be on the left. Turn left, and follow the driveway to the parking lot on the right. A good observation point west of the house faces west and the field at Antietam. The Pry House is open from Thursday to Sunday from May through November, 11:00 a.m. to 5:00 p.m., but you can walk about the grounds during regular park hours. Our next two critical decisions occurred at this location.

Stand on the high ground west of the house with the house at your back, and look west. Depending on the time of the year and the number of leaves on the trees, you should be able to see the New York and Maryland Monuments near the Antietam National Battlefield Visitor Center (see photo).

Behind you is Keedysville, and Boonsboro is about four miles beyond it to the northeast.

The Pry House and the high ground it occupies served as a place where Lee could evaluate the environment before the battle, and as the location from which McClellan observed operations and the battle from September 15 to September 17. Standing here affords you the view each commander had in 1862.

Decision—Lee Offers Battle at Sharpsburg

Robert E. Lee faced a daunting situation on the morning of September 15. The garrison at Harpers Ferry did not evacuate in response to his move west, and the operation to eliminate this obstacle was now three days behind schedule. McClellan had suddenly taken a more aggressive posture in Lee's direct front at South Mountain. By the evening of September 14, the military scales had tipped in favor of the Union. McClellan's aggressiveness at South Mountain gave the Confederate commander pause. Lee thought his enemy was now advancing "more rapidly than was convenient."[45]

The fighting at South Mountain on September 14 resulted in a Union victory. Lee determined that his forces could not hold Turner's Gap once dawn

Pry House, McClellan's forward H.Q., modern image. Matt Brant.

came, and the position was abandoned. The Confederate troops defending Crampton's Gap also fell back. Although Lee was unaware of the full extent of the Crampton's Gap defeat, he knew McLaws's and Anderson's combined force at Maryland Heights was vulnerable.

On the evening of the fourteenth, Lee sent dispatches to his commands. His army would withdraw to the Potomac by way of Sharpsburg. Lee also wrote to Jackson and asked for an estimated completion date for the Harpers Ferry operation.

Later that night, Lee sent two additional messages. The first ordered Jackson to abandon the Harpers Ferry mission and fall back to Shepherds-town and cover the army's retreat. The second ordered McLaws to abandon Maryland Heights. He and Anderson would then make their way back to Virginia however they could. Robert E. Lee's great invasion into the North was about to come to an end.

This message from Lee's headquarters illustrates the general's dilemma and intentions:

Communication to McLaws from Lee, September 14, 1862
8:00 p.m.

The day has gone against us and this army will go by Sharpsburg and cross the river. It is necessary for you to abandon your position to-night. Send your trains not required on the road to cross the river. Your troops you must have well in hand to unite with this command, which will retire by Sharpsburg. Send forward officers to explore the way, ascertain the best crossing of the Potomac, and if you can find any between you and Shepherdstown leave Shepherds-town Ford for this command. Send an officer to report to me on the Sharpsburg road, where you are and what crossing you will take. You will of course bring Anderson's division with you.[46]

Early on Monday, September 15, fortunes changed again. While initially wanting to consolidate his force at Keedysville, Lee reconsidered, seeing a better defensive position farther west beyond Antietam Creek.

Near to where you are standing, a Confederate courier found Robert E. Lee at about 8:00 a.m. The dispatch from Stonewall Jackson reads as follows:

Dispatch to Lee from Jackson, September 14, 1862
8:15 p.m.

Through God's blessing, the advance, which commenced this evening, has been successful thus far, and I look to Him for complete success to-morrow. The advance has been directed to be resumed at dawn to-morrow morning. I am thankful that our loss has been small. Your dispatch respecting the movements of the enemy and the importance of concentration has been received. Can you not connect the headquarters of the army, by signal, with General McLaws?[47]

Upon receiving Jackson's message, the Confederate commander almost instantly decided to make a stand and attempt to reunite his army at Sharpsburg. Lee ordered all of his forces to converge on the town, and he outlined his thoughts in a letter to Davis:

Communication to Davis from Lee, September 16, 1862

Learning later in the evening that Crampton's Gap on the direct road from Fredericktown to Sharpsburg had been forced, and McLaws' rear thus threatened, and believing from a report from Genl Jackson that Harper's Ferry would fall next morning, I determined to withdraw Longstreet and D. H. Hill from their positions and retire to the vicinity of Sharpsburg, where the army could be more readily united. Before abandoning the position, indications led me to believe that the enemy was withdrawing, but learning from a prisoner that Sumner's corps, which had not been engaged, was being put in position to relieve their wearied troops while the most of ours were exhausted by a fatiguing march and a hard conflict and I feared would be unable to renew the fight successfully in the morning, confirmed me in my determination. Accordingly the troops were withdrawn preceded by the trains without molestation by the enemy, and about daybreak took position in front of this place.[48]

This excerpt from Lee's after-action report also reveals his thinking:

After-Action Report by Gen. Robert E. Lee, CSA
Commanding Army of Northern Virginia

Under these circumstances, it was determined to retire to Sharps-burg, where we would be upon the flank and rear of the enemy should he move against McLaws, and where we could more readily unite with the rest of the army. This movement was efficiently and skillfully covered by the cavalry brigade of General Fitzhugh Lee, and was accomplished without interruption by the enemy, who did not appear on the west side of the pass at Boonsborough until about 8 a.m. on the following morning.

On their arrival at Sharpsburg, the commands of Longstreet and D. H. Hill were placed in position along the range of hills be-tween the town and the Antietam, nearly parallel to the course of that stream, Longstreet on the right of the road to Boonsborough and Hill on the left. The advance of the enemy was delayed by the brave opposition he encountered from Fitzhugh Lee's cavalry, and he did not appear on the opposite side of the Antietam until about 2 p.m. During the afternoon the batteries on each side were slightly engaged.[49]

This critical decision determined the location for the upcoming battle and became the next step in actually bringing the fighting on. Additionally, Lee's course of action ensured the continuation of the Maryland Campaign and made McClellan wonder why. On September 15 and 16, the Confederate commander's aggressive stance on the west bank of Antietam Creek was almost entirely bluff. But it was a good enough bluff to make McClellan contemplate what the Rebels were up to and why they were choosing to fight.

Decision—McClellan Launches His Attack

On September 15, it became evident to the Union troops advancing on the now-abandoned Confederate positions at South Mountain that they had struck the Maryland Campaign's critical first blow. McClellan had Lee's operational plans and had used them to drive the Confederate forces off South Mountain. By all indications, the Confederates were falling back, possibly as far as the Potomac. McClellan had seized the initiative from his opponent, and he sensed that an opportunity remained to follow up on the previous night's success and continue pressuring the retreating Rebel army.

Communication to Halleck from McClellan, September 14, 1862
9:40 p.m.

After a very severe engagement, the corps of Hooker and Reno have carried the heights commanding the Hagerstown road. The troops behaved magnificently. They never fought better. Franklin has been hotly engaged on the extreme left. I do not yet know the result, except that the firing indicated progress on his part. The action continued until after dark, and terminated leaving us in possession of the entire crest. It has been a glorious victory. I cannot yet tell whether the enemy will retreat during the night or appear in increased force in the morning. I am hurrying up everything from the rear, to be prepared for any eventuality. I regret to add that the gallant and able General Reno is killed.[50]

By 8:00 a.m. on September 15, McClellan and his staff shot off several dispatches to his commands indicating his intention to pursue the Confederates and attack. McClellan also sent two somewhat premature messages

View of the Antietam Battlefield from the Pry House, modern image. Matt Brant.

to Halleck that seem like a combination of rumor and speculation sprinkled with a few facts:

Communication to Halleck from McClellan, September 15, 1862
8:00 a.m.

I have just learned from General Hooker, in the advance, who states that the information is perfectly reliable that the enemy is making for Shepherdstown in a perfect panic; and General Lee last night stated publicly that he must admit they had been shockingly whipped. I am hurling everything forward to endeavor to press their retreat to the utmost.

Communication to Halleck from McClellan, September 15, 1862
10:00 a.m.

There are already about 700 rebel prisoners at Frederick, under very insufficient guard, and I shall probably send in a larger number to-day.

It would be well to have them either paroled or otherwise disposed of, as Frederick is an inconvenient place for them. Information this moment received completely confirms the rout and demoralization of the rebel army. General Lee is reported wounded and Garland killed. Hooker alone has over 1,000 more prisoners. It is stated that Lee gives his loss as 15,000. We are following as rapidly as the men can move. [51]

Alfred Pleasonton's cavalry was also on the move at first light, following orders to pursue the fleeing Rebels. The balance of the Union infantry corps was dispatched to follow the First Corps in the lead. Learning of Franklin's success at Crampton's Gap, McClellan ordered him to advance as well. McClellan received two messages from Franklin as he moved west into Pleasant Valley. The first indicated that Franklin's advance on Maryland Heights had stalled. The second stated that he believed that Harpers Ferry had fallen to the Confederates.[52]

Just after noon, Richardson, accompanied by Union cavalry, had advanced to the east bank of Antietam Creek. Upon reaching a point near where you are now standing, this force discovered that the Army of Northern Virginia was drawn up in line of battle west of Antietam Creek. Hooker joined Richardson at 2:00 p.m., and Sumner arrived an hour later. The generals quickly determined they lacked the manpower to attack the Confederate position.

McClellan himself reached this location at approximately 4:00 p.m., and he, too, determined it was impossible to attack that day. As darkness fell, the Union commander instructed the army to deploy, but he did not issue any orders to prepare for an attack the next day.

On September 16. McClellan had all his forces except Franklin's corps and Couch's and Humphreys's divisions within a few miles of his forward headquarters at the Pry House. Once McClellan awoke, he discovered a dense fog blanketing the valley. Once it lifted at about 10:00 a.m., the general continued to prepare for the coming battle. The Union Army of the Potomac now had fifty thousand men of all arms assembled east of the creek, and Abraham Lincoln and the War Department issued the following mandate: "God bless you and all with you. Destroy the rebel army if possible."[53]

In his after-action report, McClellan bemoaned the advantages of his opponent's position:

1863 After-Action Report
by Maj. Gen. George B. McClellan, USA
Commanding Army of the Potomac

On all favorable points the enemy's artillery was posted, and their reserves, hidden from view by the hills on which their line of battle was formed, could manoeuvre unobserved by our army, and from the shortness of their line could rapidly reinforce any point threatened by our attack. Their position, stretching across the angle formed by the Potomac and Antietam, their flanks and rear protected by these streams, was one of the strongest to be found in this region of country, which is well adapted to defensive warfare.[54]

McClellan chose to attack, and on the afternoon of the sixteenth, he issued orders for the First Corps to advance across Antietam Creek. However, McClellan seemed to contradict himself in postwar accounts.

Antietam National Battlefield, modern image. Author.

1862 After-Action Report
by Maj. Gen. George B. McClellan, USA
Commanding Army of the Potomac

The design was to make the main attack upon the enemy's left—at least to create a diversion in favor of the main attack, with the hope of something more by assailing the enemy's right—and, as soon as one or both of the flank movements were fully successful, to attack their center with any reserve I might then have on hand.[55]

1863 After-Action Report
by Maj. Gen. George B. McClellan, USA
Commanding Army of the Potomac

My plan for the impending general engagement was to attack the enemy's left with the corps of Hooker and Mansfield, supported by Sumner's and, if necessary, by Franklin's, and, as soon as matters looked favorably there, to move the corps of Burnside against the enemy's extreme right, upon the ridge running to the south and rear of Sharpsburg, and, having carried their position, to press along the

> crest toward our right, and, whenever either of these flank move-
> ments should be successful, to advance our center with all the forces
> then disposable.[56]

The most obvious result of the general's decision was that it inaugurated the Battle of Antietam. Secondarily, the choice to attack ensured that the battle would be fought at the location and day that history now records. This decision also allowed Lee to fight a defensive battle on the ground of his own choosing possessing good interior lines. Finally, McClellan's course of action was the next step in a series of decisions that not only led to the battle, but also guaranteed the continuation of the ever-evolving Maryland Campaign.

Stop 9—Antietam National Battlefield,
Visitor Center Observation Deck

5831 Dunker Church Road, Sharpsburg, Maryland 21782 (39.473919, -77.744968)

Decision—McClellan Does Not Attack

Return to your car from the Pry House, go back down the driveway, and turn right onto MD 34 W (Shepherdstown Pike). Then drive 2.3 miles and turn right onto Church Street (MD 65 N). This road is also called the Sharpsburg Pike and was the Hagerstown Pike in 1862. Continue on MD 65 N for 0.9 mile, and turn right onto Dunker Church Road at the battlefield entrance. Then turn into the parking lot of the **Antietam National Battlefield Visitor Center**. It is open seven days a week, from 9:00 a.m. to 5:00 p.m., excluding major holidays.

The observation deck at the eastern end of the visitor center is a great place to read this next decision. As you face due east, South Mountain is 6.5 miles in that direction. The Pry House is roughly 1.5 miles away in the same direction, and the meandering Antietam Creek is 1.0 mile away. The Joseph Poffenberger Farm is 1.5 miles north (to your left). Between you and the Poffenberger property are the David Miller Farm, the Cornfield, and Smoketown Road. About 0.5 mile southwest of you (on your right), you will see the sixty-foot Observation Tower at a bend in the Sunken Road. More or less in that same direction, about 1.75 miles away is the Burnside Bridge. The Potomac River is located approximately 2.75 miles west of you (directly

Miller Farm Antietam National Battlefield, modern image. Author.

behind you). The southern extension of the West Woods and Hauser's Ridge are situated between here and there.

Please note that we are not covering those critical decisions specific to the Battle of Antietam. For information on those decisions and a correlating tour, please see my book *Decisions at Antietam*.

Decision—McClellan Does Not Attack

On September 18, 1862, the cool and foggy dawn broke on the fields and farms around Sharpsburg, Maryland. As the mist slowly cleared, it revealed the death and devastation the previous day's struggle had brought. The battered Confederate soldiers braced themselves for renewed fighting. On the Union side, McClellan and his army spent that morning waiting for reinforcements to arrive. In the meantime, the Federal commander busied himself by sending communications to the War Department and his wife. While his message to Maj. Gen. H. W. Halleck was somewhat reserved, McClellan's letter to his wife, Mary Ellen, took a decidedly different tone.[57]

Communication to Halleck from McClellan, September 18, 1862
8:00 a.m.

The battle of yesterday continued for fourteen hours, and until after dark. We held all we gained, except a portion of the extreme left; that was obliged to abandon a part of what it had gained. Our losses very heavy, especially in general officers. The battle will probably be renewed to-day. Send all the troops you can by the most expeditious route.[58]

Letter to Mary Ellen from McClellan, September 18, 1862
8:00 a.m.

We fought yesterday a terrible battle against the entire rebel Army. The battle continued 14 hours & was terrific—the fighting on both sides was superb. The general result was in our favor, that is to say we gained a great deal of ground & held it. It was a success, but whether a decided victory depends on what occurs today. I hope that God has given us a great success. It is all in his hands, where I am content to leave it. The spectacle yesterday was the grandest I could conceive of; nothing could be more sublime. Those in whose judgement I rely on tell me I fought the battle splendidly and that it was a masterpiece of art.[59]

McClellan's view across the lines told him that the Confederates, while more concentrated than the day before, were still there. In twelve hours of fighting, over twelve thousand Union men became casualties, or just over 21 percent of those engaged.[60]

McClellan received an additional twelve thousand reinforcements by noon that day, including Couch's Fourth Corps division and Humphreys's Fifth Corps division. These men almost entirely replaced the Union losses from the previous day's fighting. McClellan now had somewhere between fifty thousand and sixty thousand men of all arms to use in a potential renewed attack.[61]

By some estimates, McClellan now had thirty thousand fresh infantrymen at his disposal, only one-third fewer men than he had committed to battle the day before. While McClellan did indeed have some fresh infantry, the four corps most heavily engaged the day before were in deplorable shape. The First Corps had suffered 2,590 total casualties, or 27 percent of its men;

the Second Corps suffered 5,138 total losses, or 32 percent; the Ninth Corps suffered 2,349 total casualties, or 19 percent; and the Twelfth Corps suffered 1,746 total losses, or 23 percent.

McClellan and Franklin discussed a renewal of the fighting.

William B. Franklin,
"Notes on Crampton's Gap and Antietam"
Battles and Leaders of the Civil War

Later in the day General McClellan came again to my headquarters, and there was pointed out to him a hill on the right, command-ing the wood, and it was proposed that the hill should be occupied by our artillery early the next morning, and that after shelling the wood, the attack should be made by the whole corps from the posi-tion then held by it. He assented to this, and it was understood that the attack was to be made. During the night, however, the order was countermanded. I met him about 9 o'clock on the morning of the 18th. He informed me that he countermanded the order because fifteen thousand Pennsylvania troops would soon arrive, and that upon their arrival the attack would be ordered.[62]

Burnside's Bridge, Antietam National Battlefield, modern image. Author.

Additionally, most of the Union army's artillery had enough ammunition for another engagement. However, the long-range twenty-pound Parrott rifles, essential to counter–battery fire the day before, had mostly empty caissons.[63]

Based on the evidence, McClellan had good reason to believe that Robert E. Lee's force still outnumbered his own, and that the long-expected Confederate counterattack was inevitable. If McClellan exposed himself too much, he might be playing right into the Rebel commander's hands. It appears that Lee expected another day of battle and was waiting for it, as illustrated by his unwillingness to retreat after the fighting on September 17.[64]

The Army of Northern Virginia was at this moment still north of the Potomac River. One of McClellan's objectives in the campaign was driving the Rebels from Maryland, and so long as Lee remained in the North, that part of his operational objective was not realized.[65] In his after-action report, McClellan described his thinking.

1863 After-Action Report
by Maj. Gen. George B. McClellan, USA
Commanding Army of the Potomac

After a night of anxious deliberation, and a full and careful survey of the situation and condition of our army, the strength and position of the enemy, I concluded that the success of an attack on the 18th was not certain. I am aware of the fact that under ordinary circumstances a general is expected to risk a battle if he has a reasonable prospect of success; but at this critical juncture I should have had a narrow view of the condition of the country had I been willing to hazard another battle with less than an absolute assurance of success. At that moment—Virginia lost, Washington menaced, Maryland invaded—the national cause could afford no risks of defeat. One battle lost and almost all would have been lost.

The troops were greatly overcome by the fatigue and exhaustion attendant upon the long continued and severely contested battle of the 17th, together with the long day and night marches to which they had been subjected during the previous three days. The supply trains were in the rear, and many of the troops had suffered from hunger. They required rest and refreshment. One division of Sumner's and all of Hooker's corps on the right had, after fighting most valiantly for several hours, been overpowered by numbers, driven back in great disorder, and much scattered, so that they were for the time somewhat demoralized. In Hooker's corps, according to the return made by General Meade, commanding, there were but 6,729 men present on the 18th, whereas on the morning of the 22nd there were 13,093 men present for duty in the same corps, showing that previous to and during the battle 6,364 men were separated from their command.[66]

McClellan did give orders that night to prepare for an assault on September 19, but when the Federals awoke, they discovered the Confederates were gone.

While circumspect, McClellan's decision was critical because it helped mark the conclusion of this battle. The commander's choice also ensured that no additional Union assaults would be made at Sharpsburg.

Stop 10—Boteler's Ford, West Virginia

River Road (County Road 17/1), 0.1 mile west of Trough Road (County Road 31/1), on the right when traveling east. Shepherdstown, West Virginia 25443 (39.427848, -77.778586)

Decision—Lee Withdraws to Virginia

From the visitor center at Dunker Church Road, turn left at the Sharpsburg Pike (MD 65 N). After 0.09 mile, turn right on Main Street / Shepherdstown Pike (MD 34). Travel southwest for 3.3 miles. As you enter West Virginia, MD 34 becomes WV 480. Proceed for 0.08 mile and turn left onto West German Street. After 0.07 mile German Street becomes River Road. Follow River Road for 1.0 mile until you see several wayside markers on your right. Park your car here. The actual crossing site is several hundred yards farther east but on private property.

This is part of the Shepherdstown Battlefield and the place where Union and Confederate forces regularly crossed the Potomac during the Maryland Campaign. As you face the river, you will see the remains of a building and a trail to the right of it that will take you to the river's edge. This trail is very steep, and it can be extremely slippery depending on weather conditions, so please exercise caution. As you face the river, the Antietam Battlefield Visitor Center is about 3.6 miles in that direction (northeast). Harpers Ferry is about 7.5 miles to the southeast (behind you and to the right). The town of Winchester is 26.0 miles to the southwest (behind you and to the right).

Potomac River at Boteler's \ Blackburn's Ford, West Virginia, modern image. Author.

Presumably, Lee made his decision to retreat from Maryland while in his headquarters at Sharpsburg. This site, however, provides a unique perspective on where his army withdrew back to Virginia.

Decision—Lee Withdraws to Virginia

On September 18, dawn began to reveal the damage Lee's army had suffered. Confederate stragglers now scattered all over the Maryland and Virginia countryside slowly began to rejoin the Army of Northern Virginia. Lee ordered the commissary and ammunition trains to feed his men and replenish his army with ammunition. He also concentrated his lines and braced for a new attack.[67]

That morning the Confederate commander had between 25,000 and 30,000 men present for duty, and his total casualties from the day before were between 25 and 28 percent. While his overall losses were devastating, the depletion of his leadership ranks was even more catastrophic. Lee had lost to death and wounding 3 of his 9 division commanders, 19 of his 39 brigade commanders, and 86 of his 173 regimental commanders. This is an overall casualty rate of nearly 50 percent. Of the 173 regiments Lee brought to Maryland, only 22 were now led by colonels. Twenty-two of his 39 brigades did not have a single regiment led by a colonel, and 5 of these had captains commanding. To lead this devastated force, Lee had only 27 general officers on hand.

As was the case nine months later in Pennsylvania, Lee now had thousands of severely wounded men to care for. He could either leave them on Northern soil or figure out how to transport this multitude back to Virginia.[68] The general described the condition of his army as follows:

After-Action Report by Gen. Robert E. Lee, CSA
Commanding Army of Northern Virginia

The arduous service in which our troops had been engaged, their great privations of rest and food, and the long marches without shoes over mountain roads, had greatly reduced our ranks before the action began. These causes had compelled thousands of brave men to absent themselves, and many more had done so from unworthy motives. This great battle was fought by less than 40,000 men on our side, all of whom had undergone the greatest labors and hardships in the field and on the march. Nothing could surpass the determined valor with which they met the large army of the enemy, fully supplied and equipped, and the result reflects the highest credit on the officers and men engaged.

Our artillery, though much inferior to that of the enemy in the number of guns and weight of metal, rendered most efficient and gallant service throughout the day, and contributed greatly to the repulse of the attacks on every part of the line. General Stuart, with the cavalry and horse artillery, performed the duty entrusted to him of guarding our left wing with great energy and courage, and rendered valuable assistance in defeating the attack on that part of our line.

On the 18th we occupied the position of the preceding day, except in the center, where our line was drawn in about 200 yards. Our ranks were increased by the arrival of a number of troops, who had not been engaged the day before, and, though still too weak to assume the offensive, we awaited without apprehension the renewal of the attack. The day passed without any demonstration on the part of the enemy, who, from the reports received, was expecting the arrival of re-enforcements. As we could not look for a material increase in strength, and the enemy's force could be largely and rapidly augmented, it was not thought prudent to wait until he should be ready again to offer battle.[69]

From a purely tactical perspective, Lee's position was precarious at best. While he could still fight, his escape route was now more vulnerable. One more determined push from McClellan might very well cut off his only line of retreat. Perhaps Lee finally realized that the opportunity he sought with the calculated risk of invading the North had slipped from his fingers and was drifting farther and farther from his grasp.

Brig. Gen. John Walker later recalled the day after the battle.

John Walker, "Sharpsburg"
Battles and Leaders of the Civil War

We had fought an indecisive battle, and although we were, per-haps, in as good a condition to renew the struggle as the enemy were, General Lee recognized the fact that his ulterior plans had been thwarted by this premature engagement, and after a consulta-tion with his corps commanders he determined to withdraw from Maryland. At dark on the night of the 18th the rearward movement began; and a little after sunrise of the next morning the entire Con-federate army had safely recrossed the Potomac at Shepherdstown.

Detained in superintending the removal of a number of the wounded of my division, I was among the last to cross the Potomac. As I rode into the river I passed General Lee, sitting on his horse

Potomac River at Boteler's \ Blackburn's Ford, West Virginia, modern image. Author.

in the stream, watching the crossing of the wagons and artillery. Returning my greeting, he inquired as to what was still behind. There was nothing but the wagons containing my wounded, and a battery of artillery, all of which were near at hand, and I told him so. "Thank God!" I heard him say as I rode on.[70]

On the evening of September 18, under the cover of darkness, the Confederate army slipped out of line to the Potomac River crossing at Shepherdstown to Virginia.[71] McClellan wired Halleck this proclamation: "I have the honor to report that Maryland is entirely freed from the presence of the enemy, who have been driven across the Potomac. No fears need now be entertained for the safety of Pennsylvania. I shall at once occupy Harper's Ferry."[72] Conversely, Lee sent the following in a dispatch to Davis: "During the night of the 18th, the army was accordingly withdrawn to the south side of the Potomac, crossing near Shepherdstown, without loss or molestation."[73]

One could certainly argue that the Maryland Campaign was not concluded at this point. As Lee departed Sharpsburg on September 18, he intended to cross back over the Potomac at Williamsport and continue on to Pennsylvania. In fact, the general was moving his army in that direction when his rear guard at Boteler's Ford came under attack and subsequently collapsed on the evening of the nineteenth. Lee was forced to turn his army around to address this threat. However, once he crossed over the Potomac, the campaign was over for all intents and purposes. It would take the Confederate commander five more days to reach that conclusion.

APPENDIX II

UNION ORDER OF BATTLE

Casualty statuses are listed from September 1 to September 20, 1862.

Abbreviations

k—killed, c—captured, mw—mortally wounded, w—wounded
Gen.—General
Lieut. Gen.—Lieutenant General
Maj. Gen.—Major General
Brig. Gen.—Brigadier General
Col.—Colonel
Lieut. Col.—Lieutenant Colonel
Maj.—Major
Capt.—Captain
Lieut.—Lieutenant
Sgt.—Sergeant
Surg.—Surgeon

ARMY OF THE POTOMAC
    Maj. Gen. George B. McClellan, Commanding

GENERAL STAFF
    Chief of Staff
        Brig. Gen. Randolph B. Marcy

Assistant Adjutant General
    Brig. Gen. Seth Williams
Inspector General
    Brig. Gen. Delos B. Sackett
Chief of Artillery
    Brig. Gen. Henry J. Hunt
Chief Quartermaster
    Lieut. Col. Rufus Ingalls

GENERAL HEADQUARTERS

ESCORT
Capt. James B. McIntyre
Independent Company Oneida (New York) Cavalry
    Capt. Daniel P. Mann
4th United States Cavalry, Company A
    Lieut. Thomas H. McCormick
4th United States Cavalry, Company E
    Capt. James B. McIntyre

REGULAR ENGINEER BATTALION
Capt. James C. Duane

PROVOST GUARD
Maj. William H. Wood
2nd United States Cavalry, Companies E, F, H, and K
    Capt. George A. Gordon
8th United States, Companies A, D, F, and G
    Capt. Royal T. Frank
19th United States, Company G
    Capt. Edmund L. Smith
19th United States, Company H
    Capt. Henry S. Welton

HEADQUARTERS GUARD
Maj. Granville O. Haller
93rd New York
    Lieut. Col. Benjamin C. Butler

QUARTERMASTER'S GUARD
1st United States Cavalry, Companies B, C, H, and I
    Capt. Marcus A. Reno

FIRST CORPS
(1) Maj. Gen. Joseph Hooker (w 9/17)
(2) Brig. Gen. George G. Meade

ESCORT
2nd New York Cavalry, Companies A, B, I, and K
Capt. John E. Naylor

FIRST DIVISION
(1) Brig. Gen. Rufus King (relieved 9/14)
(2) Brig. Gen. John P. Hatch (w 9/14)
(3) Brig. Gen. Abner Doubleday

First Brigade
Col. Walter Phelps Jr.
22nd New York
    Lieut. Col. John McKie Jr.
24th New York
    Capt. John D. O'Brian (w 9/17)
30th New York
    Col. William M. Searing
84th New York (14th Militia)
    Maj. William H. de Bevoise
2nd United States Sharpshooters
    Col. Henry A. V. Post (w 9/17)

Second Brigade
(1) Brig. Gen. Abner Doubleday
(2) Col. William Wainwright (w 9/14)
(3) Lieut. Col. J. William Hofmann
7th Indiana
    Maj. Ira G. Grover
76th New York
    (1) Col. William Wainwright
    (2) Capt. John W. Young
95th New York
    Maj. Edward Pye
56th Pennsylvania
    (1) Lieut. Col. J. William Hofmann
    (2) Capt. Frederick William

THIRD BRIGADE
Brig. Gen. Marsena R. Patrick
21st New York
Col. William F. Rogers
23rd New York
Col. Henry C. Hoffman
35th New York
Col. Newton B. Lord
80th New York (20th Militia)
Lieut. Col. Theodore B. Gates

FOURTH BRIGADE (IRON BRIGADE)
Brig. Gen. John Gibbon
19th Indiana
(1) Col. Solomon Meredith
(2) Lieut. Col. Alois O. Bachman (k 9/17)
(3) Capt. William W. Dudley
2nd Wisconsin
(1) Col. Lucius Fairchild (w 9/14)
(2) Lieut. Col. Thomas S. Allen (w 9/17)
(3) Capt. George B. Ely
6th Wisconsin
(1) Lieut. Col. Edward S. Bragg (w 9/17)
(2) Maj. Rufus R. Dawes
7th Wisconsin
Capt. John B. Callis

ARTILLERY
Capt. J. Albert Monroe
New Hampshire Light, 1st Battery
Lieut. Frederick M. Edgell
1st Rhode Island Light, Battery D
Capt. J. Albert Monroe
1st New York Light, Battery L
Capt. John A. Reynolds
4th United States, Battery B
(1) Capt. Joseph B. Campbell (w 9/17)
(2) Lieut. James Stewart

SECOND DIVISION
Brig. Gen. James B. Ricketts (w 9/17)

FIRST BRIGADE
  Brig. Gen. Abram Duryée
  97th New York
    Maj. Charles B. Northrup
  104th New York
    Maj. Lewis C. Skinner
  105th New York
    (1) Col. Howard Carroll (mw 9/17)
    (2) Capt. John C. Whiteside
  107th Pennsylvania
    Capt. James McThomson

SECOND BRIGADE
  (1) Col. William A. Christian
  (2) Col. Peter Lyle
  26th New York
    Lieut. Col. Richard H. Richardson
  94th New York
    Lieut. Col. Calvin Littlefield
  88th Pennsylvania
    (1) Lieut. Col. George W. Gile (w 9/17)
    (2) Capt. Henry B. Myers
  90th Pennsylvania
    (1) Col. Peter Lyle
    (2) Lieut. Col. William A. Leech

THIRD BRIGADE
  (1) Brig. Gen. George L. Hartsuff (w 9/17)
  (2) Col. Richard Coulter
  12th Massachusetts
    (1) Maj. Elisha Burbank (mw 9/17)
    (2) Capt. Benjamin F. Cook
  13th Massachusetts
    Maj. J. Parker Gould
  83rd New York (9th Militia)
    Lieut. Col. William Atterbury
  11th Pennsylvania
    (1) Col. Richard Coulter
    (2) Capt. David M. Cook
  16th Maine (not present)
    Col. A. W. Wildes

ARTILLERY
    1st Pennsylvania Light, Battery F
        Capt. Ezra W. Matthews
    Pennsylvania Light, Battery C
        Capt. James Thompson

THIRD DIVISION
    (1) Brig. Gen. John F. Reynolds
    (2) Brig. Gen. George G. Meade
    (3) Brig. Gen. Truman Seymour

FIRST BRIGADE
    (1) Brig. Gen. Truman Seymour
    (2) Col. Richard Biddle Roberts
    1st Pennsylvania Reserves
        (1) Col. Richard Biddle Roberts
        (2) Capt. William C. Talley
    2nd Pennsylvania Reserves
        Capt. James N. Byrnes
    5th Pennsylvania Reserves
        Col. Joseph W. Fisher
    6th Pennsylvania Reserves
        Col. William Sinclair
    13th Pennsylvania Reserves
    (1st Pennsylvania Rifles "Bucktails")
        (1) Col. Hugh W. McNeil (k 9/16)
        (2) Capt. Dennis McGee
SECOND BRIGADE
    Col. Albert L. Magilton
    3rd Pennsylvania Reserves
        Lieut. Col. John Clark
    4th Pennsylvania Reserves
        Maj. John Nyce
    7th Pennsylvania Reserves
        (1) Col. Henry C. Bolinger (w 9/14)
        (2) Maj. Chauncey A. Lyman
    8th Pennsylvania Reserves
        Maj. Silas M. Bailey
THIRD BRIGADE
    (1) Col. Thomas F. Gallagher (w 9/14)

(2) Lieut. Col. Robert Anderson
9th Pennsylvania Reserves
 Capt. Samuel B. Dick
10th Pennsylvania Reserves
 (1) Lieut. Col. Adoniram J. Warner (w 9/17)
 (2) Capt. Jonathan P. Smith
11th Pennsylvania Reserves
 Lieut. Col. Samuel M. Jackson
12th Pennsylvania Reserves
 Capt. Richard Gustin

ARTILLERY
 1st Pennsylvania Light, Battery A
  Lieut. John G. Simpson
 1st Pennsylvania Light, Battery B
  Capt. James H. Cooper
 5th United States, Battery C
  Capt. Dunbar R. Ransom

SECOND CORPS
Maj. Gen. William V. Sumner

ESCORT
6th New York Cavalry, Company D
 Capt. Henry W. Lyon
6th New York Cavalry, Company K
 Capt. Riley Johnson

FIRST DIVISION
(1) Maj. Gen. Israel B. Richardson (mw 9/17)
(2) Brig. Gen. John C. Caldwell
(3) Brig. Gen. Winfield S. Hancock

FIRST BRIGADE
Brig. Gen. John C. Caldwell
5th New Hampshire
 Col. Edward E. Cross (w 9/17)
7th New York
 Capt. Charles Brestel
61st and 64th New York
 (1) Col. Francis C. Barlow (w 9/17)
 (2) Lieut. Col. Nelson A. Miles

81st Pennsylvania
    Maj. H. Boyd McKeen

SECOND BRIGADE (IRISH BRIGADE)
    (1) Brig. Gen. Thomas F. Meagher (w 9/17)
    (2) Col. John Burke
    29th Massachusetts
        Lieut. Col. Joseph H. Barnes
    63rd New York
        (1) Col. John Burke
        (2) Lieut. Col. Henry Fowler (w 9/17)
        (3) Maj. Richard C. Bentley (w 9/17)
        (4) Capt. Joseph O'Neill
    69th New York
        (1) Lieut. Col. James Kelly (w 9/17)
        (2) Maj. James Cavanagh
    88th New York
        Lieut. Col. Patrick Kelly

THIRD BRIGADE
    Col. John R. Brooke
    2nd Delaware
        Capt. David L. Stricker
    52nd New York
        Col. Paul Frank
    57th New York
        (1) Lieut. Col. Philip S. Parisen (k 9/17)
        (2) Maj. Alford B. Chapman
    66th New York
        Capt. Julius Wehle
    53rd Pennsylvania
        Lieut. Col. Richards McMichael

ARTILLERY
    1st New York Light, Battery B
        Capt. Rufus D. Pettit
    4th United States, Batteries A and C
        Lieut. Evan Thomas

SECOND DIVISION
    (1) Maj. Gen. John Sedgwick (w 9/17)
    (2) Brig. Gen. Oliver O. Howard

First Brigade
  Brig. Gen. Willis A. Gorman
  15th Massachusetts
      Lieut. Col. John W. Kimball
  1st Minnesota
      Col. Alfred Sully
  34th New York
      Col. James A. Suitor
  82nd New York (2nd Militia)
      Col. Henry W. Hudson
  Massachusetts Sharpshooters, 1st Company
      Capt. John Saunders (k 9/17)
  Minnesota Sharpshooters, 2nd Company
      Capt. William F. Russell

Second Brigade (Pennsylvania Brigade)
  (1) Brig. Gen. Oliver O. Howard
  (2) Col. Joshua T. Owen
  (3) Col. DeWitt C. Baxter
  69th Pennsylvania
      Col. Joshua T. Owen
  71st Pennsylvania
      Col. Isaac J. Wistar (w 9/17)
  72nd Pennsylvania
      Col. DeWitt C. Baxter
  106th Pennsylvania
      Col. Turner G. Morehead

Third Brigade
  (1) Brig. Gen. Napoleon J. T. Dana (w 9/17)
  (2) Col. Norman J. Hall
  19th Massachusetts
      (1) Col. Edward W. Hinks (w 9/17)
      (2) Lieut. Col. Arthur F. Devereux (w 9/17)
      (3) Capt. H. G. Weymouth
  20th Massachusetts
      Col. William R. Lee
  7th Michigan
      (1) Col. Norman J. Hall
      (2) Capt. Charles J. Hunt

42nd New York
(1) Lieut. Col. George N. Bomford (w 9/17)
(2) Maj. James E. Mallon
59th New York
Col. William L. Tidball

ARTILLERY
1st Rhode Island Light, Battery A
Capt. John A. Tompkins
1st United States, Battery I
Lieut. George A. Woodruff

THIRD DIVISION
Brig. Gen. William B. French

FIRST BRIGADE
Brig. Gen. Nathan Kimball
14th Indiana
Col. William Harrow
8th Ohio
Lieut. Col. Franklin Sawyer
132nd Pennsylvania
(1) Col. Richard A. Oakford (k 9/17)
(2) Lieut. Col. Vincent M. Wilcox
7th West Virginia
Col. Joseph Snider

SECOND BRIGADE
Col. Dwight Morris
14th Connecticut
Lieut. Col. Sanford H. Perkins
108th New York
Col. Oliver H. Palmer
130th Pennsylvania
Col. Henry I. Zinn

THIRD BRIGADE
(1) Brig. Gen. Max Weber (w 9/17)
(2) Col. John W. Andrews
1st Delaware
(1) Col. John W. Andrews
(2) Lieut. Col. Oliver Hopkinson (w 9/17)

5th Maryland
>   (1) Maj. Leopold Blumenberg (w 9/17)
>   (2) Capt. William W. Bamberger (w 9/17)
>   (3) Capt. Salome Marsh (w and c 9/17)
>   (4) Capt. Ernest F. M. Faehtz

4th New York
>   Lieut. Col. John D. MacGregor

UNATTACHED ARTILLERY
>   1st New York Light, Battery G
>>   Capt. John D. Frank
>   1st Rhode Island Light, Battery B
>>   Capt. John G. Hazard
>   1st Rhode Island Light, Battery G
>>   Capt. Charles D. Owen

FOURTH CORPS / FIRST DIVISION (Arrived at Antietam 9/18)
Maj. Gen. Darius M. Couch

FIRST BRIGADE
>   Brig. Gen. Charles Devens Jr.
>   7th Massachusetts
>>   Col. David A. Russell
>   10th Massachusetts
>>   Col. Henry L. Eustis
>   36th New York
>>   Col. William H. Browne
>   2nd Rhode Island
>>   Col. Frank Wheaton

SECOND BRIGADE
>   Brig. Gen. Albion P. Howe
>   62nd New York
>>   Col. David J. Nevin
>   93rd Pennsylvania
>>   Col. James M. McCarter
>   98th Pennsylvania
>>   Col. John F. Ballier
>   102nd Pennsylvania
>>   Col. Thomas A. Rowley
>   139th Pennsylvania
>>   Col. Frank H. Collier

THIRD BRIGADE
   Brig. Gen. John Cochrane
   65th New York
       Col. Alexander Shaler
   67th New York
       Col. Julius W. Adams
   122nd New York
       Col. Silas Titus
   23rd Pennsylvania
       Col. Thomas H. Neill
   31st Pennsylvania
       Col. George C. Spear
   61st Pennsylvania
       Col. David H. Williams

ARTILLERY
   New York Light, 3rd Battery
       Capt. William Stuart
   1st Pennsylvania Light, Battery C
       Capt. Jeremiah McCarthy
   1st Pennsylvania Light, Battery D
       Capt. Michael Hall
   2nd United States, Battery G
       Lieut. John H. Butler

FIFTH CORPS
   Maj. Gen. Fitz John Porter

ESCORT
   1st Main Cavalry (detachment)
       Capt. George J. Summat

FIRST DIVISION
   Maj. Gen. George W. Morell

FIRST BRIGADE
   Col. James Barnes
   2nd Maine
       Col. Charles W. Roberts
   18th Massachusetts
       Lieut. Col. Joseph Hayes

22nd Massachusetts
 Lieut. Col. William S. Tilton
1st Michigan
 Capt. Emory W. Belton
13th New York
 Col. Elisha Marshall
25th New York
 Col. Charles A. Johnson
118th Pennsylvania
 (1) Col. Charles M. Prevost (w 9/20)
 (2) Lieut. Col. James Gwyn
Massachusetts Sharpshooters, 2nd Company
 Capt. Lewis E. Wentworth

SECOND BRIGADE
 Brig. Gen. Charles Griffin
2nd District of Columbia
 Col. Charles M. Alexander
9th Massachusetts
 Col. Patrick R. Guiney
32nd Massachusetts
 Col. Francis J. Parker
4th Michigan
 Col. Jonathan W. Childs
14th New York
 Col. James McQuade
62nd Pennsylvania
 Col. Jacob B. Sweitzer

THIRD BRIGADE
 Col. Thomas B. W. Stockton
20th Maine
 Col. Adelbert Ames
16th Michigan
 Lieut. Col. Norval E. Welch
12th New York
 Capt. William Huson
17th New York
 Lieut. Col. Nelson B. Bartram
44th New York
 Maj. Freeman Conner

83rd Pennsylvania
        Capt. Orpheus S. Woodward
Michigan Sharpshooters, Brady's Company
        Lieut. Jonas H. Titus Jr.

ARTILLERY
    Massachusetts Light, Battery C
        Capt. Augustus P. Martin
    1st Rhode Island Light, Battery C
        Capt. Richard Waterman
    5th United States, Battery D
        Lieut. Charles E. Hazlett

SHARPSHOOTERS
    1st United States
        Capt. John B. Isler

SECOND DIVISION
    Brig. Gen. George Sykes

FIRST BRIGADE
    Lieut. Col. Robert C. Buchanan
    3rd United States
        Capt. John D. Wilkins
    4th United States
        Capt. Hiram Dryer
    12th United States, 1st Battalion
        Capt. Matthew M. Blunt
    12th United States, 2nd Battalion
        Capt. Thomas M. Anderson
    14th United States, 1st Battalion
        Capt. W. Harvey Brown
    14th United States, 2nd Battalion
        Capt. David B. McKibbin

SECOND BRIGADE
    Maj. Charles S. Lovell
    1st and 6th United States
        Capt. Levi C. Bootes
    2nd and 10th United States
        Capt. John S. Poland
    11th United States
        Maj. DeLancey Floyd-Jones

17th United States
    Maj. George L. Andrews

THIRD BRIGADE
    Col. Gouverneur K. Warren
    5th New York
        Capt. Cleveland Winslow
    10th New York
        Lieut. Col. John W. Marshall

ARTILLERY
    1st United States, Batteries E and G
        Lieut. Alanson M. Randol
    5th United States, Battery I
        Capt. Stephen H. Weed
    5th United States, Battery K
        Lieut. William E. Van Reed

THIRD DIVISION (Arrived at Antietam 9/18)
    Brig. Gen. Andrew A. Humphreys

FIRST BRIGADE
    Brig. Gen. Erastus B. Tyler
    91st Pennsylvania
        Col. Edgar M. Gregory
    126th Pennsylvania
        Col. James G. Elder
    129th Pennsylvania
        Col. Jacob G. Frick
    134th Pennsylvania
        Col. Matthew S. Quay

SECOND BRIGADE
    Col. Peter H. Allabach
    123rd Pennsylvania
        Col. John B. Clark
    131st Pennsylvania
        Lieut. Col. William B. Shaut
    133rd Pennsylvania
        Col. Franklin B. Speakman
    155th Pennsylvania
        Col. Edward J. Allen

ARTILLERY
 1st New York Light, Battery C
  Capt. Almont Barnes
 1st Ohio Light, Battery L
  Capt. Lucius N. Robinson

ARTILLERY RESERVE
 Lieut. Col. William Hays
 1st Battalion New York Light, Battery A
  Lieut. Bernhard Wever
 1st Battalion New York Light, Battery B
  Lieut. Alfred von Kleiser
 1st Battalion New York Light, Battery C
  Capt. Robert Langner
 1st Battalion New York Light, Battery D
  Capt. Charles Kusserow
 New York Light, 5th Battery
  Capt. Elijah D. Taft
 1st United States, Battery K
  Capt. William M. Graham
 4th United States, Battery G
  Lieut. Marcus P. Miller

SIXTH CORPS
Maj. Gen. William B. Franklin

ESCORT
 6th Pennsylvania Cavalry, Companies B and G
  Capt. Henry P. Muirheid

FIRST DIVISION
Maj. Gen. Henry W. Slocum

FIRST BRIGADE
 Col. Alfred T. A. Tolbert
 1st New Jersey
  Lieut. Col. Mark W. Collet
 2nd New Jersey
  Col. Samuel L. Buck
 3rd New Jersey
  Col. Henry W. Brown

4th New Jersey
      Col. William B. Hatch

SECOND BRIGADE
   Col. Joseph J. Bartlett
   5th Maine
      Col. Nathaniel J. Jackson
   16th New York
      Lieut. Col. Joel J. Seaver
   27th New York
      Lieut. Col. Alexander D. Adams
   96th Pennsylvania
      Col. Henry L. Cake

THIRD BRIGADE
   Brig. Gen. John Newton
   18th New York
      Lieut. Col. George R. Myers
   31st New York
      Lieut. Col. Francis H. Pinto
   32nd New York
      Col. Roderick Matheson

ARTILLERY
   Capt. Emory Upton
   Maryland Light, Battery A
      Capt. John W. Wolcott
   Massachusetts Light, Battery A
      Capt. Josiah Porter
   New Jersey Light, Battery A
      Capt. William Hexamer
   2nd United States, Battery D
      Lieut. Edward B. Williston

SECOND DIVISION
   Maj. Gen. William F. Smith

FIRST BRIGADE
   (1) Brig. Gen. Winfield S. Hancock
   (2) Col. Amasa Cobb
   6th Maine
      Col. Hiram Burnham

43rd New York
   Maj. John Wilson
49th Pennsylvania
   Lieut. Col. William Brisbane
137th Pennsylvania
   Col. Henry M. Bossert
5th Wisconsin
   Col. Amasa Cobb

SECOND BRIGADE
   Brig. Gen. W. T. H. Brooks
   2nd Vermont
      Maj. James H. Walbridge
   3rd Vermont
      Col. Breed N. Hyde
   4th Vermont
      Lieut. Col. Charles B. Stoughton
   5th Vermont
      Col. Lewis A. Grant
   6th Vermont
      Maj. Oscar L. Tuttle

THIRD BRIGADE
   Col. William H. Irwin
   7th Maine
      Maj. Thomas W. Hyde
   20th New York
      Col. Ernst von Vegesack
   33rd New York
      Lieut. Col. Joseph W. Corning
   49th New York
      (1) Lieut. Col. William C. Alberger (w 9/17)
      (2) Maj. George W. Johnson
   77th New York
      Capt. Nathan S. Babcock

ARTILLERY
   Capt. Romeyn B. Ayres
   Maryland Light, Battery B
      Lieut. Theodore J. Vanneman
   New York Light, 1st Battery
      Capt. Andrew Cowan

5th United States, Battery F
  Lieut. Leonard Martin

NINTH CORPS
  (1) Maj. Gen. Ambrose E. Burnside
  (2) Maj. Gen. Jesse L. Reno (k 9/14)
  (3) Brig. Gen. Jacob D. Cox

ESCORT
  1st Maine, Company G
    Capt. Zebulon B. Blethen

FIRST DIVISION
  (1) Brig. Gen. Isaac Stevens (k 9/1)
  (2) Col. Benjamin C. Christ
  (3) Brig. Gen. Orlando B. Willcox

FIRST BRIGADE
  Col. Benjamin C. Christ
  28th Massachusetts
    Capt. Andrew P. Caraher
  17th Michigan
    Col. William H. Withington
  79th New York
    Lieut. Col. David Morrison
  50th Pennsylvania
    (1) Maj. Edward Overton Jr. (w 9/17)
    (2) Capt. William H. Diehl

SECOND BRIGADE
  Col. Thomas Welsh
  8th Michigan
    Lieut. Col. Frank Graves
    Maj. Ralph Ely
  46th New York
    Lieut. Col. Joseph P. Gerhardt
  45th Pennsylvania
    Lieut. Col. John I. Curtin
  100th Pennsylvania
    Lieut. Col. David A. Leckey

ARTILLERY
  Massachusetts Light, 8th Battery
    Capt. Asa M. Cook
  2nd United States, Battery E
    Lieut. Samuel N. Benjamin

SECOND DIVISION
  Brig. Gen. Samuel D. Sturgis

FIRST BRIGADE
  Brig. Gen. James Nagle
  2nd Maryland
    Lieut. Col. J. Eugene Duryée
  6th New Hampshire
    Col. Simon G. Griffin
  9th New Hampshire
    Col. Enoch Q. Fellows
  48th Pennsylvania
    Lieut. Col. Joshua K. Sigfried

SECOND BRIGADE
  Brig. Gen. Edward Ferrero
  21st Massachusetts
    Col. William S. Clark
  35th Massachusetts
    (1) Col. Edward A. Wild (w 9/14)
    (2) Maj. Sumner Carruth (w 9/17)
  51st New York
    Col. Robert B. Potter
  51st Pennsylvania
    Col. John F. Hartranft

ARTILLERY
  Pennsylvania Light, Battery D
    Capt. George W. Durell
  4th United States, Battery E
    (1) Capt. Joseph C. Clark Jr. (w 9/17)
    (2) Lieut. George Dickenson
    (3) 1st Sgt. C. F. Merkle

THIRD DIVISION
(1) Brig. Gen. Isaac P. Rodman (mw 9/17)
(2) Col. Edward Harland

FIRST BRIGADE
Col. Harrison S. Fairchild
9th New York
Lieut. Col. Edgar A. Kimball
89th New York
Maj. Edward Jardine
103rd New York
Maj. Benjamin Ringold

SECOND BRIGADE
Col. Edward Harland
8th Connecticut
(1) Lieut. Col. Hiram Appelman (w 9/17)
(2) Maj. John H. Ward
11th Connecticut
(1) Col. Henry W. Kingsbury (mw 9/17)
(2) Lieut. Col. G. A. Steadman
16th Connecticut
Col. Francis Beach
4th Rhode Island
(1) Col. William H. P. Steere (w 9/17)
(2) Lieut. Col. Joseph B. Curtis

ARTILLERY
5th United States, Battery A
Lieut. Charles P. Muhlenberg

KANAWHA DIVISION
(1) Brig. Gen. Jacob D. Cox
(2) Col. Eliakim P. Scammon

FIRST BRIGADE
Col. Eliakim P. Scammon
Col. Hugh Ewing
12th Ohio
Col. Carr B. White

23rd Ohio
    (1) Lieut. Col. Rutherford B. Hayes (w 9/14)
    (2) Maj. James M. Comly
30th Ohio
    (1) Col. Hugh Ewing
    (2) Lieut. Col. Theodore Jones (w and c 9/17)
    (3) Maj. George H. Hildt
Ohio Light Artillery, 1st Battery
    Capt. James R. McMullin
Gilmore's Company, West Virginia Cavalry
    Lieut. James Abraham
Harrison's Company, West Virginia Cavalry
    Lieut. Dennis Delaney

SECOND BRIGADE
  Col. Augustus Moor (c 09/12)
  Col. George Crook
  11th Ohio
    (1) Lieut. Col. Augustus H. Coleman (k 09/17)
    (2) Maj. Lyman J. Jackson
  28th Ohio
    Lieut. Col. Gottfried Becker
  36th Ohio
    (1) Col. George Crook
    (2) Lieut. Col. Melvin Clarke (k 9/17)
    (3) Maj. Ebenezer B. Andrews
  Schambeck's Company / Chicago Dragoons
    Capt. Frederick Schambeck
  Kentucky Light Artillery, Simmonds's Battery
    Capt. Seth J. Simmonds

UNATTACHED
  6th New York Cavalry (8 companies)
    Col. Thomas C. Devin
  Ohio Cavalry, 3rd Independent Company
    Lieut. Jonas Seamen
  3rd United States, Batteries L and M
    Capt. John Edwards Jr.
  2nd New York Artillery, Battery L
    Capt. Jacob Roemer

TWELFTH CORPS
(1) Maj. Gen. Joseph K. F. Mansfield (mw 9/17)
(2) Brig. Gen. Alpheus S. Williams

ESCORT
1st Michigan Cavalry, Company L
    Capt. Melvin Brewer

FIRST DIVISION
(1) Brig. Gen. Alpheus S. Williams
(2) Brig. Gen. Samuel W. Crawford (w 9/17)
(3) Brig. Gen. George H. Gordon

FIRST BRIGADE
(1) Brig. Gen. Samuel W. Crawford (w 9/17)
(2) Col. Joseph F. Knipe
5th Connecticut
    Capt. Henry W. Daboll
10th Maine
    Col. George L. Beal (w 9/17)
28th New York
    Capt. William H. H. Mapes
46th Pennsylvania
    (1) Col. Joseph F. Knipe
    (2) Lieut. Col. James L. Selfridge
124th Pennsylvania
    (1) Col. Joseph W. Hawley (w 9/17)
    (2) Maj. Isaac L. Haldeman
125th Pennsylvania
    Col. Jacob Higgins
128th Pennsylvania
    (1) Col. Samuel Croasdale (k 9/17)
    (2) Lieut. Col. William W. Hammersly (w 9/17)
    (3) Maj. Joel B. Wanner

THIRD BRIGADE
(1) Brig. Gen. George H. Gordon
(2) Col. Thomas H. Ruger
27th Indiana
    Col. Silas Colgrove

2nd Massachusetts
    Col. George L. Andrews
13th New Jersey
    Col. Ezra A. Carman
107th New York
    Col. Robert B. Van Valkenburg
Pennsylvania Zouaves d'Afrique
    Unknown
3rd Wisconsin
    Col. Thomas H. Ruger

SECOND DIVISION
Brig. Gen. George S. Greene

First Brigade
(1) Lieut. Col. Hector Tyndale (w 9/17)
(2) Maj. Orrin J. Crane
5th Ohio
    Maj. John Collins
7th Ohio
    (1) Maj. Orrin J. Crane
    (2) Capt. Frederick A. Seymour
66th Ohio
    Lieut. Col. Eugene Powell (w 9/17)
28th Pennsylvania
    Maj. Ario Pardee Jr.

Second Brigade
Col. Henry J. Stainrook
3rd Maryland
    Lieut. Col. Joseph H. Sudsburg
102nd New York
    Lieut. Col. James C. Lane
109th Pennsylvania
    Capt. George E. Seymore
111th Pennsylvania
    Maj. Thomas M. Walker (w 9/17)

Third Brigade
(1) Col. William B. Goodrich (k 9/17)
(2) Lieut. Col. Jonathan Austin

3rd Delaware
    (1) Maj. Arthur Maginnis (w 9/17)
    (2) Capt. William J. McKaig
Purnell (Maryland) Legion
    Lieut. Col. Benjamin L. Simpson
60th New York
    Lieut. Col. Charles R. Brundage
78th New York
    (1) Lieut. Col. Jonathan Austin (k 9/17)
    (2) Capt. Henry R. Stagg

ARTILLERY
    Capt. Clermont L. Best
    Maine Light, 4th Battery
        Capt. O'Neill W. Robinson Jr.
    Maine Light, 6th Battery
        Capt. Freeman McGilvery
    1st New York Light, Battery M
        Capt. George W. Cothran
    New York Light, 10th Battery
        Capt. John T. Bruen
    Pennsylvania Light, Battery E
        Capt. Joseph M. Knap
    Pennsylvania Light, Battery F
        Capt. Robert B. Hampton
    4th United States, Battery F
        Lieut. Edward D. Muhlenberg

CAVALRY DIVISION
    Brig. Gen. Alfred Pleasonton

FIRST BRIGADE
    Maj. Charles J. Whiting
    5th United States
        Capt. Joseph H. McArthur
    6th United States
        Capt. William P. Sanders
SECOND BRIGADE
    Col. John F. Farnsworth
    8th Illinois
        Maj. William H. Medill

3rd Indiana
    Maj. George H. Chapman
1st Massachusetts
    Capt. Caspar Crowninshield
8th Pennsylvania
    Capt. Peter Keenan

THIRD BRIGADE
    Col. Richard H. Rush
    4th Pennsylvania
        (1) Col. James H. Childs (k 9/17)
        (2) Lieut. Col. James K. Kerr
    6th Pennsylvania
        Lieut. Col. C. Ross Smith

FOURTH BRIGADE
    Col. Andrew T. McReynolds
    1st New York
        Maj. Alonzo W. Adams
    12th Pennsylvania
        Maj. James A. Congdon

FIFTH BRIGADE
    Col. Benjamin F. Davis
    8th New York
        Col. Benjamin F. Davis
    3rd Pennsylvania
        Lieut. Col. Samuel W. Owen

HORSE ARTILLERY
    2nd United States, Battery A
        Capt. John C. Tidball
    2nd United States, Batteries B and L
        Capt. James M. Robertson
    2nd United States, Battery M
        Lieut. Peter C. Hains
    3rd United States, Batteries C and G
        Capt. Horatio G. Gibson

UNATTACHED
    1st Maine Cavalry
        Col. Samuel H. Allen
    15th Pennsylvania Cavalry (detachment)
        Col. William J. Palmer

HARPERS FERRY / MARTINSBURG GARRISON
(1) Col. Dixon S. Miles (mw 09/15)
(2) Brig. Gen. Julius M. White

First Brigade
Col. Frederick D'utassy
65th Illinois
    Col. Daniel Cameron
39th New York
    Maj. Hugo Hildebrandt
111th New York
    Col. Jesse Segoine
115th New York
    Col. Simeon Sammon
15th Indiana Battery
    Capt. John Von Sehlen

Second Brigade
Col. William Trimble
125th New York
    Col. George Willard
126th New York
    Col. Eliakim Sherrill (w&c 09/13)
60th Ohio
    Lieut. Col. Noah Hixon
9th Vermont
    Col. George Stannard
3rd Maryland Potomac Home Guard
    Lieut. Col. Stephen Downey
1st Indiana Battery
    Capt. Silas Rigby
Ohio Battery
    Capt. Benjamin Potts

Third Brigade
Col. Thomas Ford
1st Maryland Potomac Home Guard (Battalion)
    Maj. John Steiner
32nd Ohio
    Col. Thomas Ford
5th New York Heavy Artillery, Bat. F
    Capt. Eugene McGrath

1st Maryland Cavalry (detachment)
    Capt. Charles Russell
7th Squadron, Rhode Island Cavalry
    Maj. A. Corliss

FOURTH BRIDGADE
    Col. William Ward
    12th New York (Militia)
        Col. William Ward
    87th Ohio
        Col. Henry Banning
    5th New York Heavy Artillery, Bat. A
        Capt. J. Graham

UNATTACHED
    1st Potomac Home Guard
        Col. William Maulsby
    1st Maryland Potomac Home Guard Cavalry
    (including Loudoun Rangers)
        Maj. Henry Cole
    12th Illinois Cavalry
        Col. Hasbrouck Davis
    8th New York Cavalry
        Col. Benjamin Davis
    2nd Illinois Artillery
        Capt. John Phillips

APPENDIX III

CONFEDERATE ORDER OF BATTLE

Casualty statuses are listed from September 1 to September 20, 1862.

Abbreviations

k—killed, c—captured, mw—mortally wounded, w—wounded
Gen.—General
Lieut. Gen.—Lieutenant General
Maj. Gen.—Major General
Brig. Gen.—Brigadier General
Col.—Colonel
Lieut. Col.—Lieutenant Colonel
Maj.—Major
Capt.—Captain
Lieut.—Lieutenant
Surg.—Surgeon

ARMY OF NORTHERN VIRGINIA
Gen. Robert E. Lee, Commanding

LEE'S HEADQUARTERS STAFF
Chief of Staff / Adjutant General
Lieut. Col. Robert H. Chilton

Assistant Adjutant General / Aide-de-Camp
    Maj. Walter H. Taylor
Assistant Adjutant General / Aide-de-Camp
    Maj. Charles S. Venable
Assistant Adjutant General
    Capt. Arthur P. Mason
Aide-de-Camp
    Maj. Charles Marshall
Aide-de-Camp / Chief Engineer
    Maj. Thomas M. R. Talcott
Aide-de-Camp
    Capt. Lathom Woodville
Chief of Ordnance
    Col. E. P. Alexander
Chief Surgeon / Medical Director
    Surg. LaFayette Guild, MD
Secretary
    Col. Armistead L. Long

LONGSTREET'S COMMAND/WING
Maj. Gen. James Longstreet

ESCORT
Independent Company, South Carolina Cavalry
    Capt. James Doby

ANDERSON'S DIVISION
(1) Maj. Gen. Richard H. Anderson (w 9/17)
(2) Brig. Gen. Roger A. Pryor

WILCOX'S BRIGADE
(1) Brig. Gen. Cadmus M. Wilcox
(2) Col. Alfred Cumming (w 9/17)
(3) Maj. Hilary A. Herbert
(4) Capt. James M. Crow
8th Alabama
    Maj. Hilary A. Herbert
9th Alabama
    (1) Maj. Jeremiah H. Johnston (w 9/17)
    (2) Capt. James M. Crow
    (3) Lieut. A. C. Chisholm

10th Alabama
    Capt. George C. Whatley (k 9/17)
11th Alabama
    Maj. John Caldwell Calhoun Sanders

MAHONE'S BRIGADE
  Col. William A. Parham
  6th Virginia
    Capt. John R. Ludlow
  12th Virginia
    Capt. John R. Lewellen (w 9/14)
  16th Virginia
    Maj. Francis D. Holliday (c 9/14)
  41st Virginia
    Lieut. Col. Joseph Minetree
  61st Virginia
    Unknown

FEATHERSTON'S BRIGADE
  (1) Brig. Gen. Winfield Scott Featherston
  (2) Col. Carnot Posey
  12th Mississippi
    Col. William H. Taylor
  16th Mississippi
    Capt. Abram M. Feltus
  19th Mississippi
    Col. Nathaniel H. Harris (w 9/17)
  2nd Mississippi Battalion (6 companies)
    Maj. William S. Wilson (mw 9/17)

ARMISTEAD'S BRIGADE
  (1) Brig. Gen. Lewis A. Armistead (w 9/17)
  (2) Col. James G. Hodges
  9th Virginia
    Capt. William J. Richardson
  14th Virginia
    Col. James G. Hodges
  38th Virginia
    Col. Edward C. Edmonds
  53rd Virginia
    (1) Capt. William G. Pollard (k 9/17)
    (2) Capt. Joseph C. Harwood

57th Virginia
  Col. David Dyer
5th Virginia Battalion
  Unknown

PRYOR'S BRIGADE (FLORIDA BRIGADE)
  (1) Brig. Gen. Roger A. Pryor
  (2) Col. John C. Hately (w 9/17)
14th Alabama
  Maj. James A. Broome
2nd Florida
  (1) Col. William D. Ballantine (w 9/17)
  (2) Lieut. Henry C. Geiger
5th Florida
  (1) Col. John C. Hately (w 9/17)
  (2) Lieut. Col. Thomas B. Lamar (w 9/17)
  (3) Maj. Benjamin F. Davis
8th Florida
  (1) Lieut. Col. Georges A. G. De Coppens (k 9/17)
  (2) Capt. Richard A. Waller (k 9/17)
  (3) Capt. William Baya
3rd Virginia
  (1) Col. Joseph Mayo Jr. (w 9/17)
  (2) Lieut. Col. Alexander D. Callcote

WRIGHT'S BRIGADE
  (1) Brig. Gen. Ambrose R. Wright (w 9/17)
  (2) Col. Robert H. Jones (w 9/17)
  (3) Col. William Gibson
44th Alabama
  (1) Lieut. Col. Charles A. Derby (k 9/17)
  (2) Maj. William F. Perry
3rd Georgia
  (1) Capt. Reuben B. Nisbit (w and c 9/17)
  (2) Capt. John T. Jones
22nd Georgia
  (1) Col. Robert H. Jones (w 9/17)
  (2) Capt. Lawrence D. Lallerstedt (w 9/17)
48th Georgia
  Col. William Gibson

ARTILLERY
Maj. John S. Saunders

Donaldsonville (Louisiana) Artillery
    Capt. Victor Maurin
Norfolk (Virginia) Artillery (Huger's Battery)
    Lieut. Charles R. Phelps
Moorman's (Virginia) Battery
    Capt. Marcellus N. Moorman
Portsmouth (Virginia) Artillery
    (1) Capt. Cary F. Grimes (k 9/17)
    (2) Lieut. John H. Thompson
Dixie (Virginia) Artillery
    Capt. William H. Chapman

JONES'S DIVISION
Brig. Gen. David R. Jones

TOOMBS'S BRIGADE
(1) Brig. Gen. Robert A. Toombs (w 9/17)
(2) Col. Henry L. Benning
2nd Georgia
    (1) Lieut. Col. William R. Holmes (k 9/17)
    (2) Maj. Skidmore Harris (w 9/17)
    (3) Capt. Abner M. Lewis
15th Georgia
    (1) Col. William T. Millican (mw 9/17)
    (2) Capt. Thomas H. Jackson
17th Georgia
    Capt. John A. McGregor
20th Georgia
    Col. John B. Cumming

DRAYTON'S BRIGADE
Brig. Gen. Thomas F. Drayton
50th Georgia
    Lieut. Col. Francis Kearse
51st Georgia
    Unknown
Philips's "Georgia" Legion (9 companies)
    Lieut. Col. Robert Thomas Cook
15th South Carolina
    Col. William D. DeSaussure
3rd South Carolina Battalion (7 companies)

(1) Lieut. Col. George S. James (k 9/14)
(2) Maj. William G. W. Rice (w 9/14)
(3) Capt. George M. Gunnels

KEMPER'S BRIGADE
Brig. Gen. James L. Kemper
1st Virginia
(1) Capt. George F. Newton (w 9/17)
(2) Maj. William H. Palmer
7th Virginia
Maj. Arthur Herbert
11th Virginia
(1) Maj. Adam Clement (w 9/14)
(2) Capt. Phillip S. Ashby
17th Virginia
Col. Montgomery D. Corse (w 9/17)
24th Virginia
Col. William R. Terry

PICKETT'S / GARNETT'S BRIGADE
Brig. Gen. Richard B. Garnett
8th Virginia
Col. Eppa Hunton
18th Virginia
Maj. George C. Cabell
19th Virginia
(1) Col. John B. Strange (k 9/14)
(2) Lieut. William N. Wood
(3) Capt. J. L. Cochran
(4) Capt. Benjamin J. Brown
28th Virginia
Capt. William L. Wingfield
56th Virginia
(1) Col. William D. Stuart
(2) Capt. John B. McPhail Jr. (w 9/14)

JENKINS'S BRIGADE
Col. Joseph Walker
1st South Carolina (Volunteers)
Lieut. Col. Daniel Livingston (w 9/17)
2nd South Carolina Rifles
Col. Robert A. Thompson

5th South Carolina
    Capt. Thomas C. Beckham
6th South Carolina
    Capt. Edward B. Cantey (w 9/17)
4th South Carolina Battalion (5 companies)
    Lieut. W. T. Field
Palmetto (South Carolina) Sharpshooters (12 companies)
    (1) Capt. Alfred H. Foster (w 9/17)
    (2) Capt. Franklin W. Kirkpatrick

JONES'S / G. T. ANDERSON'S BRIGADE
    Col. George T. Anderson
    1st Georgia (Regulars)
        (1) Col. William J. Magill (w 9/17)
        (2) Capt. Richard A. Wayne
    7th Georgia
        Col. George H. Carmical
    8th Georgia
        Col. John R. Towers
    9th Georgia
        Lieut. Col. John C. L. Mounger (w 9/17)
    11th Georgia (5 companies)
        Maj. Francis H. Little

ARTILLERY
    Wise (Virginia) Artillery
        Capt. James S. Brown

HOOD'S DIVISION
    Brig. Gen. John B. Hood

HOOD'S "TEXAS" / WOFFORD'S BRIGADE
    Col. William T. Wofford
    18th Georgia
        Lieut. Col. Solon Z. Ruff
    Hampton's (South Carolina) Legion
        Lieut. Col. Martin W. Gary
    1st Texas
        Lieut. Col. Philip A. Work
    4th Texas
        Lieut. Col. Benjamin F. Carter

5th Texas
    Capt. Ike N. M. Turner
Law's Brigade
    Col. Evander M. Law
    4th Alabama
        (1) Lieut. Col. Owen K. McLemore (mw 9/14)
        (2) Capt. Lawrence H. Scruggs (w 9/17)
        (3) Capt. William M. Robbins
    2nd Mississippi
        (1) Col. John M. Stone (w 9/17)
        (2) Lieut. William C. Moody
    11th Mississippi
        (1) Col. Philip F. Liddell (mw 9/16)
        (2) Lieut. Col. Samuel F. Butler (mw 9/17)
        (3) Maj. Taliaferro S. Evans (k 9/17)
        (4) Capt. Francis M. Green
    6th North Carolina
        Maj. Robert F. Webb (w 9/17)

Artillery
    Maj. Bushrod W. Frobel
    German (South Carolina) Artillery
        Capt. William K. Bachman
    Palmetto (South Carolina) Artillery
        Capt. Hugh R. Garden
    Rowan (North Carolina) Artillery
        Capt. James Reilly

Evans's Brigade
    (1) Brig. Gen. Nathan G. Evans
    (2) Col. Peter F. Stevens (w 9/17)
    17th South Carolina
        Col. Fitz W. McMaster
    18th South Carolina
        Col. William H. Wallace
    22nd South Carolina
        Maj. Miel Hilton
    23rd South Carolina
        Lieut. E. R. White
    Holcombe (South Carolina) Legion
        Col. Peter F. Stevens

Macbeth (South Carolina) Artillery
Capt. Robert Boyce

RESERVE ARTILLERY

WASHINGTON (LOUISIANA) ARTILLERY
Col. James B. Walton
1st Company
Capt. Charles W. Squires
2nd Company
Capt. John B. Richardson
3rd Company
Capt. Merritt B. Miller
4th Company
Capt. Benjamin F. Eshleman

LEE'S BATTALION
Col. Stephen D. Lee
Ashland (Virginia) Artillery
Capt. Pichegru Woolfolk Jr.
Bedford (Virginia) Artillery
Capt. Tyler C. Jordan
Brooks (South Carolina) Artillery (Rhett's Battery)
Lieut. William Elliott
Eubank's (Virginia) Battery
Capt. John L. Eubank
Madison (Louisiana) Light Artillery
Capt. George V. Moody
Parker's (Virginia) Battery
Capt. William W. Parker

JACKSON'S COMMAND/WING
Maj. Gen. Thomas J. Jackson

ESCORT
Company H, 4th Virginia Cavalry (Black Horse Troop)
Capt. Robert Randolph
White's Virginia Cavalry (3 companies)
Capt. Elijah V. White

EWELL'S / LAWTON'S DIVISION
    (1) Brig. Gen. Alexander Lawton (w 9/17)
    (2) Brig. Gen. Jubal A. Early

LAWTON'S BRIGADE
    (1) Col. Marcellus Douglass (k 9/17)
    (2) Maj. John H. Lowe
    (3) Col. John H. Lamar
    13th Georgia
        Capt. D. A. Kidd
    26th Georgia
        Col. Edmund N. Atkinson
    31st Georgia
        (1) Lieut. Col. John T. Crowder (w 9/17)
        (2) Maj. John H. Lowe
    38th Georgia
        (1) Capt. William H. Battey (k 9/17)
        (2) Capt. Peter Brennan
        (3) Capt. John W. McCurdy
    60th Georgia
        Maj. Waters B. Jones
    61st Georgia
        (1) Col. John H. Lamar
        (2) Maj. Archibald P. McRae (k 9/17)
        (3) Capt. James D. van Valkenburg

TRIMBLE'S BRIGADE
    (1) Capt. W. F. Brown (k 9/01)
    (2) Col. James A. Walker (w 9/17)
    15th Alabama
        Capt. Isaac B. Feagin (w 9/17)
    12th Georgia
        (1) Capt. James G. Rogers (k 9/17)
        (2) Capt. John T. Carson
    21st Georgia
        (1) Maj. Thomas C. Glover (w 9/17)
        (2) Capt. James C. Nisbet
    21st North Carolina
        Capt. F. P. Miller (k 9/17)
    1st North Carolina Battalion Sharpshooters

HAYS'S BRIGADE
>Brig. Gen. Harry T. Hays
>5th Louisiana
>>Col. Henry Forno
>6th Louisiana
>>(1) Col. Henry B. Strong (k 9/17)
>>(2) Lieut. Col. Nathaniel G. Offutt
>7th Louisiana
>>Col. Davidson B. Penn (w 9/17)
>8th Louisiana
>>Lieut. Col. Trevanion D. Lewis (w 9/17)
>14th Louisiana
>>Lieut. Col. David Zable (w 9/17)

EARLY'S BRIGADE
>(1) Brig. Gen. Jubal A. Early
>(2) Col. William Smith (w 9/17)
>13th Virginia
>>Capt. Frank V. Winston
>25th Virginia
>>Capt. Robert D. Lilley
>31st Virginia
>>Col. John S. Hoffman
>44th Virginia
>>Capt. David W. Anderson (w 9/17)
>49th Virginia
>>(1) Col. William Smith
>>(2) Lieut. Col. Jonathan C. Gibson (w 9/17)
>52nd Virginia
>>Col. Michael G. Harman
>58th Virginia
>>Capt. H. W. Wingfield

ARTILLERY
>Maj. Alfred R. Courtney
>Johnson's (Virginia) Battery
>>Capt. John R. Johnson
>Louisiana Guard Artillery
>>Capt. Louis E. D'Aquin

A. P. HILL'S LIGHT DIVISION
Maj. Gen. Ambrose P. Hill

BRANCH'S BRIGADE
  (1) Brig. Gen. Lawrence O. Branch (k 9/17)
  (2) Col. James H. Lane
  7th North Carolina
      Col. Edward G. Haywood
  18th North Carolina
      Lieut. Col. Thomas J. Purdie
  28th North Carolina
      (1) Col. James H. Lane
      (2) Maj. William J. Montgomery
  33rd North Carolina
      Lieut. Col. Robert F. Hoke
  37th North Carolina
      Capt. William G. Morris

GREGG'S BRIGADE
  Brig. Gen. Maxcy Gregg (w 9/17)
  1st South Carolina (Provisional Army)
      (1) Maj. Edward McCrady Jr.
      (2) Col. Daniel H. Hamilton Sr.
  1st South Carolina Rifles
      Lieut. Col. James M. Perrin (w 9/17)
  12th South Carolina
      (1) Col. Dixon Barnes (mw 9/17)
      (2) Lieut. Col. Cadwallader Jones
      (3) Maj. William H. McCorkle
  13th South Carolina
      Col. Oliver E. Edwards
  14th South Carolina
      Lieut. Col. William D. Simpson

ARCHER'S BRIGADE
  Brig. Gen. James J. Archer (ill 9/17)
  Col. Peter Turney
  5th Alabama Battalion
      Capt. Charles M. Hooper
  19th Georgia
      Maj. James H. Neal
  1st Tennessee (Provisional Army)
      Col. Peter Turney
  7th Tennessee

(1) Maj. Samuel G. Shepard
(2) Lieut. George A. Howard
14th Tennessee
(1) Col. William McComb (w 9/17)
(2) Lieut. Col. James W. Lockert

FIELD'S BRIGADE
Col. John M. Brockenbrough
40th Virginia
Lieut. Col. Fleet W. Cox
47th Virginia
Lieut. Col. John W. Lyell
55th Virginia
Maj. Charles N. Lawson
22nd Virginia Battalion (6 companies)
Maj. Edward P. Tayloe

THOMAS'S BRIGADE
Col. Edward L. Thomas
14th Georgia
Col. R. W. Folsom
35th Georgia
Lieut. Col. Bolling H. Holt
45th Georgia
Maj. Washington L. Grice
49th Georgia
Lieut. Col. Seaborn M. Manning

PENDER'S BRIGADE
Brig. Gen. William Dorsey Pender
16th North Carolina
Lieut. Col. William A. Stowe
22nd North Carolina
Maj. Christopher C. Cole
34th North Carolina
Lieut. Col. John McDowell
38th North Carolina
Lieut. Col. Robert F. Armfield

ARTILLERY
Lieut. Col. Reuben L. Walker
Pee Dee (South Carolina) Artillery
Capt. David G. McIntosh

Crenshaw's (Virginia) Battery
> Capt. William G. Crenshaw

Fredericksburg (Virginia) Artillery
> Capt. Carter M. Braxton

Purcell (Virginia) Artillery
> Capt. William R. J. Pegram

Lecher's (Virginia) Artillery
> Capt. Greenlee Davidson

JACKSON'S / JONES'S DIVISION
(1) Brig. Gen. John R. Jones (w 9/17)
(2) Brig. Gen. William E. Starke (k 9/17)
(3) Col. Andrew J. Grigsby

STONEWALL'S / WINDER'S BRIGADE
(1) Col. Andrew J. Grigsby
(2) Lieut. Col. Robert D. Gardner (w 9/17)
(3) Maj. Hazael J. Williams
4th Virginia
> Lieut. Col. Robert D. Gardner

5th Virginia
> (1) Maj. Hazael J. Williams
> (2) Capt. E. L. Curtis (w 9/17)

27th Virginia
> Capt. Frank C. Wilson

33rd Virginia
> (1) Capt. Jacob Golladay (w 9/17)
> (2) Lieut. David Walton

JONES'S BRIGADE
(1) Capt. John E. Penn (w 9/17)
(2) Capt. A. C. Page (w 9/17)
(3) Capt. Robert W. Withers
21st Virginia
> Capt. Archer C. Page

42nd Virginia
> (1) Capt. Robert W. Withers
> (2) Capt. D. W. Garrett

48th Virginia
> Capt. John H. Candler

1st (Irish) Virginia Battalion (5 companies)
 Lieut. Charles A. Davidson

TALIAFERRO'S BRIGADE
 (1) Col. Edward T. H. Warren
 (2) Col. James W. Jackson (w 9/17)
 (3) Col. James L. Sheffield
 47th Alabama
  (1) Col. James W. Jackson
  (2) Maj. James M. Campbell
 48th Alabama
  Col. James L. Sheffield
 10th Virginia
  Col. Edward T. H. Warren
 23rd Virginia
  Lieut. Col. Simeon T. Walton
 37th Virginia
  Lieut. Col. John F. Terry (w 9/17)

STARKE'S BRIGADE
 (1) Brig. Gen. William E. Starke (k 9/17)
 (2) Col. Jesse M. Williams (w 9/17)
 (3) Col. Leroy A. Stafford (w 9/17)
 (4) Col. Edmund Pendleton
 1st Louisiana
  (1) Lieut. Col. Michael Nolan
  (2) Capt. William E. Moore
 2nd Louisiana
  Col. Jesse M. Williams
 9th Louisiana
  (1) Col. Leroy A. Stafford
  (2) Lieut. Col. William R. Peck
 10th Louisiana
  Capt. Henry D. Monier
 15th Louisiana
  Col. Edmund Pendleton
 Coppens's (First Louisiana Zouaves) Battalion
  Capt. M. Alfred Coppens

ARTILLERY
 Maj. Lindsay M. Shumaker
 Alleghany (Virginia) Artillery
  Capt. Joseph Carpenter

Baltimore (Maryland) Artillery
   Capt. John B. Brockenbrough
Danville (Virginia) Artillery
   Capt. George Wooding
Hampden (Virginia) Artillery
   Capt. William H. Caskie
Lee (Virginia) Battery
   Capt. Charles I. Raine
Rockbridge (Virginia) Artillery
   Capt. William T. Poague

UNATTACHED DIVISIONS

MCLAWS'S DIVISION
   Maj. Gen. Lafayette McLaws

KERSHAW'S BRIGADE
   Brig. Gen. Joseph B. Kershaw
   2nd South Carolina
      (1) Col. John D. Kennedy (w 9/17)
      (2) Maj. Franklin Gaillard
   3rd South Carolina
      Col. James D. Nance
   7th South Carolina
      (1) Col. David W. Aiken (w 9/17)
      (2) Capt. John S. Hard
   8th South Carolina
      Lieut. Col. Axalla J. Hoole

COBB'S BRIGADE
   (1) Brig. Gen. Howell Cobb
   (2) Lieut. Col. Christopher C. Sanders
   (3) Lieut. Col. William MacRae
   16th Georgia
      Lieut. Col. Philip Thomas
   24th Georgia
      Maj. Robert E. McMillan (w 9/17)
   Cobb's (Georgia) Legion
      Lieut. Col. Luther Glenn
   15th North Carolina
      Lieut. Col. William MacRae

SEMMES'S BRIGADE
    Brig. Gen. Paul J. Semmes
    10th Georgia
        (1) Maj. Willis C. Holt (w 9/17)
        (2) Capt. William Johnston (w 9/17)
        (3) Capt. Philologus H. Loud (w 9/17)
    53rd Georgia
        (1) Lieut. Col. Thomas Sloan (mw 9/17)
        (2) Capt. Samuel W. Marshborne
    15th Virginia
        (1) Capt. Emmett M. Morrison (w and c 9/17)
        (2) Capt. Edward J. Willis
    32nd Virginia
        Col. Edgar B. Montague

BARKSDALE'S BRIGADE
    Brig. Gen. William Barksdale
    13th Mississippi
        Lieut. Col. Kennon McElroy (w 9/15)
    17th Mississippi
        Lieut. Col. John C. Fiser
    18th Mississippi
        (1) Maj. James C. Campbell (w 9/17)
        (2) Lieut. Col. William H. Luse
    21st Mississippi
        (1) Capt. John Sims
        (2) Col. Benjamin G. Humphreys

ARTILLERY
    (1) Maj. Samuel P. Hamilton
    (2) Col. Henry C. Cabell
    Manly's Battery (1st North Carolina, Battery A)
        Capt. Basil C. Manly
    Pulaski (Georgia) Artillery
        Capt. John P. W. Read
    Richmond (Fayette) Artillery
        Capt. Miles C. Macon
    Richmond Howitzers, 1st Company
        Capt. Edward S. McCarthy
    Troup (Georgia) Artillery
        Capt. Henry H. Carlton

D. H. HILL'S DIVISION
Maj. Gen. Daniel H. Hill

RIPLEY'S BRIGADE
(1) Brig. Gen. Roswell S. Ripley (w 9/17)
(2) Col. George P. Doles
4th Georgia
    (1) Col. George P. Doles
    (2) Maj. Robert S. Smith (k 9/17)
    (3) Capt. William H. Willis
44th Georgia
    Capt. John C. Key
1st North Carolina
    Lieut. Col. Hamilton A. Brown
3rd North Carolina
    (1) Col. William L. De Rosset (w 9/17)
    (2) Maj. Stephen D. Thurston (w 9/17)

RODES'S BRIGADE
Brig. Gen. Robert E. Rodes (w 9/17)
3rd Alabama
    Col. Cullen A. Battle
5th Alabama
    Maj. Edwin L. Hobson
6th Alabama
    (1) Col. John B. Gordon (w 9/17)
    (2) Lieut. Col. James N. Lightfoot (w 9/17)
12th Alabama
    (1) Col. Bristor B. Gayle (k 9/14)
    (2) Lieut. Col. Samuel B. Pickens (w 9/14)
    (3) Capt. Exton Tucker (k 9/17)
    (4) Capt. W. L. Maroney (w 9/17)
    (5) Capt. Adolph Proskauer (w 9/17)
26th Alabama
    Col. Edward A. O'Neal (w 9/17)

GARLAND'S BRIGADE
Brig. Gen. Samuel Garland Jr. (k 9/14)
Col. Duncan K. McRae (w 9/17)
5th North Carolina
    (1) Col. Duncan K. McRae (w 9/17)
    (2) Capt. Thomas M. Garrett

12th North Carolina
> Capt. Shugan Snow

13th North Carolina
> (1) Lieut. Col. Thomas Ruffin Jr. (w 9/17)
> (2) Capt. Joseph H. Hyman

20th North Carolina
> Col. Alfred Iverson Jr.

23rd North Carolina
> (1) Col. Daniel H. Christie
> (2) Lieut. Col. Robert D. Johnston

ANDERSON'S BRIGADE
> (1) Brig. Gen. George B. Anderson (mw 9/17)
> (2) Col. Charles C. Tew (k 9/17)
> (3) Col. Risden T. Bennett (w 9/17)
> (4) Col. Daniel Harvey Christie

2nd North Carolina
> (1) Col. Charles C. Tew (k 9/17)
> (2) Maj. John Howard (w 9/17)
> (3) Capt. Gideon M. Roberts

4th North Carolina
> (1) Col. Bryan Grimes
> (2) Capt. William T. Marsh (k 9/17)
> (3) Capt. Edwin A. Osborn (w 9/17)
> (4) Capt. Daniel P. Latham (k 9/17)

14th North Carolina
> (1) Col. Risden T. Bennett (w 9/17)
> (2) Lieut. Col. William A. Johnson (w 9/17)
> (3) Maj. Andrew W. Sillers

30th North Carolina
> (1) Col. Francis M. Parker (w 9/17)
> (2) Maj. William W. Sillers

RAIN'S / COLQUITT'S BRIGADE
> Col. Alfred H. Colquitt

13th Alabama
> (1) Col. Birkett D. Fry (w 9/17)
> (2) Lieut. Col. William H. Betts (w 9/17)
> (3) Maj. Algernon S. Reaves (w 9/17)

6th Georgia
> (1) Lieut. Col. James M. Newton (k 9/17)

(2) Maj. Philemon Tracy (k 9/17)

(3) Lieut. Eugene P. Bennett

23rd Georgia

(1) Col. William P. Barclay (k 9/17)

(2) Lieut. Col. Emory F. Best (w 9/17)

(3) Maj. James H. Huggins (w 9/17)

27th Georgia

(1) Col. Levi B. Smith (k 9/17)

(2) Lieut. Col. Charles T. Zachry (w 9/17)

(3) Capt. William H. Rentfro

28th Georgia

(1) Maj. Tully Graybill (w 9/17)

(2) Capt. Nehemiah J. Garrison (w 9/17)

(3) Capt. George W. Warthen

ARTILLERY

Maj. Scipio F. Pierson

Hardaway's (Alabama) Battery

Capt. Robert A. Hardaway

Jefferson Davis (Alabama) Artillery

Capt. James W. Bondurant

Jones's (Virginia) Battery

Capt. William B. Jones

King William (Virginia) Artillery

Capt. Thomas H. Carter (w 9/17)

WALKER'S DIVISION

Brig. Gen. John G. Walker

WALKER'S BRIGADE

(1) Col. Vannoy H. Manning (w 9/17)

(2) Col. Edward D. Hall

3rd Arkansas

Capt. John W. Reedy

27th North Carolina

Col. John R. Cooke

46th North Carolina

(1) Col. Edward D. Hall

(2) Lieut. Col. William A. Jenkins

48th North Carolina
(1) Col. Robert C. Hill
(2) Lieut. Col. Samuel H. Walkup
30th Virginia
Lieut. Col. Robert S. Chew (w 9/17)
French's (Virginia) Battery
Capt. Thomas B. French
2nd Georgia Battalion

RANSOM'S BRIGADE
Brig. Gen. Robert Ransom Jr.
24th North Carolina
Lieut. Col. John L. Harris
25th North Carolina
Col. Henry M. Rutledge
35th North Carolina
Col. Matt W. Ransom
49th North Carolina
Lieut. Col. Leroy M. McAfee
Branch's (Virginia) Battery
Capt. James R. Branch

ARTILLERY RESERVE
Brig. Gen. William N. Pendleton

BROWN'S BATTALION
Col. J. Thompson Brown
Powhatan (Virginia) Artillery
Capt. Willis J. Dance
Richmond (Virginia) Howitzers, 2nd Company
Capt. David Watson
Richmond (Virginia) Howitzers, 3rd Company
Capt. Benjamin H. Smith Jr.
Salem (Virginia) Artillery
Capt. Abraham Hupp
Williamsburg (Virginia) Artillery
Capt. John A. Coke

CUTTS'S BATTALION
Lieut. Col. A. S. Cutts
Blackshear's (Georgia) Battery
Capt. James A. Blackshear

Irwin (Georgia) Artillery
Capt. John Lane
Lloyd's (North Carolina) Battery
Capt. Whitmel P. Lloyd
Patterson's (Georgia) Battery
Capt. George M. Patterson
Ross's (Georgia) Battery
Capt. Hugh M. Ross

JONES'S BATTALION
Maj. H. P. Jones
Morris (Virginia) Artillery
Capt. Richard C. M. Page
Orange (Virginia) Artillery
Capt. Jefferson Peyton
Turner's (Virginia) Battery
Capt. William H. Turner
Long Island (Virginia) Battery
Capt. Abram Wimbish

NELSON'S BATTALION
Maj. William Nelson
Amherst (Virginia) Artillery
Capt. Thomas J. Kirkpatrick
Fluvanna (Virginia) Artillery
Capt. John J. Ancell
Huckstep's (Virginia) Battery
Capt. Charles T. Huckstep
Johnson's (Virginia) Battery
Capt. Marmaduke Johnson
Milledge (Georgia) Artillery
Capt. John Milledge

MISCELLANEOUS BATTERIES
Cutshaw's (Virginia) Battery
Capt. Wilford A. Cutshaw
Magruder (Virginia) Artillery
Capt. Thomas J. Page Jr.
Rice's (Virginia) Battery / 8th Star
New Market (Virginia) Artillery
Capt. William H. Rice
Dixie (Virginia) Artillery
Capt. G. B. Chapman

CAVALRY
Maj. Gen. James E. B. Stuart

HAMPTON'S BRIGADE
    Brig. Gen. Wade Hampton
    1st North Carolina
        Col. Laurence S. Baker
    2nd South Carolina
        Col. Matthew C. Butler
    10th Virginia
    Cobb's (Georgia) Legion
        (1) Lieut. Col. Pierce M. B. Young (w 9/13)
        (2) Maj. William G. Delony
    Jeff Davis (Mississippi) Legion
        Lieut. Col. William T. Martin

LEE'S BRIGADE
    Brig. Gen. Fitzhugh Lee
    1st Virginia
        Lieut. Col. Luke T. Brien
    3rd Virginia
        (1) Lieut. Col. John T. Thornton (k 9/17)
        (2) Capt. Thomas Owens
    4th Virginia
        Col. Williams C. Wickham
    5th Virginia
        Col. Thomas L. Rosser
    9th Virginia
        Col. William Henry "Rooney" Fitzhugh Lee (w 9/15)

ROBERTSON'S / MUNFORD'S BRIGADE
    Col. Thomas T. Munford
    2nd Virginia
        Lieut. Col. Richard H. Burks
    6th Virginia
        Col. Thomas S. Flournoy
    7th Virginia
        Capt. Samuel B. Myers
    12th Virginia
        Col. Asher W. Harman
    17th Virginia Battalion

HORSE ARTILLERY
    Capt. John Pelham
    Chew's (Virginia) Battery
        Capt. R. Preston Chew
    Hart's (South Carolina) Battery
        Capt. James F. Hart
    Pelham's (Virginia) Battery
        Capt. John Pelham

APPENDIX IV

STRENGTHS AND CASUALTIES OF CONFEDERATE AND UNION FORCES

The figures contained in the following tables are compiled from these sources:

United States War Department, *The War of the Rebellion: Official Records of the Union and Confederate Armies* (hereafter cited as *OR*), (Washington, DC: United States Government Printing Office, 1887), vol. 19, pt. 1, pp. 67, 183–204, 548–49, 810–13.

D. Scott Hartwig, *To Antietam Creek: The Maryland Campaign of September 1862* (Baltimore: Johns Hopkins University Press, 2012), 542, 674–86.

Walter Herron Taylor, *Four Years with General Lee* (New York: D. Appleton, 1878), 71–75.

Ezra A. Carman, *The Maryland Campaign of 1862*, ed. Thomas G. Clemens (El Dorado Hills, CA: Savas Beatie, 2012), 1:567–620.

Daniel J. Vermilya, *Perceptions, Not Realities: The Strength, Experience, and Condition of the Army of the Potomac at Antietam* (Sharpsburg, MD: Save Historic Antietam Foundation, 2012*)*, 23.

C. W. Whitehair, *Escape across the Potomac* (Infinity, 2009), 134–35.

Thomas A. McGrath, *Shepherdstown: Last Clash of the Antietam Campaign* (Lynchburg, VA: Schroeder, 2013), 64, 211–17.

1862 Maryland Campaign Strength and Casualty Details

Union Army of the Potomac

Union Overview

Source ➡	McClellan	Hartwig		
Corps ⬇	After-action report - 1863	PFD 09-02	K.W.M. -So. Mtn.	Present on 09-17
First - Hooker	14,856	16,536	923	10,903
Second - Sumner	18,813	18,282	0	17,716
Fourth - Couch (Div)	NA	6,400	0	NA
Fifth - Porter	12,930	8,639	0	9,589
Sixth - Franklin	12,300	13,841	533	11,862
Ninth - Reno - Cox\Burnside	13,819	16,621	889	14,650
Twelfth - Mansfield	10,126	13,161	0	8,861
Cav. - Pleasonton	4,320	4,812	0	4,543
Reserve Artil.	NA	950	0	950
Total	87,164	99,242	2,345	79,074

Source ➡	Carman\OR			Vermilya
Corps ⬇	Engaged on 09-17	Casualties	%	Present on 09/17
First - Hooker	9,438	2,590	27.44%	9,438
Second - Sumner	16,065	5,138	31.98%	16,065
Fourth - Couch (Div)	NA	9	0.00%	0
Fifth - Porter	3,224	109	3.38%	8,000
Sixth - Franklin	2,585	439	16.98%	11,865
Ninth - Reno - Cox\Burnside	12,693	2,349	18.51%	12,693
Twelfth - Mansfield	7,631	1,746	22.88%	7,631
Cav. - Pleasonton	4,320	30	0.69%	4,320
Reserve Artil.	* NA	0	0.00%	NA
Total	55,956	12,410	22.18%	70,012

** Available 09-18	43,546

* Included in Fifth Corps totals

** This number does not include the more than 12,000 men in Couch's and Humphrey's Divisions

Union Detail

South Mountain - September 14

AotP Divisions	PFD	Engaged	KWM	KWM %
First Corps				
First - Doubleday	3,920	3,920	495	12.63%
Second - Ricketts	3,193	3,193	35	1.10%
Third - Meade	3,247	3,147	392	12.46%
Second Corps				
First - Richardson	4,275	NA	0	0.00%
Second -Sedgwick	5,681	NA	0	0.00%
Third - French	5,740	NA	0	0.00%
Artillery-Unatt.	369	NA	0	0.00%
Fourth Corps				
First - Couch	6,400	NA	0	0.00%
Fifth Corps				
First - Morell	6,100	NA	0	0.00%
Second - Sykes	3,489	NA	0	0.00%
Third - Humphreys	6,400	NA	0	0.00%
Artillery Res.	950	NA	0	0.00%
Sixth Corps				
First - Slocum	6,532	6,532	513	7.85%
Second - Smith	7,309	0	19	0.26%
Ninth Corps				
First - Wilcox	3,603	3,603	355	9.85%
Second - Sturgis	3,923	3,923	157	4.00%
Third - Rodman	2,934	0	20	0.68%
Kanawha - Cox	3,510	3,510	356	10.14%
Twelfth Corps				
First - Williams	4,735	NA	0	0.00%
Second - Greene	2,504	NA	0	0.00%
Artillery-Unatt.	392	NA	0	0.00%
Cavalry				
Cavalry	4544	4544	1	0.02%
General Staff			3	

Antietam - September 17

AotP Divisions	PFD	Engaged	KWM	KWM %
First Corps				
First - Doubleday	3,425	3,425	812	23.71%
Second - Ricketts	3,158	3,158	1,204	38.13%
Third - Meade	2,855	2,855	573	20.07%
Second Corps				
First - Richardson	4,275	4,275	1,165	27.25%
Second -Sedgwick	5,681	5,681	2,210	38.90%
Third - French	5,740	5,740	1,750	30.49%
Artillery-Unatt.	369	369	10	2.71%
Fourth Corps				
First - Couch	6,400	0	9	0.14%
Fifth Corps				
First - Morell	6,100	0	0	0.00%
Second - Sykes	3,489	3,224	98	3.04%
Third - Humphreys	6,400	0	0	0.00%
Artillery Res.	950	950	11	1.16%
Sixth Corps				
First - Slocum	6,019	0	65	1.08%
Second - Smith	7,290	2,585	373	14.43%
Ninth Corps				
First - Wilcox	3,248	3,248	338	10.41%
Second - Sturgis	3,766	3,354	679	20.24%
Third - Rodman	2,914	2,914	1,077	36.96%
Kanawha - Scammon	3,154	3,154	255	8.08%
Twelfth Corps				
First - Williams	4,735	4,735	1,077	22.75%
Second - Greene	2,504	2,504	651	26.00%
Artillery-Unatt.	392	392	17	4.34%
Cavalry				
Cavalry	4543	4543	30	0.66%
General Staff			6	

Shepherdstown - September 19&20

AotP Divisions	PFD	Engaged	KWM	KWM %
First Corps				
First - Doubleday	2,613	NA	0	0.00%
Second - Ricketts	1,954	NA	0	0.00%
Third - Meade	2,282	NA	0	0.00%
Second Corps				
First - Richardson	3,110	NA	0	0.00%
Second -Sedgwick	3,471	NA	0	0.00%
Third - French	3,990	NA	0	0.00%
Artillery-Unatt.	359	NA	0	
Fourth Corps				
First - Couch	6,391	NA	0	0.00%
Fifth Corps				
First - Morell	6,100	6,100	349	5.72%
Second - Sykes	3,126	3,224	15	0.47%
Third - Humphreys	6,400	NA	0	0.00%
Artillery Res.	939	950	3	0.32%
Sixth Corps				
First - Slocum	5,954	NA	0	0.00%
Second - Smith	2,212	NA	0	0.00%
Ninth Corps				
First - Wilcox	2,910	NA	0	0.00%
Second - Sturgis	2,675	NA	0	0.00%
Third - Rodman	1,837	NA	0	0.00%
Kanawha - Scammon	2,899	NA	0	0.00%
Twelfth Corps				
First - Williams	3,658	NA	0	0.00%
Second - Greene	1,853	NA	0	0.00%
Artillery-Unatt.	375	NA	0	0.00%
Cavalry				
Cavalry	4,513	4513	3	0.07%

Confederate Army of Northern Virginia

Confederate Overview

Source ➡	Walter Taylor	Hartwig					
Divisions ⬇	"Four Years With General Lee"	Present 09-2-62	PFD-So. Mtn. & Harpers Ferry	KWM-So. Mtn. & Harpers Ferry	PFD 09-17 (Est.)	Non Combat Losses	Non Combat Losses %
R.H. Anderson	3,500	11,024	7,601	177	4,000	6,847	62%
DR Jones	2,430	9,034	6,563	953	3,392	4,943	55%
Hood	3,852	3,839	2,970	24	2,304	1,332	35%
Evans Brig.	2,200	1,058	550	216	399	443	42%
S.D. Lee Batt.	*	*	*	*	318		
Washington Artil.	*	590	0	0	596	0	0%
Ewell (Lawton)	3,400	6,246	5,186	0	4,127	2,119	34%
A.P. Hill	3,400	8,464	5,824	69	3,014	5,481	65%
Jackson (J.R. Jones)	3,852	5,578	3,882	0	2,094	3,476	62%
McLaws	2,893	7,759	4,432	962	3,312	3,524	45%
Walker	3,200	5,159	4,555	4	3,946	1,209	23%
D.H. Hill	3,000	9,842	8,314	1,000	5,790	3,057	31%
Cav. Stuart	*	5,313	5,000	0	4,500	813	15%
Reserve Artil.	*	1,299	700	0	621	678	52%
Cav. & Artil. Est.	8,000	NA	NA	NA	NA	NA	NA
Total	39,727	75,205	55,577	3,405	38,413	33,922	45%

Source ➡	Carman		
Divisions ⬇	Engaged 09-17	KWM Antietam	%
R.H. Anderson	4,000	1,278	31.95%
D.R. Jones	3,392	758	22.35%
Hood	2,304	1,025	44.49%
Evans Brig.	399	84	21.05%
S.D. Lee Batt.	318	85	26.73%
Washington Artil.	278	34	12.23%
Ewell (Lawton)	4,127	1,338	32.42%
A.P. Hill	2,568	417	16.24%
Jackson (J.R. Jones)	2,094	648	30.95%
McLaws	2,961	1,119	37.79%
Walker	3,994	1,120	28.04%
D.H. Hill	5,795	2,310	39.86%
Cav. Stuart	4,500	49	1.09%
Reserve Artil.	621	51	8.21%
Cav. & Artil. Est.	NA	NA	NA
Total	37,351	10,316	27.62%

* Available 09-18	27,035

* This figure does not include the 6000 Confederate stragglers that reportedly joined Lee's army on the 18th.

Confederate Detail

South Mountain & Harpers Ferry - September 13 to 15

AoNV Divisions	PFD	Engaged	KWM	KWM %
Longstreet				
R.H. Anderson	7,601	7,601	177	2.33%
D.R. Jones	6,563	6,563	953	14.52%
Hood	2,970	2,970	24	0.81%
Evans Brig.	550	550	216	39.27%
S.D. Lee Batt.	*	*	*	*
Washington Artil.	0	0	0	0
Jackson				
Ewell (Lawton)	5,186	5,186	0	0.00%
A.P. Hill	5,824	5,824	69	1.18%
Jackson (J.R. Jones)	3,882	3,882	0	0.00%
Unattached				
McLaws	4,432	4,432	962	21.71%
Walker	4,555	4,555	4	0.09%
D.H. Hill	8,314	8,314	1,000	12.03%
Cav. Stuart	5,000	5,000	0	0.00%
Reserve Artil.	700	700	0	0.00%

Antietam - September 17

AoNV Divisions	PFD	Engaged	KWM	KWM %
Longstreet				
R.H. Anderson	4,000	4,000	1,278	31.95%
D.R. Jones	3,392	3,392	758	22.35%
Hood	2,304	2,304	1,025	44.49%
Evans Brig.	399	399	84	21.05%
S.D. Lee Batt.	318	318	85	26.73%
Washington Artil.	596	278	34	12.23%
Jackson				
Ewell (Lawton)	4,127	4,127	1,338	32.42%
A.P. Hill	3,014	2,568	417	16.24%
Jackson (J.R. Jones)	2,094	2,094	648	30.95%
Unattached				
McLaws	3,312	2,961	1,119	37.79%
Walker	3,946	3,994	1,120	28.04%
D.H. Hill	5,790	5,795	2,310	39.86%
Cav. Stuart	4,500	4,500	49	1.09%
Reserve Artil.	621	621	51	8.21%

Shepherdstown- September 19&20

AoNV Divisions	PFD	Engaged	KWM	KWM %
Longstreet				
R.H. Anderson *	2,722	450	5	1.11%
D.R. Jones	2,634	NA	0	0.00%
Hood	1,279	NA	0	0.00%
Evans Brig.	315	NA	0	0.00%
S.D. Lee Batt.	233	NA	0	0.00%
Washington Artil.	562	NA	0	0.00%
Jackson				
Ewell (Lawton) *	2,789	300	9	3.00%
A.P. Hill *	2,597	2,597	292	11.24%
Jackson (J.R. Jones)	1,446	NA	0	0.00%
Unattached				
McLaws	2,193	NA	0	0.00%
Walker	2,826	NA	0	0.00%
D.H. Hill *	3,480	100	0	0.00%
Cav. Stuart *	4,451	4,451	0	0.00%
Reserve Artil.	570	570	2	0.35%

* Estimated

Harpers Ferry Garrison

Harpers Ferry Overview

Unit ⬇	PFD 09/13/62	Killed or Wounded	Missing or Captured	Casualties KW %
General Staff	7	1	6	14.29%
First Brigade - D'utassy	3,454	47	3,407	1.36%
Second Brigade - Trimble	4,357	81	4,276	1.86%
Third Brigade - Ford	1,352	79	1,139	5.84%
Fourth Brigade - Ward	1,710	1	1,709	0.06%
Unattached	3,294	2	1,999	0.06%
Total	14,174	211	12,536	1.49%

Harpers Ferry Detail

	Present	Killed or Wounded	Missing or Captured
General Staff	**7**	**1**	**6**
FIRST BRIGADE			
Col. Frederick D'utassy	1	0	1
65th Illinois - Col. Daniel Cameron	817	7	810
39th New York - Maj. Hugo Hildebrandt	545	15	530
111th New York - Col. Jesse Segoine	981	11	970
115th New York - Col. Simeon Sammon	989	11	978
15th Indiana Battery - Capt. John Von Sehlen	121	3	118
First Birgade Total	**3,454**	**47**	**3,407**
SECOND BRIGADE			
Col. William Trimble	1	0	1
125th New York - Col. George Willard	922	3	919
126th New York - Col. Eliakim Sherrill	1,031	55	976
60th Ohio - Lieut. Col. Noah Hixon	913	8	905
9th Vermont - Col. George Stannard	747	3	744
3rd Maryland Potomac Home Guard - Lieut. Col. Stephen Downey	546	12	534
1st Indiana Battery - Capt. Silas Rigby	113	0	113
Ohio Battery - Capt. Benjamin Potts	84	0	84
Second Birgade Total	**4,357**	**81**	**4,276**
THIRD BRIGADE			
Col. Thomas Ford	1	0	1
1st Maryland Potomac Home Guard (Battalion) - Maj. John Steiner	307	6	313
32nd Ohio - Col. Thomas Ford	742	68	674
5th New York Heavy Artillery, Bat. F - Capt. Eugene McGrath	133	2	131
1st Maryland Cavalry (detachment) - Capt. Charles Russell	23	3	20
7th Squadron, Rhode Island Cavalry - Maj. A. Corliss	146	0	0
Third Birgade Total	**1,352**	**79**	**1,139**
FOURTH BRIGADE			
Col. William Ward	1	0	1
12th New York (militia) - Col. William Ward	560	0	560
87th Ohio - Col. Henry Banning	1,015	1	1,014
5th New York Heavy Artillery, Co. A - Capt. J. Graham	134	0	134
Fourth Birgade Total	**1,710**	**1**	**1,709**
UNATTACHED			
1st Maryland Potomac Home Guard - Col. William P. Maulsby	478	0	478
1st Maryland Potomac Home Guard Cavalry (including Loudoun Rangers) - Maj. Henry Cole	136	0	0
12th Illinois Cavalry - Col. Hasbrouck Davis	702	2	157
8th New York Cavalry - Col. Benjamin Davis	706	0	92
2nd Illinois Artillery - Capt. John Phillips	100	0	100
Unattached - Orderlies, men in hospital and hospital staff	1172	0	1,172
Unattached Total	**3294**	**2**	**1,999**
Garrison Total	**14,174**	**211**	**12,536**

Cavalry Breakout

1st Maryland Potomac Home Guard Cavalry - Maj. Henry Cole	124
Loudoun Rangers	12
12th Illinois Cavalry - Col. Hasbrouck Davis *	575
8th New York Cavalry - Col. Benjamin Davis	614
7th Squadron, Rhode Island Cavalry - Maj. A. Corliss	146
Total	1,471

*Col. Arno Voss is also listed as Comander of 12th Ill., and as the officer who led the breakout

NOTES

Introduction

1. Joseph L. Harsh, *Sounding the Shallows: A Confederate Companion for the Maryland Campaign of 1862* (Kent, OH: Kent State University Press, 2000), 24–27; United States War Department, The War of the Rebellion: Official Records of the Union and Confederate Armies (Washington, DC: United States Government Printing Office, 1874–1880), vol. 19, pt. 2, pp. 626–27. Hereafter, this source will be cited in the following format: *OR*, vol. 19, pt. 2, pp. 626–27.

2. Joseph L. Harsh, *Taken at the Flood: Robert E. Lee and Confederate Strategy in the Maryland Campaign of 1862* (Kent, OH: Kent State University Press, 1999), 476.

3. Understanding the numbers available to Lee is challenging to say the least. The 41,000 number listed in the *OR* is referred to as "imperfect" and possibly understated. Using the numbers listed in appendix IV, Lee should have had only 28,000 men available to him after the Battle of Antietam. We know a large number of stragglers joined Lee's army after the battle on the seventeenth. It is possible that number of stragglers was as high as 13,000 men. *OR*, vol. 19, pt. 2, p. 621. See also appendix IV of this book for details on strength.

4. *OR*, vol. 19, pt. 2, pp. 626–27.

5. *OR*, vol. 19, pt. 2, p. 627.

6. *OR*, vol. 19, pt. 2, pp. 628–29.

7. *OR*, vol. 19, pt. 2, pp. 342–43; *OR*, vol. 51, pt. 1, pp. 854–59.

8. George McClellan to Marry Ellen McClellan, September 25, 1862, in *The Civil War Papers of George B. McClellan: Selected Correspondence, 1860–1865*, ed. Stephen W. Sears, (New York: Da Capo, 1992), 481–82.

9. Determining how many men McClellan could potentially bring to the next fight is a problematic exercise. Of the 164,000 soldiers, 72,000 were in or near the Washington fortifications. Subtracting approximately 15 percent from the 92,000 *OR* figure to account for noncombatants, you get a figure of closer to 78,000 troops available to McClellan on September 20. Using Vermilya's most conservative "present for duty" numbers on September 17 in appendix IV, subtracting the casualties, and adding the reinforcements of Humphreys and Couch, you get a number just over 70,000. *OR*, vol. 19, pt. 2, p. 336. See also appendix IV of this book for details on strength.

10. The communications referred to date from September 21, 1862, to September 27, 1862. *OR*, vol. 19, pt. 2, p. 339–63.

11. *OR*, vol. 19, pt. 1, p. 72; Stephen W. Sears, *Lincoln's Lieutenants: The High Command of the Army of the Potomac* (Boston: Houghton Mifflin Harcourt, 2017), 424–25, 433–36; *OR*, vol.1 9, pt. 2, 336–545.

12. Stephen W. Sears, *George B. McClellan: The Young Napoleon* (New York: Da Capo, 1999), 339–40; *OR*, vol. 19, pt. 2, p. 545–46.

13. James Murfin, *The Gleam of Bayonets: The Battle of Antietam and Robert E. Lee's Maryland Campaign, September 1862* (Baton Rouge: Louisiana State University Press, 1964), 55–60.

14. Murfin, *Gleam of Bayonets*, 55–60.

15. Edward Porter Alexander, *Military Memoirs of a Confederate: A Critical Narrative* (New York: Charles Scribner's Sons, 1907), 110–11.

16. James M. McPherson, *The Illustrated Battle Cry of Freedom: The Civil War Era* (New York: Oxford University Press, 2003), 329–35, 339–47, 352–54, 436–42.

17. McPherson, Illustrated Battle Cry of Freedom, 367.

18. Horace Greeley, "A Prayer for Twenty Millions," *New York Tribune*, August 20, 1862.

19. Jennifer L. Weber, *Copperheads: The Rise and Fall of Lincoln's Opponents in the North* (New York: Oxford University Press, 2006), 52.

20. James Michael Martinez, *Carpetbaggers, Cavalry, and the Ku Klux Klan: Exposing the Invisible Empire during Reconstruction* (Lanham, MD: Rowman and Littlefield, 2007), 41.

21. J. G. Randall and Richard Current, *Lincoln the President*, vol. 2, *Midstream to the Last Full Measure* (New York: Da Capo, 1997), 132–34.

22. J. Cutler Andrews, *The North Reports the Civil War* (Pittsburgh: University of Pittsburgh Press, 1955), 270; Stephen W. Sears, *Landscape Turned Red: The Battle of Antietam* (New Haven, CT: Ticknor and Fields, 1983), 7.

23. Steven E. Woodworth, *Davis & Lee at War* (Lawrence: University Press of Kansas, 1995), 130, 180.

24. *OR*, vol. 51, pt. 2, p. 615.

Chapter 1

1. Ethan S. Rafuse, *Antietam, South Mountain, & Harpers Ferry: A Battlefield Guide* (Lincoln: University of Nebraska Press. 2008), 3; James Longstreet, *From Manassas to Appomattox: Memoirs of the Civil War in America* (1896; repr., New York, William S. Konecky Associates, 1992), 193–95.

2. D. Scott Hartwig, *To Antietam Creek: The Maryland Campaign of September 1862* (Baltimore: Johns Hopkins University Press, 2012), 57–58, 686. See appendix IV of this book for details on strength.

3. Older references listing the Confederate order of battle during the campaign attach McLaws's and Walker's Divisions to Longstreet's Command. These sources also attach D. H. Hill's division to Jackson's Command. In more contemporary references all three units are listed as "unattached." To say the least, this command structure was somewhat fluid and often confusing. During the campaign some divisions were interchanged within the Confederate command. For example, D. H. Hill was under Jackson early on in the campaign but removed at some point in the view of army command. However, Jackson still saw D. H. Hill as being under his authority by September 9. This explains why Jackson's and Lee's headquarters both sent copies of Special Orders 191 to D. H. Hill. Ezra A. Carman, *The Maryland Campaign of September 1862: Ezra A. Carman's Definitive Study of the Union and Confederate Armies at Antietam*, ed. Joseph Pierro (Hoboken, NJ: Taylor and Francis, 2008), 415–34. See also appendix III of this book for details on the Confederate order of battle.

4. Hartwig, *To Antietam Creek*, 83.

5. *OR*, vol. 19, pt. 2, pp. 590–91; Hartwig, *To Antietam Creek*, 82–83.

6. Joseph L. Harsh, Taken at the Flood: Robert E. Lee and Confederate Strategy in the Maryland Campaign of 1862 (Kent, OH: Kent State University Press, 1999), 44–45; Ezra Carman, *The Maryland Campaign of September 1862*, ed. Thomas G. Clemens, vol. 1, *South Mountain* (El Dorado Hills, CA: Savas Beatie, 2010, 2012), 83.

7. Stephen W. Sears, *Chancellorsville* (Boston: Houghton Mifflin Harcourt, 1996), 32–35; Matt Spruill III and Matt Spruill IV, *Decisions at Second Manassas: The Fourteen Critical Decisions That Defined the Battle* (Knoxville: University of Tennessee Press, 2018), 103–4.

8. Confederate general Joe Johnston fell back from Centerville in March 1862 for several reasons. They included logistical issues and the fact that his flanks were vulnerable to any turning movement by the Army of the Potomac. Craig L. Symonds, *Joseph E. Johnston: A Civil War Biography* (New York: W. W. Norton, 1992), 142–43.

9. Hartwig, *To Antietam Creek*, 50–51; Harsh, *Taken at the Flood*, 48.

10. Carman, *Maryland Campaign of September 1862*, 1:131. See also appendix IV of this book for details on strength and casualties. Harsh, *Taken at the Flood*, 21.

11. *OR*, vol. 19, pt. 2, pp. 589–90.

12. Harsh, *Taken at the Flood*, 21–25; *OR*, vol. 19, pt. 2, pp. 590–91; Sears, *Landscape Turned Red*, 63–67.

13. Harsh, *Taken at the Flood*, 77, 80–82, 195–96.

14. James Murfin, *Gleam of Bayonets*, 64–71; *OR*, vol. 19, pt. 2, pp. 590–91, 593–94, 598–99; Rafuse, *Antietam, South Mountain, & Harpers Ferry*, 3–4; Carman, *Maryland Campaign of September 1862*, 1:45–50.

15. *OR*, vol. 19, pt. 2, p. 600.

16. In an 1886 letter from E. C. Gordon to William Allan, Gordon described a conversation he had with Lee. The full quote was in reference to the so-called Lost Dispatch. Douglas Southall Freeman, *Lee's Lieutenants: A Study in Command* (New York: Charles Scribner's Sons, 1942), 2:716–17.

17. Harsh, *Taken at the Flood*, 85–86, 97–98; Carman, *Maryland Campaign of September 1862*, 1:89–94.

18. Stephen B. Oates, *With Malice Toward None* (New York: Harper and Row, 1977), 304–6, 315–17; Sears, *Landscape Turned Red*, 10; Hartwig, *To Antietam Creek*, 1.

19. Several messages from Halleck in the *OR* refer to his concern for the capital. His message to McClellan on the thirteenth seems to be the most earnest. *OR*, vol. 19, pt. 2, p. 280–81.

20. Stephen E. Ambrose, *Halleck: Lincoln's Chief of Staff* (Baton Rouge: Louisiana State University Press, 1962), 82; "A Barbarian Invasion of the North," *New York Times*, September 3, 1862, p. 4, *New York Times* Archive, https://www.nytimes.com/1862/09/03/archives/a-barbarian-invasion-of-the-north.html; George Templeton Strong, entry for September 13, 1862, in *The Diary of George Templeton Strong*, ed. Allan Nevins and Milton H. Thomas (New York: Macmillan, 1962), 203; *OR*, vol. 19, pt. 2, p. 182.

21. Sears, *Landscape Turned Red*, 9–17; Murfin, *Gleam of Bayonets*, 72–77; Carman, *Maryland Campaign of September 1862*, 1:131; Gideon Welles, entry for September 1, 1862, in The Civil War Diary of Gideon Welles, Lincoln's Secretary of the Navy: The Original Manuscript Edition, ed. William E. Gienapp and Erica L. Gienapp (Chicago: University of Illinois Press, 2014), 24–26.

22. Warner, Ezra J., *Generals in Blue: Lives of the Union Commanders* (Baton Rouge: Louisiana State University, 1964), 376–77; Peter Cozzens, *General John Pope: A Life for the Nation* (Champaign: University of Illinois Press, 2000), 1.

23. Sears, *Lincoln's Lieutenants*, 332; Sears, *Landscape Turned Red*, 79.

24. William Marvel, *Burnside* (Chapel Hill: University of North Carolina Press, 1991), 110–11; Sears, *McClellan: The Young Napoleon*, 265.

25. *OR*, vol. 19, pt. 2, p. 169.

26. Hartwig, *To Antietam Creek*, 131; Curt Anders, *Henry Halleck's War: A Fresh Look at Lincoln's Controversial General-in-Chief* (Carmel: Guild Press of Indiana, 1999), 251–53, 258–59; *OR*, vol. 12, pt. 3, p. 808; *OR*, vol. 19, pt. 2, p. 169.

27. Warner, *Generals in Blue*, 234–35, 378–80; Geoffrey Perret, *Lincoln's War: The Untold Story of America's Greatest President as Commander in Chief* (New York: Random House, 2004), 211; William Roscoe Thayer, *John Hay: In Two Volumes* (Boston: Houghton, Mifflin, 1915), 1:128.

28. *OR*, vol. 53, pt. 1, p. 786.

29. *OR*, vol. 53, pt. 2, p. 189–90.

30. Hartwig, To Antietam Creek, 132

31. George Brinton McClellan, *McClellan's Own Story: The War for the Union, the Soldiers Who Fought It, the Civilians Who Directed It and His*

Relations to It and to Them (New York: C. L. Webster, 1887), 551; *OR*, vol. 19, pt. 2, pp. 169, 182; *OR*, vol. 19, pt. 1, p. 786; Hartwig, *To Antietam Creek*, 132; Carman, *Maryland Campaign of September 1862*, 1:134.

32. The details of events during this time frame are voluminous, and no one source contains them all. Murfin, *Gleam of Bayonets*, 71–85; *OR*, vol. 12, pt. 2, pp. 82–84; *OR*, vol. 12, pt. 3, pp. 741, 769–74, 787–88, 796–98; *OR*, vol. 19, pt. 2, pp. 169, 182–83, 189–90; Cozzens, *General John Pope*, 195–96; Welles, entries for September 1, 1862, to September 7, 1862, in *Civil War Diary*, 24–33.

33. See the introduction for details on actions after the Battle of Antietam.

34. Daniel J. Vermilya, Perceptions, Not Realities: The Strength, Experience, and Condition of the Army of the Potomac at Antietam (Sharpsburg, MD: Save Historic Antietam Foundation, 2012); Hartwig, *To Antietam Creek*, 138–40; Carman, *Maryland Campaign: Ezra A. Carman's Definitive Study*, 397–414. See also appendix II of this manuscript for details on the Union order of battle, and appendix IV for details on troop strength.

35. The argument for this current version of the Army of the Potomac being constructed from five separate commands can be found in Vermilya's "Perceptions, Not Realities." His addition to reach this number includes the Army of Virginia, the Army of the Potomac, and the Ninth Corps, which was basically made up of three separate units. Vermilya, *Perceptions, Not Realities*, 8.

36. Lee believed that the Union army would take weeks, not days to organize itself and partake in offensive operations. In a September 16 message to Confederate secretary of war George W. Randolph, Lee, who was in Sharpsburg, stated that the Union army was "advancing more rapidly than was convenient from Fredericktown." Harsh, *Taken at the Flood*, 32–33, *OR*, vol. 19, pt. 1, p. 140; *OR*, vol. 19, pt. 2, p. 590.

37. Warner, *Generals in Blue*, 195–97; Sears, *Lincoln's Lieutenants*, 285–86; Anders, *Henry Halleck's War*, 3–8; Ambrose, *Halleck*, 3–8; Bvt. Maj. Gen. George W. Cullum, Biographical Register of the Officers and Graduates of the U.S. Military Academy at West Point, N.Y. (Boston: Houghton, Mifflin, 1891), 1:733–40.

38. Murfin, *Gleam of Bayonets*, 106–7, 111; *OR*, vol. 19, pt. 2, pp. 603–5; Douglas Southall Freeman and Richard Harwell, *Lee: An Abridgment in One Volume of the Four-Volume "R. E. Lee" by Douglas Southall Freeman*, 1st Touchstone ed. (New York: Simon and Schuster, 1997), 247–49.

39. McClellan, *McClellan's Own Story*, 550; *OR*, vol. 19, pt. 2, p. 254.

40. See appendix IV of this work for information on armies' strengths and casualties. *OR*, vol. 19, pt. 1, pp. 549, 787–88.

41. *OR*, vol. 19, pt. 2, p. 189; Sears, *Landscape Turned Red*, 89–90.

42. Charles River Editors, Harpers Ferry: The History of the Federal Armory That Became One of America's Most Famous National Parks (Ann Arbor, MI: Charles River Editors, 2015), 11–14.

43. *OR*, vol. 19, pt. 2, p. 189.

44. For the evacuation of Winchester, see *OR*, vol. 12-3, p. 800. On September 11, 1862, McLaws and Anderson were near Burkittsville, Maryland, and a path east was available to Miles along the track of the Baltimore and Ohio Railroad. For positions on September 11, see W. H. Mattern and E. A. Carman, cartographers, *Theatre of Operations, Maryland Campaign, September 1862*, 1862, 28 x 36 cm, Library of Congress, https://www.loc.gov/item/2009584566/.

45. Who commanded the cavalry breakout is a matter of some debate. Technically, two officers, Col. Hasbrouck Davis and Col. Arno Voss, were senior to Grimes Davis. Grimes Davis gets the lion's share of the credit for the operation perhaps because he was a West Pointer, and the breakout and subsequent capture of Longstreet's reserve ordnance train was largely his idea. Additionally, Grimes Davis used his southern accent to fool Confederate teamsters into redirecting the ordnance train. Sears, *Landscape Turned Red*, 151–52; Carman, *Maryland Campaign of September 1862*, 1:254–56; *OR*, vol. 19, pt. 1, pp. 629–31.

46. Chester G. Hearn, *Six Years of Hell: Harpers Ferry During the Civil War* (Baton Rouge: Louisiana State University Press, 1996), 293–96.

47. *OR*, vol. 19, pt. 2, pp. 280–81; Ambrose, *Halleck*, 82–83.

48. Benjamin Franklin Wade and US Congress Joint Committee on the Conduct of the War, *Report of the Joint Committee on the Conduct of the War: Army of the Potomac* (Washington, DC: United States Government Printing Office, 1863), 478.

49. Edwin B. Coddington, *The Gettysburg Campaign: A Study in Command* (New York: Charles Scribner's Sons, 1968), 92, 130–33; Glen Tucker, *High Tide at Gettysburg: The Pennsylvania Campaign* (Gettysburg, PA: Stan Clark Military Books, 1958), 71–72, 79.

50. Harsh, *Taken at the Flood*, 110–12.

51. Hartwig, *To Antietam Creek*, 125–26.

52. *OR*, vol. 19, pt. 2, pp. 604–5.

53. Throughout history, a number of military texts have included the phrase "No plan survives first contact with the enemy" or variations thereof. The original quote, "No plan of operations extends with any certainty beyond the first contact with the main hostile force," is credited to Field Marshal Helmuth Karl Bernhard Graf von Moltke (October 26, 1800–April 24, 1891), who was chief of staff of the Prussian Army. Helmuth von Moltke, *Moltke on the Art of War: Selected Writings*, ed. Daniel Hughes (New York: Random House Ballantine, 1993), viii.

54. For positions on September 9 and 10, see Mattern and Carman, *Theatre of Operations, Maryland Campaign*.

55. Whether Lee knew on September 9 that McClellan was commanding the Union field army is debatable, as is the notion that Lee was taking actions based on that information. If we use September 7, indicated by Hartwig, as the date McClellan was ordered to oversee the force pursuing the Confederates, it is hard to believe Lee would have had this knowledge less than two days later. In a letter to his sister dated September 7, Lee's adjutant, Col. Walter Taylor, made no mention of McClellan, referring only to "the Army of Pope." John Walker indicated that when he had conversed with Lee on September 7, Lee spoke about McClellan as if he was in command. There is some evidence that by September 9, people in Frederick, including some Confederates, believed that McClellan was indeed in command of the field army. It is also very likely that they confused the news that McClellan had taken charge of the Washington defenses on September 2 with the idea that he was commanding the actual field army. Lee might or might not have made the same assumption. Hartwig, *To Antietam Creek*, 132; Walter Taylor to Mary Lou Taylor (sister), Friday, September 7, 1862, in *Lee's Adjutant: The Wartime Letters of Colonel Walter Herron Taylor, 1862–1865*, ed. R. Lockwood Tower (Columbia: University of South Carolina Press, 1995), 42–43; William W. Hassler, "*The Civil War Letters of General William Dorsey Pender to His Wife*," *Georgia Review* 17, no. 1 (1963): 68, http://www.jstor.org/stable/41395942; John G. Walker, "Jackson's Capture of Harper's Ferry," in *Battles and Leaders of the Civil War*, ed. Robert Underwood Johnson and Clarence Clough Buel (New York: Century, 1887), 2:605–6; "Four Days Experience with the Rebels in Frederick," *Civilian & Telegraph* (Cumberland, MD), September 18, 1862.

56. *OR*, vol. 19, pt. 2, pp. 597–600; Longstreet, *From Manassas to Appomattox*, 205–8.

57. Coddington, *Gettysburg Campaign*, 92, 130–33; Tucker; *High Tide at Gettysburg*, 71–72, 79.

58. Based on Lee's communications it is reasonable to assume his primary goal was to drive the Union forces away and capture them only if circumstances allowed.

59. There are three known surviving versions of Special Orders 191. The first version has ten articles/paragraphs and is considered to be the complete Lost Dispatch. The second version, found by Union soldiers on September 13 with D. H. Hill's name at the bottom, has only eight articles/paragraphs. The third version, which Jackson sent to D. H. Hill and Hill saved, also has only eight articles/paragraphs. Neither the copy McClellan would eventually possess nor the copy D. H. Hill preserved includes the first two paragraphs discussing Lee's order that no troops enter Frederick and Maj. Walter Taylor's mission. *OR*, vol. 19, pt. 1, 42–43; *OR*, vol. 19, pt. 2, 603–5; Harsh, *Taken at the Flood*, 154–57.

60. *OR*, vol. 19, pt. 2, pp. 603–4; Longstreet described the meeting with Lee and Jackson in his autobiography. Longstreet, *From Manassas to Appomattox*, 201–3.

61. Halleck's belief that the Confederates would double back on Washington, DC, is illustrated in his September 13 communication to McClellan. *OR*, vol. 19, pt. 2, pp. 280–81. For the positions of Franklin's Sixth Corps on September 13, see Mattern and Carman, *Theatre of Operations, Maryland Campaign*.

62. "Sugarloaf Mountain—History," Sugarloaf Mountain—Stronghold, Inc., updated 2003, http://sugarloafmd.com/sl_history.html, Link dead as of November 22, 2021; "History of the Blue Ridge," Friends of the Blue Ridge Mountains, updated July 22, 2020, https://friends ofblueridge.org/our-mountains/mountains-history/#:~:text=The%20 Blue%20Ridge%2C%20part%20of,South%20Africa's%20Barberton%20 greenstone%20belt.

63. Paul J. Scheips, "Union Signal Communications Innovation and Conflict," *Civil War History* 9, no. 4 (December 1963): 399–421.

64. Hartwig, *To Antietam Creek*, 108, 131, 163–64; *OR*, vol. 19, pt. 1, pp. 117–18; *OR*, vol. 19, pt. 2, pp. 184–87.

65. Hartwig, To Antietam Creek, 107–9; *OR*, vol. 19, pt. 2, pp. 200–201; Abner Hard, History of the Eighth Cavalry Regiment, Illinois Volunteers, during the Great Rebellion (Aurora, IL.: self-pub., 1868), 174.

66. For positions from September 6 to 9, see Mattern and Carman, *Theatre*

of Operations, Maryland Campaign. For a record of communication for the same time period, see *OR*, vol. 19, pt. 2, p. 189–224.

67. "Intelligence: Human Intelligence," *Central Intelligence Agency—News & Information*, last updated April 30, 2013, https://www.cia.gov/news -information/featured-story-archive/2010-featured-story-archive /intelligence-human-intelligence.html, Link dead as of November 22, 2021.

68. Harsh, *Taken at the Flood*, 107–8; Hartwig, To Antietam Creek, 127; Sears, *Landscape Turned Red*, 107; Edwin C. Fishel, The Secret War for the Union: The Untold Story of Military Intelligence in the Civil War (Boston: Houghton Mifflin, 1996), 342.

69. Fishel, Secret War for the Union, 213–15; Sears, Landscape Turned Red, 103–5.

70. *OR*, vol. 19, pt. 2, pp. 205, 218–19.

71. *OR*, vol. 19, pt. 2, pp. 218–19, vol. 51, pt. 1, sec. 2, pp. 802–3. For Union positions on September 9, see Mattern and Carman, *Theatre of Operations, Maryland Campaign.*

72. Laurence H. Freiheit, Boots and Saddles: Cavalry during the Maryland Campaign of September 1862 (Iowa City: Camp Pope Publishing, 2012), 453; Hartwig, To Antietam Creek, 177.

73. *OR*, vol. 19, pt. 2, pp. 221–23, vol. 51, pt. 1, sec. 2, pp. 802–3.

74. Hartwig, *To Antietam Creek*, 177–78, 184–85, 193; Freiheit, *Boots and Saddles*, pp. 180–82.

75. *OR*, vol. 19, pt. 2, pp. 247, 249, 256–57, 266.

76. For positions from September 11, see Mattern and Carman, *Theatre of Operations, Maryland Campaign.*, Maryland Campaign, September 1862.

77. *OR*, vol. 19, pt. 2, p. 216.

78. Hartwig, *To Antietam Creek,*. 109, 193–94.

79. *OR*, vol. 19, pt. 1, p. 209.

80. Recent scholarship conflicts as to the exact time the Lost Order was found. Hartwig indicates approximately 9:00 a.m., while Stotelmyer identifies a time closer to noon. As there was no US standard time in 1862, it is not unreasonable to state that any time cited by an individual could be off by as much as an hour. Hartwig, *To Antietam Creek*, 281; Steven R. Stotelmyer, *Too Useful to Sacrifice: Reconsidering George B. McClellan's Generalship in the Maryland Campaign from South Mountain to Antietam* (El Dorado Hills, CA: Savas Beatie, 2019), 22–23.

81. For soldiers' positions on September 13, see Mattern and Carman, *Theatre of Operations, Maryland Campaign*; *OR*, vol. 19, pt. 1, 209, pt. 2, pp. 474–81; Sears, *Landscape Turned Red*, 111–13; Freeman, *Lee's Lieutenants*, 2:718; Stotelmyer, *Too Useful to Sacrifice*, 19, 23–24.

82. Sykes's Fifth Corps division was above Rockville, and Humphreys had not yet left Washington. For positions on September 13, see Mattern and Carman, *Theatre of Operations, Maryland Campaign.*

83. The main evidence for the time McClellan received the Lost Order is his communication sent to Lincoln on the thirteenth. It was previously supposed that the time stamp on that communication (12 m.) indicated he sent the message at 12:00 meridian, or noon. However, more recent evidence indicates the message's time stamp was in fact midnight. *OR*, vol. 19, pt. 2, p. 281; Hartwig, *To Antietam Creek*, 283–84; Stotelmyer, *Too Useful to Sacrifice*, 30.

84. Stephen W. Sears, *Controversies and Commanders: Dispatches from the Army of the Potomac* (Boston: Houghton Mifflin Harcourt, 1999), 114.

85. There is some debate as to how much the Lost Order made a difference in the campaign. While earlier studies like Stephen Sears's cite the dispatch as significant, more recent studies argue that its finding had little effect on the course of the campaign. Donald R. Jermann, *Antietam: The Lost Order* (Gretna, LA: Pelican, 2006), 9; Sears, *Landscape Turned Red*, 114–15; Stotelmyer, *Too Useful to Sacrifice*, 44.

86. There are three surviving versions of SO 191 that we know of. The first version has ten articles\paragraphs. This is considered to be the complete version of the Lost Dispatch. The second version, found by Union soldiers on September 13 with D.H. Hill's name at the bottom, has only eight articles\paragraphs. The third version, sent from Jackson to D.H. Hill and saved by Hill, also has only eight articles\paragraphs. The first two paragraphs discussing Lee's order that no troops enter Frederick and Maj. Walter Taylor's mission are not included on the copy McClellan would eventually possess nor the one preserved by D.H. Hill. Photos of the McClellan version show the opening paragraph labeled with the Roman Numeral "III." *OR*, vol. 19, pt. 1, pp.42-43, vol. 19, pt. 2, pp. 603-605; Harsh, *Taken at the Flood*, pp. 154-7

87. *OR*, vol. 19, pt. 2, pp. 257, 269, 272–73.

88. Harsh, *Taken at the Flood*, 239; *OR*, vol. 19, pt. 2, pp. 603–4.

89. Details of the Union communications relating to McClellan's knowledge of Confederate troop strength and positions may be found in a

voluminous series of documents in the *Official Records*. These items' dates range from September 10 to September 13. *OR*, vol. 19, pt. 2, pp. 230–89; *OR*, vol. 51, pt. 1, sec. 2, pp. 823–25.

90. For positions on September 13, see Mattern and Carman, *Theatre of Operations, Maryland Campaign*; Murfin, *Gleam of Bayonets*, 161–62.

91. Historians debate whether McClellan could have moved more of his forces closer to the gaps that night (see Stotelmyer, *Too Useful to Sacrifice*, chapter 1). The bottlenecks of Frederick, the National Road, and the Catoctin Mountains certainly made this feat difficult to execute, but in my view, it was not impossible. Murfin, *Gleam of Bayonets*, 162.

92. *OR*, vol. 19, pt. 1, p. 42.

93. *OR*, vol. 19, pt. 2, p. 281.

94. *OR*, vol. 19, pt. 2, pp. 281–82.

95. In both his August 1863 report on the Maryland Campaign and his report on the Army of the Potomac of the same date, McClellan repeated the following sentence: "On the 13th an order fell into my hands, issued by General Lee, which fully disclosed his plans, and I immediately gave orders for a rapid and vigorous forward movement." The sentence is also repeated verbatim in *McClellan's Own Story*. *OR*, vol. 19, pt. 1, p. 42; George Brinton McClellan, *Report of Major-General George B. McClellan, upon the Organization of the Army of the Potomac, and Its Campaigns in Virginia and Maryland, from July 26, 1861, to November 7, 1862* (Boston: Boston Courier, 1864), 117–18; McClellan, *McClellan's Own Story*, 572.

96. In *Taken at the Flood*, Joseph Harsh argues that the importance of Special Orders 191 has been overstated, adding, "The information in the lost orders did not materially affect the movements of the Federal army on the 13th, except to cause Pleasonton and Burnside to approach Turner's Gap with greater caution." Harsh, *Taken at the Flood*, 252; *OR*, vol. 19, pt. 1, pp. 42–43, 45; *OR*, vol. 19, pt. 2, pp. 281–82, 271–73; McClellan, *McClellan's Own Story*, 572–75.

97. *OR*, vol. 19, pt. 1, p. 140.

98. Sears, *Landscape Turned Red*, 95–96.

99. Edward Clifford Gordon, "Memorandum of a Conversation with R. E. Lee," in *Lee the Soldier, ed. Garry Gallagher* (Lincoln: University of Nebraska Press, 1996), 25–27.

100. *OR*, vol. 19, pt. 1, pp. 1019–20.

101. *OR*, vol. 19, pt. 1, p. 817.

102. *OR*, vol. 19, pt. 1, p. 140.

103. Harsh, *Taken at the Flood*, 234–37, 242–44.

104. Jermann, *Antietam: The Lost Order*, 140–44.

105. Longstreet, *From Manassas to Appomattox*, 219–20.

106. John David Hoptak, *The Battle of South Mountain* (Charleston, SC: History Press, 2011), 35–36, 64–65; Carman, *Maryland Campaign: Ezra A. Carman's Definitive Study*, 135–36; Longstreet, *From Manassas to Appomattox*, 220. See also appendix IV of this work for details on troop strength.

107. Where Lee might have decided to fall back to is a matter of speculation. The Sharpsburg scenario does assume Lee and Longstreet discussed it and that Lee recognized its natural strength prior to September 15. This is by no means certain.

108. This math assumes the presence of total number of soldiers present for duty on the seventeenth plus the soldiers of the Harpers Ferry garrison and all of Franklin's and Couch's men. There is some doubt as to the usefulness of the Harpers Ferry garrison, as those troops are often cited as very inexperienced. See appendix IV for details on troop strength.

Chapter 2

1. Hoptak, *Battle of South Mountain*, 9.

2. Warner, *Generals in Blue*, 373–74; "The Saving of the Declaration of Independence," *New York Times*, July 2, 1905, SM4; Cullum, *Biographical Register*, 2:196–97.

3. Pleasonton is officially listed as having five brigades of cavalry in the order of battle. However, these units were widely dispersed and assigned to a variety of duties other than scouting. See appendix II for the Union order of battle.

4. *OR*, vol. 19, pt. 1, pp. 208–10, 814–18; *OR*, vol. 51, pt. 1, sec. 2, pp. 829–30; Carman, *Maryland Campaign: Ezra A. Carman's Definitive Study*, 143.

5. Jacob D. Cox, *Military Reminiscences of the Civil War, vol. 1, April 1861–November 1863* (New York: Charles Scribner's Sons, 1900), 276–79.

6. Jacob D. Cox, "Forcing Fox's Gap and Turner's Gap," in *Battles and Leaders of the Civil War*, ed. Robert Underwood Johnson and Clarence Clough Buel (New York: Century, 1887), 2:58–86.

7. John Michael Priest, *Before Antietam: The Battle for South Mountain* (Shippensburg, PA: White Mane Books, 1992), 129–34; *OR*, vol. 19, pt. 1, pp. 208–10, 814–18, 1019–20; Jacob D. Cox, "The Battle of Antietam," in *Battles and Leaders of the Civil War*, ed. Robert Underwood Johnson and Clarence Clough Buel (New York: Century, 1887), 2:582–86. See also appendix IV for details on troop strength.

8. Hartwig, *To Antietam Creek*, 331.

9. Hoptak, *Battle of South Mountain*, 67–68, 85.

10. Cox, *Military Reminiscences*, 1:287.

11. *OR*, vol. 19, pt. 1, pp. 427–28.

12. Rafuse, *Antietam, South Mountain, & Harpers Ferry*, 175, 179, 180–83.

13. Bradley M. Gottfried, *The Maps of Antietam: An Atlas of the Antietam (Sharpsburg) Campaign, Including the Battle of South Mountain, September 2–20, 1862* (El Dorado Hills, CA: Savas Beatie, 2012), 36, 40.

14. Warner, *Generals in Blue*, 159–60; Mark A. Snell, *From First to Last: The Life of Major General William B. Franklin* (New York: Fordham University Press, 2002), 1–2, 28, 36–52, 68–70, 147–48; Cullum, *Biographical Register*, 2:152–54.

15. There is some question as to whether Couch was reporting to Franklin or to McClellan. Evidence suggests that McClellan was issuing orders directly to Couch. See McClellan's dispatch to Franklin on the evening of the thirteenth. *OR*, vol. 19, pt. 1, pp. 45–46; Sears, *Landscape Turned Red*, 101–2. For positions on September 13, see Mattern and Carman, *Theatre of Operations, Maryland Campaign*.

16. *OR*, vol. 19, pt. 2, pp. 280–81; *OR*, vol. 19-1, pp. 25–27; Ethan S. Rafuse, *McClellan's War: The Failure of Moderation in the Struggle for the Union* (Bloomington: Indiana University Press, 2005), 289, 293.

17. In his 11:00 p.m. dispatch to Halleck, McClellan indicated that there was a chance that Miles at Harpers Ferry still held out. McClellan also alluded to the possibility that several of the commands outlined in Special Orders 191 were in his front. Additionally, in his September 13 message to Franklin, McClellan noted that firing suggested Harpers Ferry still held out. *OR*, vol. 19, pt. 2, pp. 28–82; *OR*, vol. 19-1, pp. 44–45.

18. By counting the troops, we know the size of this potential force as compared with Lee's. However, as McClellan still believed Lee's army outnumbered his, he would not have had this perspective.

19. *OR*, vol. 19, pt. 1, pp. 45–46; Rafuse, *Antietam, South Mountain, & Harpers Ferry*, 197–99. The 30,000 number includes Franklin's troops

(11,862), Couch's troops (6,400), and the total number of servicemen of the Harpers Ferry garrison (14,000). See appendix IV of this book for details on troop strength.

20. McClellan sent Franklin two messages that day. The first is in volume 19-2 of the *Official Records,* and the second is in volume 51-1, sec. 2. Opinions differ as to whether these constituted one communication or two. *OR,* vol. 19, pt. 1, pp. 45–46; *OR,* vol. 51, pt. 1, sec. 2, pp. 826–27; Harsh, *Sounding the Shallows,* 16. If you draw a straight line on a map from Buckeystown to Burkittsville, the distance is eleven miles. If you follow the roads, the distance is as much as fifteen miles.

21. *OR,* vol. 19, pt. 1, pp. 45.

22. *OR,* vol. 19, pt. 1, pp. 45.

23. Snell, *From First to Last,* 173–87.

24. Joseph J. Bartlett, "Crampton's Pass: The Start of the Great Maryland Campaign," *National Tribune,* December 19, 1889.

25. Bartlett, "Crampton's Pass"; Timothy J. Reese, *Sealed with Their Lives: The Battle for Crampton's Gap, Burkittsville, Maryland, September 14, 1862* (Baltimore: Butternut and Blue, 1998), 40, 42–44, 67–70, 83; *OR,* vol. 19, pt. 1, pp. 46–47, 374–75, 870.

26. Based on the testimony of Julius White, it seems the garrison's officers saw no indication that relief was imminent. *OR,* vol. 19, pt. 1, p. 744. See Jackson's dispatch to Lee on the surrender of Harpers Ferry, *OR,* vol. 19, pt. 1, p. 951.

27. Based on the 8:00 p.m. dispatch from Chilton to McLaws, Lee had made up his mind to retreat. Franklin's lack of pressure on his command no doubt convinced McLaws to hold out. *OR,* vol. 51-2, pp. 618–19; Hartwig, *To Antietam Creek,* 477.

28. Hartwig, *To Antietam Creek,* 205–6; Sears, *Landscape Turned Red,* 122; Cullum, *Biographical Register,* 1:334–35.

29. Recent scholarship indicates that some one thousand black contrabands were also present at Harpers Ferry at the time of its capture. Alexander Rossino, "The Contrabands of Harpers Ferry," *Savas Beatie Blog,* September 3, 2019, https://www.savasbeatie.com/savas-beatie-blog/the-contrabands-of-harpers-ferry-new-blog-by-author-alexander-rossino/?fbclid=IwAR1wTOt2mReX18ayufb_QfRFyz71zIbKHAbT-rDjMVB7yU5oLIjM-x_Yt58. For the after-action reports of Colonel Ford and Stonewall Jackson, see *OR,* vol. 19, pt. 1, pp. 541–46, 952–55. See also appendix IV of this work for details on troop strength.

30. Carman, *Maryland Campaign: Ezra A. Carman's Definitive Study*, 125–26; S. C. Gwynne, *Rebel Yell: The Violence, Passion, and Redemption of Stonewall Jackson* (New York: Scribner, 2014), 458; Dennis E. Frye, *Antietam Shadows: Mystery, Myth and Machination* (Sharpsburg, MD: Antietam Rest, 2018), 103–4.

31. *OR*, vol. 19, pt. 1, pp. 523–31, 757.

32. Hartwig, *To Antietam Creek*, 207; *OR*, vol. 19, pt. 1, p. 549. See appendix IV for details on casualties.

33. The number of artillery pieces captured at Harpers Ferry gives us some indication as to what Miles had available. However, reports are at odds with one another. Additionally, there are a number of indicators that by September 15 the Union batteries were either very low on ammunition or out of it. Henry Kyd Douglas, "Stonewall Jackson in Maryland," in *Battles and Leaders of the Civil War*, ed. Robert Underwood Johnson and Clarence Clough Buel (New York: Century, 1887), 2:627; *OR*, vol. 19, pt. 1, pp. 527–28, 538–39, 548–49, 564.

34. Julius White, "The Surrender of Harper's Ferry," in *Battles and Leaders of the Civil War*, ed. Robert Underwood Johnson and Clarence Clough Buel (New York: Century, 1887), 2:613; Carman, *Maryland Campaign: Ezra A. Carman's Definitive Study*, 122.

35. *OR*, vol. 19, pt. 1, p. 539.

36. *OR*, vol. 19, pt. 1, p. 793.

37. *OR*, vol. 19, pt. 1, p. 800.

38. Henry Kyd Douglas, *I Rode with Stonewall: Being Chiefly the War Experiences of the Youngest Member of Jackson's Staff from the John Brown Raid to the Hanging of Mrs. Surratt* (Chapel Hill: University of North Carolina Press, 1940), 162.

39. Of all the Confederate units at Harpers Ferry, McLaws's/Anderson's fought the most and faced the longest and most difficult route to join the rest of the army at Sharpsburg. McLaws wrote in his after-action report that his exhausted command left the vicinity of Harpers Ferry on the morning of the sixteenth and did not arrive at Sharpsburg until the early morning hours of the seventeenth. *OR*, vol. 19, pt. 1, pp. 47, 857.

40. Gordon, "Memorandum of a Conversation with R. E. Lee," 25–27; *OR*, vol. 19, pt. 1, p. 140.

41. Longstreet, *From Manassas to Appomattox*, 227; *OR*, vol. 19, pt. 2, pp. 608–9; *OR*, vol. 51, pt. 2, p. 618–9; Murfin, *Gleam of Bayonets*, 186–92;

Carman, *Maryland Campaign: Ezra A. Carman's Definitive Study*, 169–73; Harsh, *Taken at the Flood*, 294.

42. *OR*, vol. 51, pt. 2, p. 618-9

43. Harsh, *Taken at the Flood*, 292.

44. Hartwig, *To Antietam Creek*, 481–84.

45. *OR*, vol. 19, pt. 1, p. 951.

46. This number is an estimate based on the men in Longstreet's and D. H. Hill's commands. See appendix III for the Confederate order of battle, and see appendix IV for details on troop strength.

47. Longstreet, *From Manassas to Appomattox*, 233–34; Harsh, *Taken at the Flood*, 330.

48. Harsh, *Taken at the Flood*, 301; Sears, *Landscape Turned Red*, 167–69.

49. It seems logical that Lee was still looking to accomplish the political and military objectives he set at the beginning of the campaign. Murfin, *Gleam of Bayonets*, 64–69; Hartwig, *To Antietam Creek*, 51.

50. *OR*, vol. 19, pt. 1, p. 140.

51. Recent research by Dennis Frye traces this quote by Lee to Douglas Southall Freeman, who cited a 1911 book by William H. Morgan entitled *Personal Reminiscences of the War of 1861–5*. Morgan, who was not at Antietam during the battle, indicated he heard the quote from some of his fellow soldiers in the Eleventh Virginia. Frye, *Antietam Shadows*, 21–25; Douglas Southall Freeman, *R. E. Lee: A Biography* (New York: Charles Scribner's Sons, 1936), 2:378; Harsh, *Taken at the Flood*, 334, 344, 354–55.

52. Sears, *Landscape Turned Red*, 160–61.

53. McClellan, *McClellan's Own Story*, 613–15.

54. Sears, *Landscape Turned Red*, 162–64; Rafuse, *McClellan's War*, 303–8; Stotelmyer, *Too Useful to Sacrifice*, 94, 140.

55. McClellan, *McClellan's Own Story*, 584–87.

56. *OR*, vol. 19, pt. 2, p. 289.

57. *OR*, vol. 19, pt. 2, p. 294.

58. This is a perfect example of information that made its way to McClellan during the campaign that combined some small bits of truth with rumor and speculation. It is fair to note that Lee was probably riding in his ambulance during this time. This circumstance would go a long way to explain why he was reported as wounded. *OR*, vol. 19, pt. 2, pp. 295–96.

59. *OR*, vol. 19, pt. 1, p. 47; *OR*, pt. 2, p. 296.

60. Murfin, *Gleam of Bayonets*, 199, 204–6; Carman, *Maryland Campaign: Ezra A. Carman's Definitive Study*, 175–80; Walter H. Hebert, *Fighting Joe Hooker* (Indianapolis: Bobbs-Merrill, 1944), 137–38.

61. See appendix IV of this work for details on troop strength. Hartwig, *To Antietam Creek*, 515, 582, 585–88, 594; Gottfried, *Maps of Antietam*, 116–18.

62. *OR*, vol. 19, pt. 1, p. 52. See appendix IV of this work for details on troop strength.

63. McClellan, *McClellan's Own Story*, 588.

64. *OR*, vol. 19, pt. 2, pp. 307–8; Hartwig, *To Antietam Creek*, 436; Carman, *Maryland Campaign of September 1862*, 1:343; Rafuse, *McClellan's War*, 282.

65. *OR*, vol. 19, pt. 1, pp. 30, 216–19; Cox, "Battle of Antietam," 2:633.

66. Frye, *Antietam Shadows*, 144–47.

Chapter 3

1. David Hunter Strother, entry for September 18, 1862, in *A Virginia Yankee in the Civil War: The Diaries of David Hunter Strother*, ed. Cecil D. Eby (Chapel Hill: University of North Carolina Press, 1961), 112.

2. Harsh, *Sounding the Shallows*, 21; Murfin, *Gleam of Bayonets*, 295–96.

3. *OR*, vol. 19, pt. 2, p. 322.

4. McClellan, *McClellan's Own Story*, 612–13.

5. See appendices II and IV for details on casualties.

6. For positions at the end of the battle, see United States War Department, map 14, in Atlas of the Battlefield of Antietam, Prepared under the Direction of the Antietam Battlefield Board, Lieut. Col. Geo. W. Davis, U.S.A., President, Gen. E. A. Carman, U.S.V., Gen. H. Heth, C.S.A. Surveyed by Lieut. Col. E. B. Cope, Engineer, H. W. Mattern, Assistant Engineer, of the Gettysburg National Park. Drawn by Charles H. Ourand. Position of Troops by Gen. E. A. Carman. Published by Authority of the Secretary of War, Under the Direction of the Chief of Engineers, U.S. Army, 1908 (Washington, DC: Government Printing Office, 1908), https://www.loc.gov/item/2008621532/; Gottfried, *Maps of Antietam*, 235.

7. Carman, *Maryland Campaign: Ezra A. Carman's Definitive Study*, 365–66.

8. See appendix IV for details on casualties.

9. *OR*, vol. 19, pt. 1, p. 65.

10. See appendix IV for details on casualties and appendix II for the Union order of battle.

11. William B. Franklin, "Notes on Crampton's Gap and Antietam," in *Battles and Leaders of the Civil War*, ed. Robert Underwood Johnson and Clarence Clough Buel (New York: Century, 1887), 2:597.

12. Stotelmyer, *Too Useful to Sacrifice*, 54.

13. The casualty rates are from those divisions engaged on the seventeenth. Division commanders killed or wounded include Ricketts, Richardson, Sedgwick, Rodman, and Crawford. See appendix II and appendix IV for further details.

14. See Humphreys's after-action report, *OR*, vol. 19, pt. 1, pp. 368–74. See appendix IV of this work for details on casualties and appendix II for the Union order of battle.

15. Kevin Pawlak, *"Railroads—Tracks to the Antietam: The Railroad Supplies the Army of the Potomac, September 18, 1862,"* Emerging Civil War, posted October 27, 2018, https://emergingcivilwar.com/2018/10/27/railroads-tracks-to-the-antietam-the-railroad-supplies-the-army-of-the-potomac-september-18-1862/?fbclid=IwAR3SRmkuuzAzDvsD_rOOrktikPTiDkLZBdswRbbccrrWiL8wxYAtFfE3QGw; *OR*, vol. 19-1, pp. 205–7.

16. Communications in the *Official Records* provide no specific details on what numbers McClellan believed he faced on September 18. But accounts Cox and McClellan wrote after the fighting would seem to lend credence to the notion that McClellan still believed Lee had a significant force at his disposal. Cox, "Battle of Antietam," 2:658; *OR*, vol. 19, pt. 1, pp. 65–66.

17. Harsh, *Taken at the Flood*, 440.

18. Carman, *Maryland Campaign: Ezra A. Carman's Definitive Study*, 365.

19. *OR*, vol. 19, pt. 1, p. 66.

20. James Longstreet, "The Invasion of Maryland," in *Battles and Leaders of the Civil War*, ed. Robert Underwood Johnson and Clarence Clough Buel (New York: Century, 1887), 2:670.

21. John B. Hood, *Advance and Retreat: Personal Experiences in the United States and Confederate States Armies* (New Orleans: Published for the Hood Orphan Memorial Fund, G. T. Beauregard, 1880), 45.

22. Harsh, *Taken at the Flood*, 431.

23. Douglas, *I Rode with Stonewall*, 174.

24. *OR*, vol. 19, pt. 1, p. 151.

25. Harsh, *Taken at the Flood*, 430.

26. Lee's desire to get past the Union right and attack might also have been an escape plan. Sears, *Landscape Turned Red*, 274–75; Harsh, *Taken at the Flood*, 441–43.

27. Harsh, *Taken at the Flood*, 431–33. See appendix IV of this book for details on casualties.

28. John G. Walker, "Sharpsburg," in *Battles and Leaders of the Civil War,* ed. Robert Underwood Johnson and Clarence Clough Buel (New York: Century, 1887), 2:682.

29. Harsh, *Taken at the Flood*, 444–47.

30. *OR*, vol. 19, pt. 1, p. 68.

31. Confederate States of America, Army of Northern Virginia, *Reports of the Operations of the Army of Northern Virginia: From June 1862, to and Including the Battle at Fredericksburg, Dec. 13, 1862* (Richmond, VA: R. M. Smith 1864), 1:36.

32. The totality of men and supplies captured by Confederates at Harpers Ferry was 12,000 prisoners, 13,000 small arms, 73 cannon, 305 pairs of shoes, a number of wagons, and food and other stores. This haul no doubt greatly aided Lee's army and embarrassed the Union. Yet the cost at which it was purchased was very high, and it did not significantly impact the outcome of the war. Harsh, *Taken at the Flood*, 321; *OR*, vol. 19, pt. 1, pp. 955, 981.

Conclusion

1. *OR*, vol. 19, pt. 1, pp. 212, 339–40, 830–31.

2. *OR*, vol. 19, pt. 1, pp. 212, 479; Harsh, *Taken at the Flood*, 452–54, 462.

3. Thomas A. McGrath, *Shepherdstown: Last Clash of the Antietam Campaign* (Lynchburg, VA: Schroeder, 2013), 65–67, 83; Harsh, *Taken at the Flood*, 459–61; Freeman, *Lee's Lieutenants*, 2:232.

4. Carman, *Maryland Campaign: Ezra A. Carman's Definitive Study*, 371–75; *OR*, vol. 19, pt. 1, pp. 338–41, 348–49, 982.

5. *OR*, vol. 19, pt. 1, p. 330.

6. Harsh, *Taken at the Flood*, 475–76; *OR*, vol. 19, pt. 2, pp. 626–27, 628–29.

7. Rather than focusing on various details from the two disparate perspectives on McClellan after the Battle of Antietam, I recommend reading the following: Sears, *Landscape Turned Red*, chapters 9 and 10; Stotelmyer, *Too Useful to Sacrifice*, chapter 5.

8. Based on the communications in the *Official Records*, two things seem certain. The administration and the War Department believed McClellan was getting all the supplies he needed. McClellan, on the other hand, indicated that the opposite was true. For details on the extensive communications between McClellan and Washington, see United States Congress Joint Committee on the Conduct of the War, *Report of the Joint Committee on the Conduct of the War, Part I, Army of the Potomac, 1863*, United States Congressional Serial Set, Issue 1152 (Washington, DC: Government Printing Office, 1865), 492–565; McClellan, *McClellan's Own Story*, 613–15; *OR*, vol. 19, pt. 2, pp. 336–545.

9. *OR*, vol. 19, pt. 1, p. 13.

10. *OR*, vol. 19, pt. 1, p. 72; Sears, *Lincoln's Lieutenants*, 424–25, 433–36; *OR*, vol. 19, pt. 2, 336–545.

11. James M. McPherson, *The Illustrated Battle Cry of Freedom: The Civil War Era* (New York: Oxford University Press, 2003), 491–92; John Hay, entry for September 25, 1864, in *Inside Lincoln's White House: The Complete Civil War Diary of John Hay, ed.* Michael Burlingame and John R. T. Ettlinger (Carbondale: Southern Illinois University Press, 1997), 232.

12. *OR*, vol. 19, pt. 2, p. 545

13. *OR*, vol. 19, pt. 2, pp. 545–46; McPherson, *Battle Cry of Freedom*, 483.

14. McClellan, *McClellan's Own Story*, 642.

15. The five battles are Turner's and Fox's Gaps, Crampton's Gap, Harpers Ferry, Antietam, and Shepherdstown. Often, the three South Mountain battles are considered to be one. As the engagements at Turner's and Fox's Gaps were some six miles from Crampton's Gap and no units at any one location were in a position to support those at another, the battles were essentially two separate engagements. And while both engagements shared the strategic goal of splitting Lee's army, the Sixth Corps at Crampton's Gap had an exclusive objective—namely, the relief of Harpers Ferry. Lastly, while the Confederate forces under the command of Lafayette McLaws fought at both Harpers Ferry and Crampton's, most accounts treat those battles as separate engagements.

16. See appendix IV for details on casualties.

17. *OR*, vol. 19, pt. 2, p. 622.

18. Hartwig, *To Antietam Creek*, 686. See appendix IV of this book for details on casualties.

19. See "Transcript of the Proclamation," National Archives: Online Exhibits, accessed Nov. 2021, https://www.archives.gov/exhibits/featured -documents/emancipation-proclamation/transcript.html.

Appendix I

1. *OR*, vol. 19, pt. 2, pp. 590–91.

2. *OR*, vol. 19, pt. 2, pp. 590–91.

3. Harsh, *Taken at the Flood*, 64.

4. *OR*, vol. 19, pt. 2, p. 591.

5. *OR*, vol. 19, pt. 2, pp. 592–93.

6. Douglas, "Stonewall Jackson in Maryland," 2:620.

7. *Diary of George Templeton Strong*, 177.

8. Perret, *Lincoln's War*, 211; Thayer, *John Hay*, 1:128.

9. Civil War Papers of George B. McClellan, 435.

10. Hartwig, *To Antietam Creek*, 177–78, 184–85, 193; Freiheit, *Boots and Saddles*, 180–82.

11. Hard, *History of the Eighth Cavalry*, 174.

12. *"Monocacy National Battlefield / Best Farm,"* National Park Service, accessed September 25, 2020, https://www.nps.gov/mono/learn/history culture/best_farm.htm.

13. Longstreet, *From Manassas to Appomattox*, 201–4.

14. The copy of Special Orders 191 that made its way to McClellan did not contain the first two paragraphs shown here. *OR*, vol. 19, pt. 1, pp. 42–43; *OR*, pt. 2, pp. 602–3.

15. Hartwig, *To Antietam Creek*, 109, 193–94.

16. *OR*, vol. 19, pt. 2, pp. 270–71.

17. Stotelmyer, *Too Useful to Sacrifice*, 22–23.

18. For positions on September 13, see Mattern and Carman, *Theatre of Operations, Maryland Campaign*.

19. *OR*, vol. 19, pt. 2, p. 270.

20. *OR*, vol. 19, pt. 2, p. 281.

21. *OR*, vol. 19, pt. 1, p. 42.

22. For positions on September 12, see Mattern and Carman, *Theatre of Operations, Maryland Campaign*. See appendix IV of this work for details on troop strength.

23. *OR*, vol. 19, pt. 1, pp. 1018–19.

24. *OR*, vol. 19, pt. 1, 1018–19.

25. Cox, *Military Reminiscences*, 276–79.

26. See appendix IV for details on armies' strength.

27. *OR*, vol. 19, pt. 1, pp. 209–10.

28. Hoptak, *Battle of South Mountain*, 67–68, 85.

29. Cox, *Military Reminiscences*, 287.

30. *OR*, vol. 19, pt. 1, pp. 426–27.

31. *OR*, vol. 19, pt. 2, pp. 280–81; *OR*, vol. 19-1, pp. 25–27; Rafuse, *McClellan's War*, 289, 293.

32. McClellan sent two messages to Franklin on that day. The first message is in volume 19-2 of the *Official Records*, and the second is in volume 51-1. Opinions differ as to whether these constituted one communication or two. *OR*, vol. 19, pt. 1, pp. 45–46; *OR*, vol. 51, pt. 1, sec. 2, pp. 826–27.

33. This number is the combined total of Franklin's, Couch's, and Miles's forces. See appendix IV for details on armies' strength.

34. Snell, *From First to Last*, 173–76.

35. *OR*, vol. 19, pt. 1, p. 870.

36. *OR*, vol. 19, pt. 1, pp. 374–75.

37. *OR*, vol. 19, pt. 2, pp. 603–4.

38. *OR*, vol. 19, pt. 2, p. 254.

39. *OR*, vol. 19, pt. 2, pp. 280–81.

40 *OR*, vol. 19, pt. 1, p. 4.

41. Recent scholarship also indicates that some one thousand black contrabands were present at Harpers Ferry at the time of its capture. Rossino, "Contrabands of Harpers Ferry." For Colonel Ford's and Stonewall Jackson's after-action reports, see *OR*, vol. 19, pt. 1, pp. 541–46, 952–55. See also appendix IV of this book for details on troop strength.

42. *OR*, vol. 19, pt. 1, pp. 527–28.

43. *OR*, vol. 19, pt. 1, p. 793.

44. Who commanded the breakout is a matter of some debate. Technically,

two officers, Col. Hasbrouck Davis and Col. Arno Voss, were senior to Grimes Davis. As Grimes Davis was a West Pointer, and the plan was largely his idea, and he was the one who used his southern accent to fool the Confederate teamsters into redirecting the ordnance train, he gets the lion's share of the credit. It is also unclear how many Confederate wagons the Union cavalry captured. The number is cited as between 40 and 104. Sears, *Landscape Turned Red*, 151–52; Carman, *Maryland Campaign*, 1:254–56; *OR*, vol. 19, pt. 1, pp. 629–31; Hartwig, *To Antietam Creek*, 541, 551.

45. *OR*, vol. 19, pt. 1, p. 140.

46. *OR*, vol. 51, pt. 2, p. 618–19.

47. *OR*, vol. 19, pt. 1, p. 951.

48. *OR*, vol. 19, pt. 1, p. 140.

49. *OR*, vol. 19, pt. 1, pp. 147–48.

50. *OR*, vol. 19, pt. 2, p. 289.

51. *OR*, vol. 19, pt. 2, pp. 294–95.

52. *OR*, vol. 19, pt. 1, p. 47; *OR*, pt. 2, p. 296.

53. *OR*, vol. 19, pt. 1, p. 53.

54. *OR*, vol. 19, pt. 1, p. 54.

55. *OR*, vol. 19, pt. 1, p. 30.

56. *OR*, vol. 19, pt. 1, p. 55.

57. Harsh, *Sounding the Shallows*, 21; Murfin, *Gleam of Bayonets*, 295–96.

58. *OR*, vol. 19, pt. 2, p. 322.

59. McClellan, *McClellan's Own Story*, 612.

60. See appendices II and IV for details on casualties.

61. Carman, *Maryland Campaign: Ezra A. Carman's Definitive Study*, 365–66.

62. Franklin, "Crampton's Gap and Antietam," 2:597.

63. Pawlak, "Railroads—Tracks to the Antietam"; *OR*, vol. 19-1, pp. 205–7.

64. No communications in the *Official Records* contain specific details about the numbers of enemy troops McClellan believed he faced on the eighteenth. Accounts Cox and McClellan wrote afterward seem to lend credence to the idea that McClellan still believed Lee had a significant force available to him. Cox, "Battle of Antietam," 2:658; *OR*, vol. 19, pt. 1, pp. 65–66.

65. Stotelmyer, *Too Useful to Sacrifice*, 54.

66. *OR*, vol. 19, pt. 1, pp. 65–66.

67. Harsh, *Taken at the Flood*, 431.

68. Harsh, *Taken at the Flood*, 431–33. See appendix IV of this book for details on casualties.

69. *OR*, vol. 19, pt. 1, p. 151.

70. John G. Walker, "Sharpsburg," in *Battles and Leaders of the Civil War*, ed. Robert Underwood Johnson and Clarence Clough Buel (New York: Century, 1887), 2:682.

71. Harsh, *Taken at the Flood*, 444–47.

72. *OR*, vol. 19, pt. 1, p. 68.

73. Confederate States of America, *Operations of the Army of Northern Virginia*, 36.

BIBLIOGRAPHY

Alexander, Edward Porter. *Military Memoirs of a Confederate: A Critical Narrative.* New York: Charles Scribner's Sons, 1907.

Ambrose, Stephen E. *Halleck: Lincoln's Chief of Staff.* Baton Rouge: Louisiana State University Press, 1962.

Anders, Curt. *Henry Halleck's War: A Fresh Look at Lincoln's Controversial General-in-Chief.* Carmel: Guild Press of Indiana, 1999.

Anderson, Thomas M. "The Reserves at Antietam." *Century Illustrated Monthly Magazine* 32 (May–October 1886).

Andrews, J. Cutler. *The North Reports the Civil War.* Pittsburgh: University of Pittsburgh Press, 1955.

"A Barbarian Invasion of the North." *New York Times,* September 3, 1862, p. 4. *New York Times* Archive. https://www.nytimes.com/1862/09/03/archives/a-barbarian-invasion-of-the-north.html.

Bartlett, Joseph J. "Crampton's Pass: The Start of the Great Maryland Campaign." *National Tribune,* December 19, 1889.

Carman, Ezra A. *The Maryland Campaign of 1862.* Edited by Thomas G. Clemens. 3 vols. El Dorado Hills, CA: Savas Beatie, 2010, 2012.

———. *The Maryland Campaign of September 1862: Ezra A. Carman's Definitive Study of the Union and Confederate Armies at Antietam.* Edited by Joseph Pierro. Hoboken, NJ: Taylor and Francis, 2008.

Charles River Editors. *Harpers Ferry: The History of the Federal Armory That Became One of America's Most Famous National Parks.* Ann Arbor, MI: Charles River Editors, 2015.

Coddington, Edwin B. *The Gettysburg Campaign: A Study in Command.* New York: Charles Scribner's Sons, 1968.

Confederate States of America, Army of Northern Virginia. *Reports of the Operations of the Army of Northern Virginia: From June 1862, to and Including the Battle at Fredericksburg, Dec. 13, 1862.* Vol. 1. Richmond, VA: R. M. Smith, 1864.

Cox, Jacob D. "Forcing Fox's Gap and Turner's Gap." In *Battles and Leaders of the Civil War,* edited by Robert Underwood Johnson and Clarence Clough Buel. Vol. 2, 583-590. New York: Century, 1887.

———. *Military Reminiscences of the Civil War.* Vol. 1, *April 1861–November 1863.* New York: Charles Scribner's Sons, 1900.

———. "The Battle of Antietam." In *Battles and Leaders of the Civil War,* edited by Robert Underwood Johnson and Clarence Clough Buel. Vol. 2, 630-660. New York: Century, 1887.

Cozzens, Peter. *General John Pope: A Life for the Nation.* Champaign: University of Illinois Press, 2000.

Cullum, Bvt. Maj. Gen. George W. *Biographical Register of the Officers and Graduates of the U.S. Military Academy at West Point N.Y.* Vols. 1 and 2. Boston: Houghton, Mifflin, 1891.

Douglas, Henry Kyd. *I Rode with Stonewall, Being Chiefly the War Experiences of the Youngest Member of Jackson's Staff from the John Brown Raid to the Hanging of Mrs. Surratt.* Chapel Hill: University of North Carolina Press, 1940.

———. "Stonewall Jackson in Maryland." In *Battles and Leaders of the Civil War,* edited by Robert Underwood Johnson and Clarence Clough Buel. Vol. 2, 620-629. New York: Century, 1887.

Downey, Brian R., and contributors. Antietam on the Web. Updated December 31, 2018. http://antietam.aotw.org/.

Early, Jubal A. *Lieutenant General Jubal A. Early, Confederate States of America.* 1912. Reprinted, Oxfordshire, United Kingdom, Acheron, 2012.

Fishel, Edwin C. *The Secret War for the Union: The Untold Story of Military Intelligence in the Civil War.* Boston: Houghton Mifflin, 1996.

"Four Days Experience with the Rebels in Frederick." *Civilian & Telegraph* (Cumberland, MD), September 18, 1862.

Franklin, William B. "Notes on Crampton's Gap and Antietam." In *Battles and Leaders of the Civil War*, edited by Robert Underwood Johnson and Clarence Clough Buel. Vol. 2, 591-597. New York: Century, 1887.

Freeman, Douglas Southall. *Lee's Lieutenants: A Study in Command*. Vol. 2. New York: Charles Scribner's Sons, 1942.

Freeman, Douglas Southall, and Richard Harwell. *Lee: An Abridgment in One Volume of the Four-Volume "R. E. Lee" by Douglas Southall Freeman*. 1st Touchstone ed. New York: Simon and Schuster, 1997.

Freiheit, Laurence H. *Boots and Saddles: Cavalry during the Maryland Campaign of September 1862*. Iowa City: Camp Pope Publishing, 2012.

Frye, Dennis E. *Antietam Shadows: Mystery, Myth and Machination*. Sharpsburg, MD: Antietam Rest, 2018.

Gallagher, Garry, ed. *Lee the Soldier*. Lincoln: University of Nebraska Press, 1996.

Gillon, Steven M. *10 Days That Unexpectedly Changed America*. New York: Broadway Books, 2006.

Gordon, Edward Clifford. *"Memorandum of a Conversation with R. E. Lee."* In *Lee the Soldier*, ed. Garry Gallagher, 25-27. Lincoln: University of Nebraska Press, 1996.

Gottfried, Bradley M. *The Maps of Antietam: An Atlas of the Antietam (Sharpsburg) Campaign, Including the Battle of South Mountain, September 2–20, 1862*. El Dorado Hills, CA: Savas Beatie, 2012.

Greeley, Horace. "A Prayer for Twenty Millions." *New York Tribune*, August 20, 1862.

Gwynne, S. C. *Rebel Yell: The Violence, Passion, and Redemption of Stonewall Jackson*. New York: Scribner, 2014.

Hard, Abner. *History of the Eighth Cavalry Regiment, Illinois Volunteers, during the Great Rebellion*. Aurora, IL: Self-published, 1868.

Harsh, Joseph L. *Sounding the Shallows: A Confederate Companion for the Maryland Campaign of 1862*. Kent, OH: Kent State University Press, 2000.

———. *Taken at the Flood: Robert E. Lee and Confederate Strategy in the Maryland Campaign of 1862*. Kent, OH: Kent State University Press, 1999.

Hartwig, D. Scott. "To Antietam Creek: The Maryland Campaign of 1862." Lecture given September 17, 2014, at US Army Heritage and Education

Center. YouTube Video. https://www.youtube.com/watch?v=4Amf
TmouQFM.

———. *To Antietam Creek: The Maryland Campaign of September 1862.* Baltimore: Johns Hopkins University Press, 2012.

Hassler, Warren W., Jr. *General George B. McClellan: Shield of the Union.*
Westport, CT: Greenwood, 1957.

Hassler, William W. "The Civil War Letters of General William Dorsey
Pender to His Wife." *Georgia Review* 17, no. 1 (1963): 68. http://www
.jstor.org/stable/41395942.

Hay, John. *Inside Lincoln's White House: The Complete Civil War Diary of John
Hay.* Edited by Michael Burlingame and John R. T. Ettlinger. Carbondale: Southern Illinois University Press, 1997.

Hearn, Chester G. *Six Years of Hell: Harpers Ferry during the Civil War.* Baton Rouge: Louisiana State University Press, 1996.

"History of the Blue Ridge." Friends of the Blue Ridge Mountains. Updated July 22, 2020. https://friendsofblueridge.org/our-mountains
/mountains-history/#:~:text=The%20Blue%20Ridge%2C%20part%20
of,South%20Africa's%20Barberton%20greenstone%20belt.

Hood, John B. *Advance and Retreat: Personal Experiences in the United States
and Confederate States Armies.* New Orleans: Published for the Hood Orphan Memorial Fund, G. T. Beauregard, 1880.

Hoptak, John David. *The Battle of South Mountain.* Charleston, SC: History
Press, 2011.

"Intelligence: Human Intelligence." Central Intelligence Agency—News
& Information. Last updated April 30, 2013. https://www.cia.gov/news
-information/featured-story-archive/2010-featured-story-archive
/intelligence-human-intelligence.html. Link dead as of November 22,
2021.

Jermann, Donald R. *Antietam: The Lost Order.* Gretna, LA: Pelican, 2006.

Longstreet, James. *From Manassas to Appomattox: Memoirs of the Civil War in
America.* 1896. Reprint. New York: William S. Konecky Associates, 1992.

———. "The Invasion of Maryland," in *Battles and Leaders of the Civil War,*
ed. Robert Underwood Johnson and Clarence Clough Buel. Vol. 2, 663-
674. New York: Century, 1887.

Martinez, James Michael. *Carpetbaggers, Cavalry, and the Ku Klux Klan:
Exposing the Invisible Empire during Reconstruction.* Lanham, MD:
Rowman and Littlefield, 2007.

Marvel, William. *Burnside*. Chapel Hill: University of North Carolina Press, 1991.

Mattern, H. W., and E. A. Carman, cartographers. *Theatre of Operations, Maryland Campaign, September 1862*. 1862. 28 x 36 cm. Library of Congress. https://www.loc.gov/item/2009584566/.

McClellan, George Brinton. *McClellan's Own Story: The War for the Union, the Soldiers Who Fought It, the Civilians Who Directed It and His Relations to It and to Them*. New York: C. L. Webster, 1887.

———. *Report of Major-General George B. McClellan, upon the organization of the Army of the Potomac, and its campaigns in Virginia and Maryland, from July 26, 1861, to November 7, 1862*. Boston: Boston Courier, 1864.

McGrath, Thomas A. *Shepherdstown: Last Clash of the Antietam Campaign*. Lynchburg, VA: Schroeder, 2013.

McPherson, James M. *The Illustrated Battle Cry of Freedom: The Civil War Era*. New York: Oxford University Press, 2003.

"Monocacy National Battlefield / Best Farm." National Park Service, accessed September 25. 2020, https://www.nps.gov/mono/learn/historyculture/best_farm.htm.

Murfin, James. *The Gleam of Bayonets: The Battle of Antietam and Robert E. Lee's Maryland Campaign, September 1862*. Baton Rouge: Louisiana State University Press, 1964.

Nolan, Alan T. *Lee Considered: General Robert E. Lee and Civil War History*. Chapel Hill: University of North Carolina Press, 1991.

Oates, Stephen B. *With Malice toward None*. New York: Harper and Row, 1977.

Pawlak, Kevin. "Railroads—Tracks to the Antietam: The Railroad Supplies the Army of the Potomac, September 18, 1862." Emerging Civil War. Posted October 27, 2018. https://emergingcivilwar.com/2018/10/27/railroads-tracks-to-the-antietam-the-railroad-supplies-the-army-of-the-potomac-september-18-1862/?fbclid=IwAR3SRmkuuzAzDvsD_rOOrktikPTiDkLZBdswRbbccrrWiL8wxYAtFfE3QGw.

Perret, Geoffrey. *Lincoln's War: The Untold Story of America's Greatest President as Commander in Chief*. New York: Random House, 2004.

Priest, John Michael. *Antietam: The Soldiers' Battle*. 1989. Reprint. Havertown, PA: Savas, 2014.

———. *Before Antietam: The Battle for South Mountain*. Shippensburg, PA: White Mane Books, 1992.

Rafuse, Ethan S. *Antietam, South Mountain, & Harpers Ferry: A Battlefield Guide*. Lincoln: University of Nebraska Press, 2008.

———. *McClellan's War: The Failure of Moderation in the Struggle for the Union*. Bloomington: Indiana University Press, 2005.

Randall, J. G., and Richard Current. *Lincoln the President*. Vol. 2, *Midstream to the Last Full Measure*. New York: Da Capo, 1997.

Reese, Timothy J. *Sealed with Their Lives: The Battle for Crampton's Gap, Burkittsville, Maryland, September 14, 1862*. Baltimore: Butternut and Blue, 1998.

Rossino, Alexander. "The Contrabands of Harpers Ferry." *Savas Beatie Blog*. September 3, 2019. https://www.savasbeatie.com/savas-beatie -blog/the-contrabands-of-harpers-ferry-new-blog-by-author-alexander -rossino/?fbclid=IwAR1wTOt2mReX18ayufb_QfRFyz71zIbKHAbT -rDjMVB7yU5oLIjM-x_Yt58.

"The Saving of the Declaration of Independence." *New York Times*, July 2, 1905.

Sears, Stephen W., ed. *Chancellorsville*. Boston: Houghton Mifflin Harcourt, 1996.

———. *Controversies and Commanders: Dispatches from the Army of the Potomac*. Boston: Houghton Mifflin Harcourt, 1999.

———. *George B. McClellan: The Young Napoleon*. New York: Da Capo, 1999.

———. *Landscape Turned Red: The Battle of Antietam*. New Haven, CT: Ticknor and Fields, 1983.

———. *Lincoln's Lieutenants: The High Command of the Army of the Potomac*. Boston: Houghton Mifflin Harcourt, 2017.

———. *The Civil War Papers of George B. McClellan: Selected Correspondence, 1860–1865*. New York: Da Capo, 1992.

Scheips, Paul J. "Union Signal Communications Innovation and Conflict." *Civil War History* 9, no. 4 (December 1963): 399–421.

Snell, Mark A. *From First to Last: The Life of Major General William B. Franklin*. New York: Fordham University Press, 2002.

Spruill, Matt, III, and Matt Spruill IV. *Decisions at Second Manassas: The Fourteen Critical Decisions That Defined the Battle*. Knoxville: University of Tennessee Press, 2018.

Stotelmyer, Steven R. *Too Useful to Sacrifice: Reconsidering George B. McClellan's Generalship in the Maryland Campaign from South Mountain to Antietam*. El Dorado Hills, CA: Savas Beatie, 2019.

Strong, George Templeton. *The Diary of George Templeton Strong*. Edited by Allan Nevins and Milton H. Thomas. New York: Macmillan, 1962.

Strother, Hunter. Entry for September 18, 1862. In *A Virginia Yankee in the Civil War: The Diaries of David Hunter Strother*, edited by Cecil D. Eby. Chapel Hill: University of North Carolina Press, 1961.

"Sugarloaf Mountain—History." Sugarloaf Mountain—Stronghold, Inc. Updated 2003. http://sugarloafmd.com/sl_history.html. Link dead as of November 22, 2021.

Symonds, Craig L. *Joseph E. Johnston: A Civil War Biography*. New York: W. W. Norton, 1992.

Tate, Thomas K. *General Edwin Vose Sumner, USA: A Civil War Biography*. Jefferson, NC: McFarland, 2013.

Taylor, Walter Herron. *Four Years with General Lee*. New York: D. Appleton, 1878.

———. *Lee's Adjutant: The Wartime Letters of Colonel Walter Herron Taylor, 1862–1865*. Edited by R. Lockwood Tower. Columbia: University of South Carolina Press, 1995.

Thayer, William Roscoe. *John Hay: In Two Volumes*. Boston: Houghton, Mifflin, 1915.

"Transcript of the Proclamation." National Archives: Online Exhibits. Accessed Nov. 2021. https://www.archives.gov/exhibits/featured-documents /emancipation-proclamation/transcript.html.

Tucker, Glen. *High Tide at Gettysburg: The Pennsylvania Campaign*. Gettysburg, PA: Stan Clark Military Books, 1958.

United States Congress Joint Committee on the Conduct of the War. *Report of the Joint Committee on the Conduct of the War, Part I, Army of the Potomac, 1863*. United States Congressional Serial Set, Issue 1152. Washington, DC: Government Printing Office, 1865.

United States War Department. *Atlas of the Battlefield of Antietam, Prepared Under the Direction of the Antietam Battlefield Board, Lieut. Col. Geo. W. Davis, U.S.A., President, Gen. E. A. Carman, U.S.V., Gen. H. Heth, C.S.A. Surveyed by Lieut. Col. E. B. Cope, Engineer, H. W. Mattern, Assistant Engineer, of the Gettysburg National Park. Drawn by Charles H. Ourand. Position of Troops by Gen. E. A. Carman. Published by Authority of the Secretary of War, Under the Direction of the Chief of Engineers, U.S. Army, 1908*. Washington, DC: Government Printing Office, 1908. https://www.loc.gov/item/2008621532/.

United States War Department. *The War of the Rebellion: Official Records of the Union and Confederate Armies.* 128 vols. Washington, DC: United States Government Printing Office, 1874–80.

Vermilya, Daniel J. Perceptions, *Not Realities: The Strength, Experience, and Condition of the Army of the Potomac at Antietam.* Sharpsburg, MD: Save Historic Antietam Foundation, 2012.

von Moltke, Helmuth. *Moltke on the Art of War: Selected Writings.* Edited by Daniel Hughes. Random House Ballantine, 1993.

Wade, Benjamin Franklin, and US Congress Joint Committee on the Conduct of the War. *Report of the Joint Committee on the Conduct of the War: Army of the Potomac.* Washington, DC: United States Government Printing Office, 1863.

Walker, John G. "Jackson's Capture of Harper's Ferry." In *Battles and Leaders of the Civil War,"* edited by Robert Underwood Johnson and Clarence Clough Buel. 604-611.New York: Century, 1887.

———. "Sharpsburg." In *Battles and Leaders of the Civil War,"* edited by Robert Underwood Johnson and Clarence Clough Buel. 675-682. New York: Century, 1887.

Warner, Ezra J. *Generals in Blue: Lives of the Union Commanders.* Baton Rouge: Louisiana State University, 1964.

———. *Generals in Gray: Lives of the Confederate Commanders.* Baton Rouge: Louisiana State University, 1959.

Weber, Jennifer L. *Copperheads: The Rise and Fall of Lincoln's Opponents in the North.* New York: Oxford University Press, 2006.

Welles, Gideon. *The Civil War Diary of Gideon Welles, Lincoln's Secretary of the Navy: The Original Manuscript Edition.* Edited by William E. Gienapp and Erica L. Gienapp. Chicago: University of Illinois Press, 2014.

Whitehair, C. W. *Escape across the Potomac.* Conshohocken, PA: Infinity Publishing, 2009.

White, Julius. "The Surrender of Harper's Ferry." In *Battles and Leaders of the Civil War,* edited by Robert Underwood Johnson and Clarence Clough Buel. Vol. 2, 611-615. New York: Century, 1887.

Woodworth, Steven E. *Davis & Lee at War.* Lawrence: University Press of Kansas, 1995.

INDEX

Command decisions are listed in *italics*.